100 THINGS WWE FANS SHOULD KNOW & DO BEFORE THEY DIE

Bryan Alvarez

30 YEARS
TRIUMPH
BOOKS

Library of Congress Cataloguing-in-Publication Data

Names: Alvarez, Bryan, author.
Title: 100 things WWE fans should know and do before they die / Bryan Alvarez.
Other titles: One hundred things WWE fans should know and do before they die
Description: Chicago, Illinois : Triumph Books LLC, [2019]
Identifiers: LCCN 2019013061 | ISBN 9781629376936
Subjects: LCSH: World Wrestling Entertainment, Inc.—Miscellanea. | Wrestling-United States—History. | Wrestling matches—United States—History. | Wrestlers—United States.
Classification: LCC GV1195 .A44 2019 | DDC 791.6/4-dc23
LC record available at https://lccn.loc.gov/2019013061

This book is available in quantity at special discounts for your group or organization. For further information, contact:
    Triumph Books LLC
    814 North Franklin Street
    Chicago, Illinois 60610
    (312) 337-0747
    www.triumphbooks.com

Printed in U.S.A.
ISBN: 978-1-62937-693-6
Design by Patricia Frey
Photos courtesy of AP Images unless otherwise indicated

To Vince

Contents

Foreword

I have known Bryan Alvarez for more than 15 years, and he is one of my closest friends. That said, I don't have a clue how we became friends, and we've only actually met in person four, maybe five times. I think we first connected online through our mutual friend Jeff Marek. Jeff worked for Live Audio Wrestling and knew Bryan as a fellow wrestling journalist, and Jeff was the guy who first got me set up online with my website, StormWrestling.com. Through Jeff we interacted a little bit online and I think I appeared on the old Eyada Internet radio show Bryan used to do with Dave Meltzer. When I "retired" from full-time wrestling and left the WWE in 2005, we started doing a regular podcast together on the Wrestling Observer/Figure Four website, which we still do today. From doing the podcast, we've become great friends, and we've even had a wrestling match against each other. The match was for the local Seattle indy promotion Bryan was working for at the time, and I worked under a mask as the Ideal Canadian. I primarily took the booking as a means to fly to Seattle to meet Bryan for the first time and have someone else pay for the trip. Bryan picked up the win that night, which was no doubt the pinnacle of his pro wrestling career, while a mere embarrassing footnote in mine.

If I can be serious for a minute: I do have a world of respect for Bryan Alvarez. He has been a wrestling fan for 30 years, a journalist covering pro wrestling for 20, and an active pro wrestler for more than a decade. He is also an accomplished author, having co-written *The Death of WCW* with R.D. Reynolds. I can't think of a single other individual who has his depth of experience and knowledge in all of these fields, which is why he is the perfect person to write *100 Things WWE Fans Should Know & Do Before They Die*.

While the title is pretty self-explanatory, I don't think it conveys the true extent of this book's usefulness. For a current WWE fan (or pro wrestling fan in general), it is both an amazing learning tool for things you need to know as well as a great bucket list of things you need to do. The things to know will allow you to understand the history of the industry and its important figures without having to devote the majority of your life to reading 100 different biographies and history-of-wrestling books. If you take up the challenge to do all of the recommended things described in this book, I guarantee you they will be the highlight of your wrestling fandom.

I consider myself a die-hard wrestling fan after more than 35 years as a fan and almost 30 years as a pro wrestler, and I wish I'd had a few copies of this book during that time to pass around to my family and friends. I wish this book had been around when my oldest daughter first started becoming a wrestling fan. It would have been beneficial for both her and me. Pro wrestling is not easily explained to a non-wrestling fan. Pro wrestling needs context, and to fully understand the WWE product today you need to at least have a basic understanding of how we got to where we are now. This book provides that context.

Lance Storm is a pro wrestler best known for his work in World Wrestling Entertainment (WWE), Extreme Championship Wrestling (ECW), and World Championship Wrestling (WCW). After retiring from full-time wrestling, he began running a pro wrestling school, the Storm Wrestling Academy, in Calgary, Alberta, Canada. He also co-hosts the Figure Four Daily *podcast on WrestlingObserver.com.*

Introduction

My first book, *The Death of WCW*, co-written with R.D. Reynolds, was published in 2004. Years later, I was convinced to update and expand that book for an anniversary edition, and then to voice the audiobook for Audible.com. In both instances, I vowed never to write (or voice) another book again. Despite what you might hear in commercials that air on *Wrestling Observer Live*, writing a book is not easy.

So, when I was approached to write *100 Things WWE Fans Should Know & Do Before They Die*, I reminded myself of that vow. But the folks at Triumph Books, including my future editor Adam Motin, were so helpful and professional and easy to deal with that before I knew it, I was writing another book.

The Death of WCW was originally intended to be a list of stupid things that no successful wrestling company would ever do, and the punch line was that WCW did all of those things. But during the writing process, I realized I was writing a history of the company more than I was creating a list, and the project morphed into what it became.

History has a way of repeating itself.

This book happens to be a list of things to know and do, but based on the entries you can learn about everything from the reason the WWWF was formed to how the company managed to sign a $2.3 billion television deal 55 years later. In between those stories you can learn about the biggest stars in wrestling, moments that changed the course of wrestling history, the greatest victories both real and fake, the most devastating tragedies, and so much more.

In the end, I'm so glad I wrote this book, because it gave me a chance to research the professional wrestling promotion I've been watching since I was 13 years old, and which helped direct the course of my life. I hope it brings back memories, perhaps teaches you some things, and brings you many hours of enjoyment.

One final note: this book assumes the reader has a passing knowledge of words and phrases specific to the world of pro wrestling. If you do come across something you're not sure about, check the "Wrestling Terms You Should Know" section toward the back of the book.

100 THINGS
WWE FANS
SHOULD KNOW & DO
BEFORE THEY DIE

1 Vince McMahon

Of course, the very first name that must be mentioned in any book about WWE is that of Vincent Kennedy McMahon. He also happens to be the person most difficult to encapsulate in just a few pages.

Vince McMahon Jr. is the chairman, CEO, and majority shareholder of today's World Wrestling Entertainment. His grandfather, Jess McMahon, promoted boxing and very occasionally pro wrestling at Madison Square Garden in New York City. His father, Vincent James McMahon, was co-founder alongside Toots Mondt of what was then known as the World Wide Wrestling Federation, in 1963.

McMahon Jr. didn't meet his biological father until he was 12 years old. The elder McMahon had left the family and Vince Jr. was raised by his mother and a series of stepfathers. Upon meeting McMahon Sr., Vince began attending events at the Garden and became interested in following his father into the business. He wanted to be a wrestler but the elder McMahon, who was wary of him even being involved in a behind-the-scenes capacity in wrestling, strongly discouraged him from doing so. (Vince Sr. was appalled when his son bleached his hair blond to look like his idol, Dr. Jerry Graham.) It wasn't until long after his father passed away that McMahon Jr., in his early 50s at the time, began to promote himself as a wrestler, ultimately making himself, for a few days, the World Wrestling Federation champion.

As a promoter, McMahon Jr. changed the business forever. Up until the early 1980s, wrestling was largely a territorial business. The United States was divided into a number of different regional territories, including New York, St. Louis, Los Angeles, Memphis, the Carolinas, etc. Many territories had their own local stars and local television contracts, and unless wrestling fans regularly traveled to other parts of the country, studied wrestling magazines, or had friends to correspond with, they generally knew little about what happened outside of their home territory. Wrestlers could work programs and then pack up and move on to a new territory if they began to get stale.

By the mid-1970s the writing was on the wall with the advent of nationwide cable television. There had been nationally broadcast pro wrestling here and there dating back to the late 1940s and early 1950s—for instance, pro wrestling on the DuMont Network, which helped make the original Gorgeous George a star—but with cable beginning to take hold it became increasingly clear that the territorial model would ultimately die, and whoever could go national with strong television first would become the king of pro wrestling.

Many tried, many failed, but Vince McMahon Jr. succeeded. He paid stations around the country to replace their local territorial wrestling shows with tapes of his World Wrestling Federation events. He purchased the Georgia Championship Wrestling time slot on Superstation TBS. He spent big money to raid the best talent from the biggest regional territories, his crown jewel being "The Incredible" Hulk Hogan. He got into bed with MTV to launch the "Rock 'n' Wrestling Connection"; he got into bed with NBC to promote *Saturday Night's Main Event* in a time slot which pre-empted *Saturday Night Live*. And he rode that momentum to create WrestleMania, his annual megashow which had its ups and downs over the years but today remains by far the most lucrative annual wrestling event there has ever been.

In the mid-1990s, McMahon faced a number of sex- and drug-related scandals that nearly put him in prison. While he escaped a sentence he did not do so unscathed and had to change the way he promoted his business. He fell behind and for a period of time got his ass kicked by World Championship Wrestling. Run by Eric

Bischoff and backed by Ted Turner's pocketbook, *WCW Monday Nitro* featured all of the stars of the 1980s who McMahon thought were too old to draw ratings. Bischoff reintroduced them to a generation of kids and teenagers looking for childhood nostalgia, whose parents had disposable income to spend on tickets, merchandise, and pay-per-view events. McMahon Jr. struggled until hitting upon a series of extremely lucky scenarios: a real-life pro wrestling screwjob that turned him into the hottest bad guy in pro wrestling; a superstar named Stone Cold Steve Austin catching fire and becoming the hottest babyface in the industry; and a feud between the two of them that turned WWF business around. Riding the wave of success, McMahon Jr. took WWF public and became a multi-millionaire and later a billionaire, and he never looked back.

While WWE has never been able to recapture the magic of the Attitude Era—the late 1990s/early 2000s glory days—it has continued to make money hand over fist, primarily due to changes in the television landscape. Throughout the 20th century, most promotions either had to pay to get their shows on the air or were paid very little money for their tapes. The success of *Monday Night RAW* and *SmackDown* ultimately led to a period where television rights fees slowly went from just another number on the balance sheet below pay-per-view revenue and ticket sales to far and away the most important number for business. In late 2018, WWE signed a five-year, $2.3 billion television deal for the rights to *RAW* and *SmackDown*. The company's value in 2018 hovered between $5 and $7 billion.

It would take a book to tell the story of Vince McMahon Jr. Through the ups and downs, successes and failures, philanthropy and scandals, good decisions and bad, he remains, without question, the greatest pro wrestling promoter of all time.

Less than 1,000 words on the life of Vince McMahon. But fear not. His story weaves itself through every other story in this book.

2 Hulk Hogan

Hulk Hogan is arguably the most famous American pro wrestler of all time. Worldwide, he would most certainly rank below El Santo in Mexico and Rikidozan in Japan, two men who transcended pro wrestling and became cultural icons; both have regularly made lists of the 10 most famous people in their respective countries, and we're not talking most famous wrestlers or sports stars, we're talking most famous *human beings*. But in America, for decades, if you asked someone on the street to name a pro wrestler, the first name many would say would be Hulk Hogan.

Entire books will be written about Hogan in the future, which won't be easy since so much of his life is wrapped in myth, tales he created partly because he's been a worker since the late 1970s, and partly because he's told so many ridiculous, larger-than-life stories during his lifetime that there's a very good chance even he has forgotten the truth.

Hogan's wrestling career itself is fairly well documented. He grew up a huge fan of both Dusty Rhodes (a massive babyface and incredible talker) and Superstar Billy Graham (an incredible personality with a larger-than-life physique) before breaking into wrestling in 1977 under Japanese American wrestler and trainer Hiro Matsuda. He had a rough go early, quit for a while, and then returned a few years later and rocketed to superstardom. For the first few years of his career he worked in Memphis, the World Wide Wrestling Federation for Vince McMahon Sr., and New Japan Pro Wrestling. But it was the AWA where he totally blew up, becoming the biggest star and draw the territory had ever seen.

In 1983, Vince McMahon began his national expansion and needed a superstar to build around. He didn't create Hogan—or

Hulk Hogan, Donald Trump, and Andre the Giant at an event to promote WrestleMania IV in 1988.

Hulkamania; he raided them from the AWA, along with most of Verne Gagne's other top stars. Hogan beat the Iron Sheik, won the WWF title, and a year later, following the success of WrestleMania I, he was the biggest pro wrestling star in all of America.

Hogan dominated the WWF throughout the rest of the 1980s and into the early 1990s. Vince McMahon Jr.'s original plan was for him to pass the torch to the Ultimate Warrior in 1990 at WrestleMania VI, but Hogan stole the spotlight in the match, the Ultimate Warrior floundered, and a year later they put the title back on Hogan. But he was on his way out for a number of reasons, not the least of which was the steroid scandal that rocked the company in the early 1990s. Hogan went on *The Arsenio Hall*

Show and outright lied about his steroid use, which was a huge scandal given Hogan had been pushed as a children's role model for a decade, preaching his mantra of training, saying your prayers, and eating your vitamins. Because of the heat, he took an almost year-long hiatus before returning and then winning the WWF championship at WrestleMania IX in 1993. But the writing was on the wall, and after dropping the title to Yokozuna at that year's King of the Ring, he left the company again.

Contrary to WWF's version of history for years, WCW did not use Ted Turner's bottomless pocketbook to lure Hogan from the WWF in an attempt to drive it out of business. Hogan actually left WWF and worked in Japan for nearly a year before finally coming to terms with WCW. He was an immediate draw for the company right out of the gate and helped boost pay-per-view and arena business. But he was pushed as a superhero, and it was inevitable that fans would tire of his act.

In 1996, against his initial wishes, Hogan was convinced to turn heel and join Scott Hall and Kevin Nash as the New World Order. He hadn't been a heel in North America in more than 15 years. The angle hit the jackpot and WCW's business grew to the point that it surpassed WWF for the first time ever and became, for a short time, the most financially successful wrestling promotion in the history of the planet. But WCW ran with a pat hand for too long, plus Hogan had serious issues with writer Vince Russo, who came aboard in 1999, which ultimately led to a defamation of character lawsuit and the end of his WCW career.

After WCW went out of business, Hogan returned to WWF for another two-year run which saw him work as both the NWO heel version of Hollywood Hogan and later the babyface red-and-yellow Hulkster. Coming off a legendary match with the Rock at WrestleMania X8, where Hogan once again stole the spotlight, he won the undisputed WWF championship from Triple H for a one-month final run. (Here's a piece of trivia: WWF then changed its name to WWE, so Hogan was, officially, the final WWF champion.) But as his run wore on, Hogan became disgruntled with being asked to do jobs and his payouts, and he left the company in 2003.

He bounced around for several years afterward, including another run in WWE, before finally heading to TNA in 2009, where he reunited with Eric Bischoff. The idea was that they were going to put all of their manpower behind making TNA competitive with WWE, including attempting to re-create the Monday Night Wars between WWE and WCW, an idea that was an epic failure since there was nothing in common between the wrestling landscapes of 1995 and 2010.

Hogan's 2014 return to WWE in a non-wrestling capacity ended abruptly a year later. I remember this evening vividly— WWE suddenly scrubbed all references to Hogan from the WWE website. It was clear something serious had happened. Sure enough, shortly thereafter the *National Enquirer* and Radar Online published stories on a Hulk Hogan tape from eight years earlier that included Hogan not only using appalling racial slurs but flat-out admitting that he was "racist to a point, y'know."

The tape in question was the famous Hulk Hogan sex tape, which had come to light years earlier. Hogan had slept with Heather Clem, the wife of radio shock jock Bubba the Love Sponge, in Bubba's bedroom with permission from Bubba, his best friend at the time. Unbeknownst to Hogan, Bubba filmed the entire thing and later told his wife that it was their ticket to retirement. The tape leaked and the website Gawker put up a series of clips. Hogan filed suit to have the tape taken down, but Gawker refused. This led to a famous and far-reaching legal battle that ended with Hogan being awarded $115 million (keep in mind, he only asked for $100 million, so you can imagine what the jury thought about Gawker). Gawker and Hogan settled for $31 million, and Gawker went out of business.

Hogan was seen as a victim in the sex tape scandal, even though technically he was still married to his wife, Linda, at the time of the recording (they later divorced). But the racial slurs were different. He was scrubbed from WWE history for years. In 2018, the company brought him back to give a speech to the locker room, but it was met poorly, particularly by the black wrestlers, who saw the speech as more a cautionary tale about how you could be filmed without your knowledge as opposed to a sincere expression of regret for what he had said. The speech was envisioned as the beginning of his return to the company, but it came off so badly that he vanished again. Finally, in November, he was brought back as the host of the Crown Jewel extravaganza in Saudi Arabia. The show was already the most controversial in WWE history, so it was somewhat fitting that the company chose that day to bring him back.

The story of Hulk Hogan and his legacy is yet to be written. He's been among the most beloved people in the business and the most reviled, and there have been ups and downs throughout his entire career. But whether remembered in a positive or negative light, what cannot be argued is he is the most famous wrestler America has ever known.

3 The First WrestleMania

Had the first WrestleMania flopped, who knows if you'd be reading this book today. The show, on March 31, 1985, was a huge gamble for the company, a potential make-it-or-break-it event.

The story of WrestleMania begins long before the first show, when Vince McMahon kicked off his national expansion. A key part of his strategy was to approach television stations around the country and offer tapes of his slickly produced WWF events. Prior to this, territorial promotions usually worked on a barter deal with the local television station (usually, but not always; some promotions paid for their television time, and some which were very successful in a market, such as Memphis wrestling, were paid for their shows by the station, although that was extremely rare). Often, the promotion would provide stations with tapes of their shows with no money changing hands. The station got free programming, and the shows would be advertisements for upcoming live events, where the promotion would make money largely off ticket sales. The bad promoters would lose money and be weeded out. The strong would survive.

In order to get his tapes played, McMahon not only offered a better-produced product; he also offered to pay big money to get his tapes on the air. If a station was doing a barter deal with a promotion and McMahon showed up willing to pay to get his show on the air, it wasn't a difficult decision to start airing WWF tapes.

The issue, of course, is that this cost a lot of money. WWF attempted to make up the cost in ticket sales for live events that would be pushed on those TV broadcasts, but by 1985 it was way behind on payments. Compounding the issue was all of the money it was paying to lure the top stars from various territories, including Verne Gagne's AWA, where McMahon raided half the roster.

In this environment, WrestleMania was conceived. The key to the success of that first WrestleMania was how big it hit with the casual audience. There were two shows on the burgeoning MTV network with angles building up the event: the July 23, 1984, "Brawl to Settle It All," where Wendi Richter beat Fabulous Moolah with Cyndi Lauper and Lou Albano in their respective corners; and the "War to Settle the Score" on February 18, 1985. The former didn't do great live business in Madison Square Garden, since it wasn't exactly the kind of feud that was going to light the hardcore wrestling fans' interest on fire, but it did a gigantic rating on MTV, a

9.0, and ended with Hulk Hogan celebrating with Richter, further establishing him as a mainstream name. The February 18 show, headlined by Hogan facing Roddy Piper, did great arena business and a 9.1 rating, the highest ever for pro wrestling on cable television, a record that will likely never be broken. Hogan beat Piper via DQ when Paul Orndorff interfered, and Mr. T, one of the hottest TV stars in the country based on his portrayal of B.A. Baracus on *The A-Team* and Clubber Lang in *Rocky III*, made the save. This set up the WrestleMania main event: Hogan and Mr. T vs. Piper and Orndorff.

WrestleMania was almost a disaster in many ways. Mr. T, whose role in the rise of WWF is historically understated, got cold feet the day of the show, concerned that one of the wrestlers would shoot on him and expose him. Everyone believed that based on his look, persona, and reputation as a bad-ass bouncer that he was the toughest man in the country. But he was an actor who portrayed a tough guy, and he knew there was resentment among the wrestlers that he walked in off a TV set and was headlining such a massive show. Worse, neither Piper nor Orndorff would agree to lose to him, and the agreement he'd made was that he'd beat one of the heels to win the match. Finally, almost at the last moment, he was talked into working and Orndorff agreed to do the job, but only to Hogan after he was accidentally hit by Cowboy Bob Orton's loaded cast.

WrestleMania business also looked dire. McMahon had rented out more than 200 buildings around the country for his closed-circuit WrestleMania gamble. The show wasn't available on PPV, only closed-circuit, and a recent closed-circuit event, the "fight" between Muhammad Ali and Antonio Inoki in 1976, was a major flop. A week out it was looking like WrestleMania would also be a massive flop; the advances were poor, and many arenas—approximately 30 percent nationwide—canceled their airings of the show.

But it all turned around in the final week. Hogan and Mr. T got a ton of mainstream attention, appearing on David Letterman's show and *Saturday Night Live*. In an unfortunate but ultimately fortuitous situation, Hogan appeared on the TV show *Hot Properties*, hosted by Richard Belzer. Belzer asked Hogan to demonstrate a wrestling hold on him. Hogan declined several times but Belzer finally talked him into it. Hogan put on what was described as a "front chinlock," but was pretty much a jiu-jitsu guillotine hold. Belzer suddenly went limp, Hogan released the hold, and Belzer collapsed, smashing the back of his head on the floor. The crowd went deathly silent, and Mr. T, off camera, quipped, "He's all right, he just sleeping." Hogan slapped his face a few times, and suddenly Belzer leaped to his feet, not having any idea where he was, and screamed, "And now, we'll be right back after this word from...you know who!" The bad news is that Belzer sued Hogan for $5 million, a lawsuit that was settled out of court for what Belzer later claimed was somewhere in the $400,000 range. The good news is the incident garnered additional mainstream publicity for WrestleMania.

In the end, WrestleMania was a hit, the most successful pro wrestling event in history up to that point, drawing 19,121 fans live to Madison Square Garden and over a million on closed-circuit, totaling nearly $5 million in revenue.

The show was a turning point for Hogan, who came out of it by far the biggest wrestling star in America. Within a few years, every major regional promoter had either gone out of business or fallen to the point that they no longer presented much competition. The wrestling world had changed forever, and there was no going back.

4 Steve Austin vs. Vince McMahon

The feud between Steve Austin and Vince McMahon changed wrestling history forever.

WWF was struggling early in the Monday Night Wars. Business was way down, and WCW was kicking its ass in the ratings. Eric Bischoff had a seemingly unlimited amount of money with which to sign whoever happened to be willing to leave WWF for the competition. While Bret Hart and Shawn Michaels were superior wrestlers for WWF, the biggest mainstream names and money-drawing superstars were on *Nitro*.

Steve Austin's career started to take off in late 1996 in a feud with Bret Hart. History recalls Austin's famous line toward Jake "The Snake" Roberts from King of the Ring in mid-1996—"Austin 3:16 says I just whipped your ass"—as a turning point, but really, it wasn't. It was a cool line, and soon "Austin 3:16" signs started showing up at arenas, but it wasn't until the Bret Hart feud that Austin began to really shine as something special in his promos.

Although Austin was getting over, the company was still attempting to build around Hart and Michaels. Austin lost to Hart at Survivor Series 1996, and WrestleMania 13 was scheduled to be the big Hart vs. Michaels rematch for the WWF championship. But things happen in wrestling, particularly when those things involve two guys who despise each other, and Mania instead featured Austin vs. Hart in an "I Quit" match. It was one of the most famous matches in WWF history, a five-star classic that Hart won after Austin passed out due to loss of blood while locked in the sharpshooter. But Austin had refused to quit, proving himself to be what he was billed as from that point forward, "one tough son of a bitch," and his career continued to skyrocket. One year later, he beat Michaels in the main event of WrestleMania XIV to win the WWF championship.

It's hard to try to imagine how big Austin might have gotten without his biggest rival.

Following the Montreal Screwjob, in which Vince McMahon orchestrated the moving of the title from Hart to Michaels, the once-friendly announcer had transformed into a hated promoter in the eyes of the fans. McMahon had flirted with being an in-ring performer in 1993, playing a heel WWF representative who was sending WWF stars to the Memphis territory in an attempt to dethrone babyface champion Jerry Lawler. Lawler was accused and then cleared of rape charges, but that ended the storyline. (It was never acknowledged on WWF television.)

While people remember Montreal as being the impetus for McMahon's heel turn, the reality is that McMahon tried very, very hard to babyface himself in the immediate aftermath of the event. All of his famous interviews, including the one where he alerted us that he didn't screw Bret, that "Bret screwed Bret," were designed to convince fans that what Vince had done was right (and, in his heart, he believed he had done the right thing) and that Hart was the villain. But the fans saw things totally in reverse, and he became a hated character.

He finally went full-bore into the Mr. McMahon character just in time to feud with Austin, who was beginning his run toward the WWF title in early 1998. There was a famous moment on the January 19, 1998, edition of *RAW* where Vince was hosting a ceremony to announce that Mike Tyson would be appearing at that year's WrestleMania. Austin interrupted, had a shoving match with Tyson that made worldwide headlines, and in the midst of it McMahon and Austin had an incredible screaming match. At that point, the now-fully heel Mr. McMahon character made it his life's goal to make sure that Austin never became the face of his World Wrestling Federation.

Of course, the rest is history. Austin won the title and feuded with McMahon throughout 1998 and most of 1999. It was the most perfect dynamic in wrestling history. Austin was the common man; the badass, beer-drinking, truck-driving redneck who rejected authority, flipped off management, and did whatever the damn hell he wanted. Mr. McMahon represented the boss who everyone hated. Unlike today, where Vince's daughter, Stephanie, is a heavily protected authority figure who might get one-upped by a babyface once a year at WrestleMania, McMahon got beat up and humiliated on—and I'm not exaggerating here—almost every single edition of *RAW*. The show would start with Vince coming up with some sort of diabolical plan to screw with Austin. Austin would outsmart McMahon, put one over on him, and usually leave him laying with a Stunner by the end of the show. Sometimes, Austin would put one over on Vince multiple times per show. Occasionally, Vince would win a battle, usually to set up a PPV match where Austin would get his revenge. If you were a normal human being who went to a job that you didn't necessarily like and hated your boss, you could come home virtually every single Monday night and live vicariously through Austin as he ridiculed, outsmarted, tortured, and humiliated his evil boss.

Never before or since has there been such a perfect dynamic, and it completely turned WWF business around to the point that McMahon was able to take the company public and, overnight, become the billionaire he'd always wanted to be.

Of course, in the end, McMahon the promoter made the critical and unforgivable error of turning Steve Austin heel at WrestleMania X-Seven on April 1, 2001. It was the opposite of right place, right time. It was the wrong place, and boy, was it ever the wrong time. WWF was at its peak, but unfortunately the wrestling business as a whole had hit the proverbial iceberg. WCW and ECW had just gone out of business or were about to. WWF had won the Monday Night Wars, but the battles had run off millions of fans in the process. The audience that got into WWF in the mid-1990s knew it was all fake, but they really wanted to believe one thing—that Vince McMahon and Steve Austin hated each other. While Austin as a heel was tremendously entertaining, the last thing those fans wanted to see was him shaking Vince's hand. The handshake and hug at the end of WrestleMania X-Seven marked the end of the Attitude Era, and for millions of fans, their days following wrestling pretty much came to an end. Luckily for WWE, the feud was such an incredible business generator that even though the company fell into a several-year lull afterward, it remained significantly more profitable post-Austin/McMahon than it was going in. And it continues to float along on the wave they kicked off to this day.

5 The Rock

If you consider worldwide recognition as a human being, the Rock is the most famous pro wrestler of all time. But his worldwide fame didn't really come from wrestling; he's been considered the single biggest movie star in the world several times over the years.

The Rock's pedigree in wrestling was second-to-none as both his father, Rocky Johnson, and grandfather, Peter Maivia, were main event wrestlers. A little-known fun fact: Peter Maivia's real name was Fanene Pita Anderson. Because Pita was Samoan, promoter Dale Anderson changed his name to Peter Maivia, after another famous Samoan star of no relation, Neff Maiava. The spellings were different; Anderson spelled it wrong, and it stuck. Years later, Neff and Peter met and became as close as brothers. Likewise, Rocky Johnson's real name wasn't Rocky Johnson. In real life, he was Wayde Bowles from Amherst, Nova Scotia. He eventually married Peter's daughter, Ata. So, when Peter and Ata had a son, Dwayne, they didn't give him the last name Bowles or Anderson or Maivia, but rather Johnson, after Peter's fake wrestling name. Then, a few years later, Peter and Ata officially changed their last names to Johnson.

Anyway, young Dwayne loved and respected wrestling for as long as he could remember and was already cutting promos on videotape at the age of 11. He excelled at football and attended the University of Miami on a full scholarship. He played the 1991 season with the Hurricanes but was injured. After graduating, he joined the CFL's Calgary Stampeders but was cut two months into the season. At that point, he decided to give wrestling a try. His family was initially against it, but eventually acquiesced. He was given a WWF tryout in 1996 and wrestled two dark matches, with Brooklyn Brawler and Chris Candido, with absolutely zero wrestling experience. He blew people away with his potential and Jim Ross signed him immediately. After his first week, some of the smartest minds in wrestling had pegged him as likely the biggest star in wrestling by the year 2000.

He beat those projections by a year.

After training in Memphis, his official WWF debut was on November 17, 1996, at the Survivor Series where, in a four-on-four elimination match, the entire rest of his team was eliminated but he came back, eliminated the remaining heels, and was the sole survivor. Fans went nuts for him. He was given the monster push, and within three months was the Intercontinental champion. But the push was a bit too heavy-handed, and it led to pockets of fans starting to turn on him.

It's funny looking back at this period, because everyone remembers that the crowd turned on the happy, smiling babyface Rocky Maivia and WWF responded by turning him heel. That did happen, to be sure. But if you're a modern fan whose idea of fans

The Rock, prior to taking on Hulk Hogan at Wrestlemania X8. (Getty Images)

turning on a guy is the reaction Roman Reigns got in 2018, the "Die, Rocky die" period is absolutely stunning in hindsight. He was overwhelmingly cheered, with only small pockets of fans turning on him. The fans were probably 90 percent behind him, but that was enough for the company back then to change directions.

Rocky Maivia was clearly extremely talented, but he was missing something. The heel turn shot him over the moon. There is a period in 1997 where you could watch "The Rock," as he was now called, seemingly on a weekly basis being twice as good as he was the week before. In my lifetime of watching wrestling, I don't think I've ever seen anyone improve so dramatically so quickly.

By the late 1990s, he might not have been the biggest star (Steve Austin had become the biggest short-term draw in wrestling history), but he was unquestionably the most charismatic performer in the business. Truth be told, the Rock being so ridiculously awesome was both a short-term positive and arguably a long-term negative.

Short-term, the combination of the Rock, Austin, and Vince McMahon was a once-in-a-lifetime (maybe several lifetimes) combination whose synergy was such that WWF went from losing $6 million in 1996 to surpassing (and ultimately crushing) WCW in 1999, becoming the biggest wrestling promotion in the history of the planet. With Austin out of action due to injury, the Rock was the babyface centerpiece of the promotion in 2000, a year in which the company did ridiculous business.

But the downside was that he was perhaps too good. There was nothing that the Rock couldn't turn to gold. He was so over that you could beat him on a weekly basis and he didn't lose an ounce of steam. You could write the stupidest, corniest, most ridiculous dialogue, and somehow the Rock would deliver it in such a way that fans would leave thinking they'd heard one of the greatest promos in wrestling history. Because he was bulletproof, WWF unfortunately concluded that the formula that worked for him was the formula that it needed to use for all of its top stars, from John Cena on down. This has resulted in a decade-plus of having top stars lose far too frequently and scripting terrible comedy promos for them. The lesson is, there is only one Dwayne Johnson.

The Rock got a glorified cameo in *The Mummy Returns* in 2001 (he was billed as co-star but got a whopping eight minutes of screen time, half of which featured a computer-generated version of him). He so impressed the producers, however, that a spinoff film, *The Scorpion King*, was written for him. This was the beginning of the end of his wrestling career. By mid-2003, he was largely out of WWE as a full-timer, and began fully transitioning into acting.

There was a lot of bitterness, both from the company and from fans, who felt he abandoned them for Hollywood. While WWE would almost certainly deny this, the reality is that his WWE contract just expired one day in 2005. Nobody called him, nobody wrote him a letter. When he confronted Vince McMahon about it, McMahon told him it was a "clerical oversight." The Rock, among the biggest names in company history and a bona-fide movie star at this point, had suddenly become a free agent due to a clerical oversight. Between August of 2004 and March of 2007, he didn't appear on a single WWE television show.

He appeared sporadically from that point forward. And then, on February 14, 2011, he returned for a two-year run spanning the WrestleManias in 2011, 2012, and 2013. In 2011, he refereed the Cena vs. Miz main event. In revenge for an incident on *RAW* where Cena gave the Rock an Attitude Adjustment, the Rock gave Cena a Rock Bottom and cost him the WrestleMania main event. The next night on *RAW*, Cena challenged the Rock to a match at the following year's WrestleMania, the first time since Hulk Hogan vs. Randy Savage that the company planned out a WrestleMania main event storyline a year in advance. The Rock and Cena headlined two straight WrestleManias, both of which broke the record for the highest-grossing wrestling shows in the history of the world, which, due to the WWE destroying its own PPV model with the WWE Network, are records that will almost certainly never be broken.

The Rock has never officially announced that he's retired from wrestling and would love to continue doing sporadic matches. However, due to suffering serious injuries during both of his WrestleMania matches with Cena (which put production of major motion pictures, including *Hercules*, on hold), he doesn't wrestle whenever he's working on a film (which is virtually always). Right place, right time, he'd return again, but as each year passes he gets a year older, and ultimately the day will come when it's no longer a good idea to wrestle. But whether he ever steps foot in the ring again, he will remain, without question, an all-time elite Hall of Famer.

6 Attend a WrestleMania

Attending a WrestleMania is probably the single biggest thing any WWE fan should do before they die.

No matter what you think of WWE, how much of it you currently watch, whether you're hardcore into it or only watch clips on YouTube, if WrestleMania comes to town, go. It's virtually impossible to have a bad time, especially if you go with a group of friends or family. It's a *RAW* or *SmackDown* taping on steroids—so to speak—where the biggest matches between the biggest stars, the biggest angles, and the biggest turns all converge for the biggest show of the year. The budget for the show is in the tens of millions of dollars, so these days it always takes place at a stadium that seats 60,000-plus (which WWE will always inflate by 10,000 to ⌐0), the entranceway and ramp are absolutely enormous, and they spare no expense on costuming, pageantry, the WrestleMania set, celebrities, etc.

You aren't always going to get what you want in terms of booking. The babyfaces don't always win at WrestleMania and the best workers aren't always in the main event. But whatever you think of the creative decisions, WWE always tries to put on a spectacular event designed to send everyone home relatively happy. Not completely happy, of course, because they need some heated angles to lead to *RAW* the following night.

And speaking of *RAW*…because WrestleMania is the biggest show of the year for WWE, the post-WrestleMania *RAW*, where they follow-up on all the finishes and start the direction for the rest of the year, is the biggest *RAW* of the year. Sometimes, as was the case with the Rock and John Cena, if you attend the *RAW* after WrestleMania you'll find out what the main event is for the following year's WrestleMania, 364 days in advance. The atmosphere is almost always incredible, because it is the one *RAW* every year where tens of thousands of fans have flown in from all over the world, and so it's easily the most hardcore and savvy (some would say annoying) crowd of the year. You'll get the craziest chants, ranging from the hilarious to the extremely aggravating. You'll get crowd reactions for babyfaces and heels sometimes completely at odds with what you'll get for any other *RAW* in any other city. You'll get once-a-year monster reactions for big angles, and you'll often get a debut or two, since WWE often calls up new stars from NXT the night after WrestleMania. It's often the one *RAW* each year you don't want to miss, and it usually does one of the better ratings of the year.

Another amazing thing about WrestleMania is something that WWE doesn't really want you to know about: over the past decade, WrestleMania weekend has turned into the biggest independent pro wrestling weekend of the year for every major non-WWE company. WWE would like you to know that it's running a Hall of

Fame ceremony on Friday, an NXT TakeOver event on Saturday, WrestleMania on Sunday, *RAW* on Monday, and *SmackDown* on Tuesday. However, if you have even a cursory knowledge of wrestling outside WWE, you will have the opportunity to attend any of more than 100 different wrestling-related events that weekend. There are meet-and-greets, Q&A's, independent conventions, and so many wrestling shows that the top indy stars in the U.S. can work nearly a dozen shows over a one-week period. Every promotion does its best business of the year over WrestleMania weekend, and many put tickets on sale during the fall of the previous year. Tickets go fast. In 2018, Ring of Honor managed to get a date at Madison Square Garden—an arena that had previously been exclusive to WWE for pro wrestling dating back to the formation of the company in 1963—head-to-head with WWE's NXT show at the Barclay's Center in New Jersey, and tickets sold out virtually immediately, almost a year prior to the show taking place.

If you are a wrestling fan to any degree at all, WrestleMania weekend is the best weekend of the year, and nothing else even comes close. There is so much wrestling available in a 50-mile radius that even picking and choosing the very best, you know you're missing out on a ton of great action every single day.

7 Bruno Sammartino

In a business where during its hottest period ever wrestlers were dying on seemingly a weekly basis, Bruno Sammartino was one of those guys who you thought would never pass away. But he did, after a two-month hospitalization, on April 18, 2018.

His in-ring moniker was "The Living Legend," and he was exactly that. He was among the most beloved wrestlers in U.S. wrestling history, and among the most beloved wrestlers anywhere in the world. He was a two-time WWWF champion, an absolute hero to his fans to the point they reacted to him losing the title for the first time in a similar way that many of us reacted when we heard he'd died—utter disbelief that such a thing could even happen. He had his ups and downs with Vince McMahon Jr. but did mend fences with the company in his final years, accepting an induction into the WWE Hall of Fame after meeting with Triple H in another moment where it felt like hell had frozen over. He lived the fullest of lives despite the fact that he almost barely lived a life at all.

Sammartino was born on October 5, 1935, in Pizzoferrato, Italy. In 1943 the Nazis invaded, and Bruno and his family were forced to hide out in a refugee camp for 14 months. The future powerhouse was just a small, sickly child at the time. His mother would regularly travel down the mountain into town for supplies, and young Bruno would sit on a rock and gaze down the hill, never knowing if she'd ever make it back. The family survived the war, but Bruno contracted rheumatic fever when he was 12, and at one point in the battle the doctor told his mother that he wasn't going to make it. She insisted to the doctor, as Bruno was covered in leeches attempting to suck the fever out of him, that she'd already lost two children and wasn't going to lose a third. Bruno lived, and attributed his survival to his mother.

Two years later he came to America, reuniting with his father, who had left the family when Bruno was one, attempting to start a new life and earn enough money to bring the family to meet him. Bruno very quickly fell in love with the weight room, probably in part as overcompensation for a childhood spent being small and weak. He lifted weights for hours every morning and ate more and more, growing into one of the strongest men in the world in the 1960s.

Bruno wanted to be a wrestler from at least the time he was in high school, but he had other dreams as well, including going to the Olympics in weightlifting. That never panned out, and in 1959 he chose wrestling over football and broke into the business with Ace Freeman in Pittsburgh. (Note: at the time, pro wrestling paid better than professional football.)

Sammartino's most famous run in wrestling was as the World Wide Wrestling Federation champion from May 17, 1963, to January 18, 1971. His reign made him a megastar and launched the WWWF. It almost never happened; Sammartino missed some dates, which he blamed on double-bookings by McMahon Sr., and he was suspended by various athletic commissions throughout the United States. Things were bad enough that he was considering going back home and becoming a carpenter. Instead, he went to work for Jack Tunney in Toronto.

For various political reasons, the National Wrestling Alliance was falling apart in the early 1960s, with promoters pulling out and creating their own world champions. When Lou Thesz beat Buddy Rogers for the title, McMahon Sr. was done. He'd used Thesz in New York in the 1950s and Thesz didn't draw well, and he thought Rogers should have remained champion. He pulled out of the NWA and created the World Wide Wrestling Federation, with Rogers as the inaugural champion (the public claim was that Rogers had beaten Antonino Rocca in a tournament in Rio De Janeiro, which never happened). McMahon and Sammartino made amends for business reasons, with McMahon paying off Sammartino's fines and thus lifting his suspensions, and Bruno agreed to come back on the condition that he won the title from Rogers. And that's exactly what happened one month later, in just 48 seconds.

Sammartino was the biggest wrestling star in the biggest wrestling and media market in the world for the next seven years,

Bruno Sammartino, arguably the most beloved performer in the history of professional wrestling.

headlining Madison Square Garden more than 130 times and selling out over half of those appearances. He was a hero to his fan base the likes of which it's hard to imagine today, where nobody is ever really allowed to get over to that degree. Even the biggest stars like John Cena and Roman Reigns are largely cogs in the machine that is World Wrestling Entertainment. When Sammartino finally lost the title to Ivan Koloff, it was such a shock that when Koloff hit his kneedrop off the top rope and the ref counted to three, Bruno thought something had gone terribly wrong and he'd lost his hearing, because the building went absolutely pin-drop silent. They didn't announce Koloff the winner for fear of a riot, and as Bruno rose to his feet and began walking to the backstage area, the silence was broken by the sobbing of fans, men and women alike.

Sammartino was talked into returning a few years later by McMahon Sr., at which point he got a more lucrative deal which included gate percentages and a more limited schedule. He had injured his back in the late 1960s and wanted to drop the WWWF title then, but McMahon wouldn't let him. By the time he finally lost to Koloff, he was really hurting physically and was mentally worn out from all the travel. It was tough to get him to agree to come back for a second run, but McMahon Sr. made it worth his while.

Sammartino's second reign was a huge business success. Perhaps the most famous story from the era involved a match with Stan Hansen where Bruno was dropped wrong on a body slam and broke his neck. Almost exactly two months later, McMahon had booked Shea Stadium for a mega show, and he needed his WWWF champion on the card. He begged Sammartino to return. Sammartino, who had been hospitalized, was told by his doctors that he'd be absolutely crazy to try to wrestle the date. But McMahon pleaded to Sammartino that if the show bombed the promoter would be finished and forced to declare bankruptcy. In a completely insane move, Sammartino worked the show. But when it was over, he wanted out.

Again, McMahon balked. He begged him to stay one more year, and he gave him not only the date that he'd lose the title to Superstar Billy Graham, but also told Graham the exact date he'd lose the title to Bob Backlund. Sammartino agreed.

Sammartino stuck around on a limited schedule after Graham beat him and had one more gigantic feud in the late 1970s and early 1980s with his real-life protege Larry Zbyszko, which did tremendous business. But his neck was bothering him a lot, and he wrapped up his wrestling career on October 4, 1981.

Sammartino returned to the now-WWF as a commentator a few years later, largely as a favor to his son and Vince McMahon Jr. But he hated the role. When he was a child he saw a wrestler die in the ring and later learned that this wrestler had been on steroids, and thus he became a staunch opponent of them. The mid-1980s WWF was filled to the brim with guys on steroids; plus, the national expansion, the "Rock 'n' Wrestling Connection," the sports entertainment before it was called sports entertainment aspect of the business—none of it appealed to him and he deeply regretted coming back. He had a major falling-out with both McMahon and his son, David (who used steroids in a decision his father never forgave him for), and walked away from every aspect of the business altogether. It was decades before Vince's son-in-law talked him into returning for the Hall of Fame.

Bruno's death was attributed to heart damage he'd sustained in his battle with rheumatic fever. He might have died much sooner, but his love of training and his hard work in the gym likely added years to his life. His death was covered all over the United States and around the world, especially in Pizzoferrato, Italy, his hometown, where a statue in his honor stands to this day.

Vince McMahon Sr.

Vincent James McMahon was the son of Roderick James "Jess" McMahon and is the father of today's Vincent Kennedy McMahon.

Roderick and Elizabeth McMahon emigrated to the United States from Western Ireland in the early 1880s and opened up a hotel. Jess McMahon was born on May 26, 1882. He was interested in sports from a young age, and by the early 1900s was promoting boxing shows with his brother, Edward, in Harlem. The McMahon family's pro wrestling dynasty kicked off on Tuesday, June 7, 1932, when McMahon promoted his first wrestling bout, featuring former New York Giant Cy Williams vs. Dr. Ralph Wilson at the Freeport Municipal Stadium in Long Island. In 1952 he created Capitol Wrestling Corporation Ltd. with partner Toots Mondt, a turn-of-the-century wrestler and later promoter who revolutionized the pro wrestling industry in the 1920s. Two years later, McMahon died of a cerebral hemorrhage at the age of 72 and his son, Vincent James McMahon, took over the family business.

Television began broadcasting on July 1, 1941, to fewer than 7,000 homes nationwide. In 1942, shortly after the U.S. entered World War II, sales of televisions and most broadcasts nationwide were suspended. Televisions at the time were operated by cathode ray tubes, and the tubes were needed for war. In 1945, after the war ended, RCA released the 630-TS television. It took about four years for the price to become affordable for the average family. But by 1949, television had taken off, with 100,000 sets being sold a week.

That year also happened to be the year pro wrestling began airing on the DuMont Network. *Wrestling from Marigold*, produced by NWA promoter Fred Kohler, was one of the first hits of broadcast television, and stars from that era, including Gorgeous George, became household names. McMahon began airing his television show on DuMont in 1955. A year later, DuMont went out of business but its New York affiliate, WABD, went independent and kept McMahon's program on the air. It was around this time that McMahon's son, Vince Jr., began tagging along with his father on trips to wrestling shows.

The 1960s and particularly 1970s were a golden era in wrestling for McMahon. The 1960s were dominated by Bruno Sammartino, and the formula was simple. The heel would get heat in the first match of the feud, which would end via countout, disqualification, or blood stoppage (in those days, the WWWF title would not change hands if the champion was deemed unable to continue due to blood loss). Bruno would then come back and win the definitive blow-off match. He drew huge money in all of WWWF's main markets in the 1960s and vanquished one heel after another. Same with his second run in the 1970s. McMahon also had a number of other colorful top stars who drew big money and gained fame through the wrestling magazines, superstars such as Mil Mascaras and, later, Andre the Giant.

The beginning of the end of the Sammartino era began on December 15, 1975, when, in the first cage match in Madison Square Garden, Sammartino pinned Ivan Koloff to finally gain revenge on Koloff for ending his first title reign years earlier. On that same evening, Superstar Billy Graham defeated Dominic DeNucci, who was pushed as Sammartino's best friend. Graham got over huge, and these two trains were set to collide. Graham beat Sammartino via countout in the first match, with Sammartino winning decisively in the second.

On April 26, 1976, history changed. Sammartino was facing Stan Hansen, and in the middle of the match Hansen lifted him up for a body slam and accidentally dumped him on his head, breaking his neck. Sammartino finished the match, losing via the usual blood stoppage. Shortly thereafter, the doctor told him he should retire.

However, two months later to the day, McMahon Sr. had booked Shea Stadium for a major show. On that same day in Japan, the most famous boxer in the world, Muhammad Ali, was facing wrestler Antonio Inoki in a mixed match. The McMahon family heavily invested in a closed-circuit deal that would have that match and the Shea Stadium show, headlined by Andre the Giant vs. Chuck Wepner, beamed to locations throughout the country. The problem was, the media was treating Ali vs. Inoki as a joke. So, McMahon went to Sammartino and begged him to face Hansen in a grudge match. Sammartino was obviously against it but McMahon begged him to do him the favor, claiming that if the show flopped, he'd be facing bankruptcy, and all the two had built together since 1963 would be lost. Sammartino, in an incredibly crazy decision, agreed to do the match. But when it was over, he wanted out for good.

The show drew 32,000 fans and a $400,000 gate, and all the newspapers attributed the success to Bruno. Four months later, McMahon had a meeting with Bruno's successor, Graham. McMahon flat-out told him when he would win the title (Spring of 1977) and the exact day he would lose it (February 20, 1978) and to whom (Bob Backlund). And that was that. Sammartino continued to defend the title through that date, upon which, as planned, Graham beat him with his feet on the ropes to win the title. His title win was not met with dead silence, but rather a near riot, and Graham fought his way to the back swinging the belt over his head, being doused with beer, swung at, and fearing for his life. But he made it.

Despite his misgivings, covered elsewhere, Graham did drop the title to Backlund on February 20, 1978, setting up the final WWWF title reign that McMahon Sr. would book before his death.

On February 21, 1980, Vince Jr. and his wife, Linda, founded Titan Sports, Inc. They were living in a trailer park at the time with their two young children, Shane and Stephanie, and McMahon was struggling to make ends meet promoting smaller towns and sometimes working odd jobs for extra cash. On June 6, 1982, he initiated a purchase of what was now World Wrestling Federation from his father and his business partners, who included Gorilla Monsoon, Phil Zacko, and Arnold Skaaland. The way McMahon Jr. tells the story, his father had no idea what his son's plans were and wouldn't have sold if he had. McMahon Jr. raised $250,000 of the $1 million sale price and was required to pay off the balance in quarterly installments, and if he missed even one payment he'd lose the company back. While the company was doing good business at the time and probably grossing $10 million per year, McMahon was essentially using company profits to make payments on his sale. It was a struggle at times and he did have to work very hard to pay it off.

McMahon Sr. stayed on in an advisory role, and for a period of time the sale itself was secret; everyone presumed the elder McMahon was still in charge. The idea that he was against his son's expansion plans seems unlikely given his behind-the-scenes role after the sale, not to mention the fact that before the sale he'd expanded into other territories himself, running shows in Los Angeles and elsewhere, and raiding Georgia Championship Wrestling. But those who were there during that period note there were disagreements between father and son. While WWE history paints McMahon Sr. as a grandfatherly figure, the truth is that many of his biggest stars over the years, including Sammartino, found evidence that he'd cheated them on payoffs or percentages, lied about the financial state of the company to get them to do him favors, and politically maneuvered based on his own self-interests. He was a cutthroat wrestling promoter like any other.

McMahon Sr. died on May 24, 1984, at the age of 69 after a battle with pancreatic cancer.

9 Nitro Debuts Against RAW

The very first *Nitro* aired on September 4, 1995, from the Mall of America in Minneapolis, Minnesota. The show was broadcast on TBS in the *Monday Night RAW* time slot on a night that *RAW* was preempted by the Westminster Dog Show.

It was, if nothing else, an exciting show. They crammed three matches into the one-hour show, took shots directly at WWF, surprised the wrestling world with the debut of Lex Luger (who had wrestled on a WWF house show the night before), and promised a major championship match the following week, something almost unheard-of on your average weekly pro wrestling telecast in 1995.

Eric Bischoff, Bobby Heenan, and former Chicago Bear (and future Four Horseman member) Steve "Mongo" McMichael did commentary. Bischoff was all right, Heenan was all right, and Mongo was absolutely horrible. Bischoff spent most of the show taking shots at WWF, but those shots were only the beginning of his crusade against Vince McMahon; he'd soon be giving away the results of matches on the taped *RAW* shows. Mongo didn't seem to have any idea what was going on and added nothing to the show.

Brian Pillman and Jushin Liger had been a classic rivalry years earlier. Their match on the first *Nitro* was hardly noteworthy and somewhat sloppy, but it did set the tone for the show, telling the world that this wasn't the land of the slow-moving dinosaurs but rather a place where smaller, athletic men were going to be providing great matches on a weekly basis. Sting vs. Ric Flair was designed to be a ratings-drawing match, since they were the two biggest stars of the NWA/WCW era up to that point in time, their rivalry moving into its seventh year. And Hulk Hogan vs. Big Bubba was a rematch from a feud that had drawn big money in the WWF in the 1980s. Hogan wrestling on free TV in 1995 was a huge deal, and it led to *Nitro* debuting with a strong 2.5 rating.

There were some big angles on the show, some obviously better than others. Scott Norton appeared to set up a match with Randy Savage for the following week. They announced that Sabu, a star from ECW, would be debuting soon. Mike Rotundo, the former IRS in WWF, was announced as returning as Michael Wallstreet. And, of course, Luger debuted.

The Luger jump was notable not only because he'd worked for WWF the night before, but also because it got people talking about who else might be thinking of jumping ship to WCW. Luger and WWF hadn't agreed to terms for a new contract and Luger told his longtime friend Sting that he was interested in coming back to WCW. Sting contacted Bischoff, who wasn't a big fan of Luger's but saw the potential in raiding him for a major surprise appearance. Luger walked out on camera to watch the Sting vs. Flair match, which was a huge shocker to even wrestlers backstage at *Nitro*. Later, after the main event, he got into the ring and had a staredown with Hogan, who he'd never had a match with in his career. Instead of saving the first meeting for PPV, it was announced that the two would square off the following week for free on *Nitro*. (Hogan won the match via disqualification.)

Week two was the first where *RAW* and *Nitro* actually went head-to-head. The concern by most that the two shows would merely split the *RAW* audience proved unfounded. Instead, a new audience emerged, which led to *Nitro* beating WWF's flagship Monday night show in the ratings (2.5 to 2.2).

Nitro's debut was considered a big success. Despite misgivings about how the company might drive off fans if they used more non-finishes like they did in the Sting vs. Flair match (no-contest when Arn Anderson ran in), the big stars, marquee matches, high-flying action, and the overall unpredictable live aspect of the show more than trumped match finishes. It took years of DQ finish after DQ finish before they finally started running off fans, and quite frankly, there were far bigger problems at that time than non-finishes. The Monday Night Wars were off to the races, and they changed the wrestling landscape forever.

10 Stone Cold Steve Austin

Stone Cold Steve Austin was the biggest WWF star of the 1990s, and the biggest short-term draw in the history of pro wrestling. His feud with Vince McMahon turned WWF business around to the degree that it went from a money-losing company to putting such a beating on World Championship Wrestling that the latter ultimately went out of business (although, to be fair, WCW was responsible for a good portion of that misfortune).

Everyone knows the general story. Austin was a great worker who never got his due in WCW and jumped ship to WWF, where he was initially pushed as the Ringmaster. The gimmick was death. Then, one day, he cut a promo on Jake "The Snake" Roberts after beating him at King of the Ring, and he rocketed to superstardom.

Except that's not exactly what happened.

The "Austin 3:16" story is one of those things that people in wrestling seem to vividly remember, but, like the Mandela Effect spelling of the Berenstain Bears (look it up), the reality is different.

The date was June 23, 1996. Austin beat Marc Mero early in the show to advance to the King of the Ring finals. The other half of the main event was, of all people, Jake "The Snake" Roberts, who beat Vader in the semis but was then squished afterward. He was selling a rib injury, and WWF president Gorilla Monsoon offered the injured Roberts the opportunity to forfeit. Jake refused. Austin targeted the ribs, hit the Stunner, and pinned him in under five minutes. Austin then cut his famous promo.

Austin didn't come out on *RAW* the next night as the hottest star in the business. In fact, he was no more over the day after that famous line than he was going in. There was maybe an Austin 3:16 sign or two in the crowd, but nothing much changed for a few months. What really burst him into the main event scene was challenging and then feuding with the returning Bret Hart starting in the fall of 1996.

Austin's catchphrase really became famous upon the marketing of the black-and-white Austin 3:16 T-shirt, which went on to become the hottest-selling T-shirt in the history of pro wrestling, grossing millions of dollars per year.

Austin was so hot by the spring of 1997 that the company pulled the trigger on a babyface turn, which occurred at WrestleMania 13 when Bret beat Austin in their famous "I Quit" match. Austin, absolutely covered in blood, was trapped in Bret's sharpshooter and refused to quit. He passed out from pain and lost the match, after which Hart refused to release the hold. In that one moment, Austin went babyface and Hart went heel, leading to one of the hottest periods creatively in company history, the summer of 1997, with the U.S. vs. Canada feud revolving around Hart, Shawn Michaels, and the Undertaker.

Austin was the recipient of both good and bad luck in his rise to the top. Originally, Triple H was going to win the King of the Ring tournament that started the ball rolling on his superstardom, but in the wake of the infamous Madison Square Garden "curtain call" incident, Hunter was punished, and Austin took his spot. WrestleMania 13 was supposed to be Hart vs. Michaels, but Michaels famously "lost his smile" and went home, allowing Austin to compete in what became one of the most famous matches of his career.

Unfortunately, at SummerSlam 1997, bad luck struck when Austin's head was too low on an Owen Hart piledriver and he suffered a broken neck and partial paralysis. Ultimately, the injury not only shortened his career but guaranteed that after he retired, he was never coming back.

But even the dark cloud of his neck injury had a silver lining. Because he couldn't wrestle, the company had to find about a thousand different creative ways to get him on TV every week in a non-wrestling role, segments that he shined in, and which got him over much bigger than if he'd just been out there wrestling matches every week.

Austin beat Michaels at WrestleMania XIV in 1998 to become the face of the company. It led to the hottest period of business in company history, all built around Austin's feud with evil heel owner Vince McMahon. His title win was what finally broke *Nitro*'s 83-week winning streak. *Nitro* won a handful of times after that, but only up until November, at which point WWF was so hot and WCW was collapsing so badly that *Nitro* never won another Monday in the ratings again.

Unfortunately, Austin's neck issues worsened, and they finally had to write him off the show in November of 1999 to get neck surgery. He'd built the company up to such a degree that even without him it continued to ride the wave of success. Despite the neck surgery, Austin was diagnosed with spinal stenosis (narrowing of the spinal canal), something he'd likely been born with, and it was clear that his career was in its final years.

Still, despite being told it would be in his best interests to retire, he continued on. The biggest turning point in his career since he

Stone Cold Steve Austin, after defeating Scott Hall at WrestleMania X8.
(Getty Images)

hit it big in 1997 occurred on April 1, 2001, at WrestleMania X-Seven. McMahon and Austin took a gamble. Sometimes gambles pay off; this one did not. The decision was made for Austin to turn heel and align himself with his most hated rival, the dastardly Mr. McMahon.

Austin as a heel was a critical success and a business disaster. He was an awesome heel, he was super entertaining, and he loved doing it. Problem is, business collapsed. To be fair, it wasn't entirely the fault of him turning heel, as the business was inevitably going to suffer to a degree with both ECW and WCW going out of business. But WCW's death in particular resulted in the loss of several million fans who were never going to switch to WWF programming; they were WCW/NWA fans and they watched through the

Stone Cold Steve Austin's 3:16 Promo

Directed to Jake "The Snake" Roberts, as told to interviewer Dok Hendrix [Michael Hayes]

"The first thing I want to be done is to get that piece of crap out of my ring. Don't just get him out of the ring, get him out of the WWF. Because I proved, son, without a shadow of a doubt, you ain't got what it takes anymore. You sit there and you thump your Bible and you say your prayers, and it didn't get you anywhere. Talk about your psalms, talk about John 3:16—Austin 3:16 says I just whipped your ass. All he's got to do is go buy him a cheap bottle of Thunderbird and try to get back some of that courage he had in his prime.

"As the King of the Ring, I'm serving notice to every one of the WWF superstars. I don't give a damn what they are, they're all on the list, and that's Stone Cold's list, and I'm fixin' to start running through all of them.

"As far as this championship match is considered, son, I don't give a damn if it's Davey Boy Smith or Shawn Michaels, Steve Austin's time has come, and when I get the shot you're looking at the next WWF champion. And that's the bottom line, because Stone Cold said so."

bitter end, and when WCW died that was the end of pro wrestling in their lives. What Austin's heel turn did was run off a sizeable percentage of fans who had started watching in the Attitude Era, who loved Stone Cold, who believed in him, who knew it was all phony but wanted to believe that, if nothing else, Austin and Vince really hated each other. When Austin turned and joined up with Vince, they checked out and moved on to something new.

Austin retired on March 30, 2003, at WrestleMania XIX in Seattle. Following his 1999 neck fusion surgery, he returned and felt great, but after two more years of hard action he was told in no uncertain terms that he needed to retire. Doctors said that one bad bump could leave him in a wheelchair, or worse. It was known heading into that WrestleMania that it was almost certainly going to be his last match, but because it's wrestling they didn't even bother announcing that or playing it up.

Austin was under immense stress, worried about his neck and also concerned that he wouldn't be able to deliver in what was probably his final match. He guzzled a full pot of coffee and one energy drink after another to the point where his heart began racing and his blood pressure went through the roof. He got on the phone and called for help, legitimately fearing he was having a heart attack, and was rushed to the hospital. Eventually, he got some food inside him and his body began to normalize. The doctors didn't want him wrestling the next day, but this was 2003, long before there was anything resembling WWE's current wellness policy, and so he went out there, was carried to an excellent final match by the Rock, and that was the end of his career.

Austin stays busy nowadays with a popular podcast. He appears sporadically for WWE, and given he's never stopped working out and was bald and goateed during his career, he always looks the same. For years there have been rumors of one more match, but he's always been adamant that he's never coming back. He remains one of the biggest stars in WWE history, an all-time legend.

John Cena

John Cena was the face of WWE for over a decade following on the heels of Stone Cold Steve Austin and the Rock. He was also one of the most controversial stars in WWE history, the biggest name in a company that had fallen greatly in popularity since the end of the Monday Night Wars, and often a scapegoat blamed for various company ills.

Cena began training in the late 1990s under Rick Bassman in Los Angeles. Ultimate Pro Wrestling, Bassman's promotion, was something of a feeder system for WWF developmental for a few years, and Cena, a freakishly shredded bodybuilder right up Vince McMahon's alley, was signed in 2001 and sent to Ohio Valley Wrestling. He was pushed right out of the gate before being called up to the main roster in June of 2002. He debuted on June 27 when he accepted an open challenge from Kurt Angle. It was a last-minute substitution, as Angle was scheduled to face the Undertaker, but the Undertaker had the flu. Someone suggested they debut Cena, McMahon agreed (provided the kid cut his hair), and Angle did a Ric Flair–level job of trying to create a star in one night before pinning him with a double chicken wing. Cena got over big with the crowd and was congratulated by several wrestlers backstage, including the toughest critic of all, the Undertaker.

Although the angle seemed like the beginning of a decade-long push, the reality is that outside of that match, Cena really didn't connect with the crowd or show any real indications that he could be the top guy. Besides his physique, his defining characteristic was that he owned more than 100 pairs of tights and nearly 100 pairs of boots and would color match them to the sports team in whatever city he wrestled in. He was working his way toward the chopping

John Cena has been the face of the WWE since the mid-2000s.

block, and there was a very good chance that he might be cut, when Stephanie McMahon and several other members of the creative team heard him in a rap battle on a tour bus in 2002. Nobody at the time thought it would lead him to massive success, but they all saw something in it and opted to give him a chance with a new character, the Doctor of Thuganomics. His career turned around as a heel white rapper, and it was the rocket that blasted him to superstardom.

His heel run lasted about a year, and in October of 2003 he turned babyface. Throughout his career he has been, to many fans, the most hated guy on the roster, yet he never officially turned heel again. While WWF babyface champions had been booed at various times in the past by pockets of fans, no babyface in company history ever got booed so hard for so long, and really, it's one of the main things, perhaps the most notable thing, that defined his time on top.

Fans have come up with a million reasons why he was booed, including the idea that people hated the white rapper gimmick. In reality, he was cheered as a white rapper for well over a year. If you look at the timeline, it was a perfect storm of events that led to him first getting booed. It all started around WrestleMania 21. He beat JBL at WrestleMania and won the world heavyweight title for the first time in his career. This probably sounds stupid, and maybe it's irrelevant, but WWE's target demographic at the time had grown up with the WWF Winged Eagle belt as the top prize. The company ditched the belt in 1998 and introduced a series of different designs from that point forward, all in an attempt to make merchandise money off toys and replicas. Cena won the title and two weeks later debuted the infamous "spinner" belt. It was a WWE championship belt all blinged out with a logo that spun. It was a monstrosity. Whether you were still bitter over the Winged Eagle or not, hardcore fans *hated* this belt.

Title aside, Cena was then drafted to *RAW*. In the buildup to WrestleMania and then following his jump to *RAW*, Cena ran through everyone. A segment of the audience became disgruntled by the company shoving this guy down their throats. Worse, while it would be unfair to say he flat-out sucked, he really wasn't a great worker; he was clumsy and sloppy at times, and he was being pushed as the top guy at a time when some of the best wrestlers in the world, guys like Eddie Guerrero, Chris Benoit, Chris Jericho, and Rey Mysterio, were either not being pushed, or worse, were not being pushed *and* being beaten by this John Cena character. The boos slowly intensified and WWE doubled down, pushing him even harder. The fans, in turn, revolted harder, and it led to a situation where he was booed for so long that booing John Cena became a gimmick, and fans would boo him for years, ultimately not even remembering why they were booing him in the first place.

In another era, WWE would have turned him heel. But things were different. It was now a publicly traded company making tons of money with several hundred million in cash on hand, and it didn't matter whether John Cena was booed or not. Despite the boos he was still the top merchandise seller, the top draw, the top ratings mover, the guy who made more of a positive difference for business than anyone else. So, he never turned.

His story week-by-week, month-by-month, and year-by-year is one for another day, another book. His legacy in the ring is that, in storyline, he won some version of the world championship 16 times, tying the made-up record first set by Ric Flair. Behind the scenes, he carried the company through a very rough period—the aftermath of the Monday Night Wars, when millions of fans had given up on pro wrestling and moved on to different passions in their lives. Cena set business records, most notably two WrestleMania matches with the Rock, the first of which helped gross $67 million and set the record for the most successful pro wrestling event in history; the second broke the record and helped gross $72 million. Because the following year's WrestleMania was the first on the WWE Network, which ultimately led to a predictable collapse of WWE PPV business, it is unthinkable that those records will ever be broken in our lifetimes.

Cena began to wind down his full-time career in 2017. Whether it is because of his absence or other factors, WWE ratings fell to near-historic lows. House show business was absolutely affected by his departure, and in the summer and fall of 2018 WWE actually *lost* money promoting house shows, something previously considered virtually impossible. Worse, his hand-picked successor, Roman Reigns, left to battle a recurrence of leukemia.

For all the talk over the years that without Cena, someone else would surely step up and take over his role as the top star, it has yet to happen. Ironically, WWE, because of newly signed lucrative television deals, is at its most profitable point in history, yet at the same time for probably the first time ever, has no male face of the company. The next chapter in pro wrestling history will be written by whoever can fill Cena's enormous shoes.

12 Macho Man Randy Savage

Macho Man Randy Savage was one of the most famous characters in the history of wrestling. With his gravelly voice, outlandish fashion sense, and larger-than-life personality both in the ring and out, he was a guy who, when he died in 2011, got a ridiculous amount of global mainstream press, largely due to so many writers and editors around the world having grown up with him as one of the key figures in the 1980s wrestling boom.

In the ring, he was one half of the greatest year-long storyline that the WWF ever booked. It started at WrestleMania III when Hulk Hogan beat Andre the Giant to retain the WWF title. A rematch was signed for *The Main Event*, an NBC special on February 5, 1988. During the match, Andre made the cover and Hogan kicked out. But the referee, alleged to be Dave Hebner, called for the bell and awarded the championship to Andre in a massive screwjob. In real life, Dave had a twin brother, Earl Hebner, who worked for Jim Crockett Promotions. WWF hired him, and the storyline of the match was that Andre's manager, Ted DiBiase, had hired some man to get plastic surgery so he could look exactly like Dave Hebner, and then paid him off to screw Hogan in the match. (It would not be the last screwjob of Earl's career.) Anyway, Andre, the new champion, then announced that he was selling the belt to DiBiase (he actually screwed up and said he was selling the tag titles). It was ruled by WWF president Jack Tunney that no one is allowed to sell the WWF title, so the championship was declared vacant. The show did a massive 33 million viewers on NBC, a number never approached before or since.

On the undercard, Randy Savage beat Intercontinental champion the Honky Tonk Man via DQ. Savage was supposed to win the title on the show, but Honky refused to do the job. In the end, it led to one of the more monumental changes in company history.

With the title held up, a tournament was scheduled for WrestleMania IV. The original plan was for DiBiase to win the tournament and the championship, which he would then drop to Hogan when Hogan was done filming the movie *No Holds Barred*. Savage would remain the No. 2 guy in the promotion as the Intercontinental champion. But since Honky refused to job, they changed the plans, and Savage was booked to win the tournament. (It was the second time in DiBiase's career that he was earmarked to become world champion but then didn't, the first being in the NWA in the early 1980s.)

Savage won the tournament, beating DiBiase in the finals after Hogan whacked DiBiase with a chair behind the referee's back. After the match, Hogan celebrated with Savage and lifted Savage's valet, the beautiful Miss Elizabeth, up onto his shoulders. The very subtle storyline was that in Savage's crowning moment, his best friend Hogan was busy touching his girl.

Hogan left to film his movie and Savage did great business feuding with DiBiase throughout the spring. At SummerSlam that year, Hogan and Savage, who were known as the Mega Powers when they teamed up, faced DiBiase and Andre in the main event. The heels had the upper hand when Elizabeth, who *never* showed skin, jumped up on the apron, yanked off her skirt, and revealed her bikini bottoms. The heels were completely distracted, leading to Savage and Hogan making a comeback and getting the win. Hogan then grabbed Elizabeth, still in her bikini bottoms, and hugged her just a little bit too long, and Savage, oh so briefly, shot him an evil glare.

The big breakup took place on February 3, 1989, on an NBC special that drew the second-largest audience of all time, 21 million viewers. It was Hogan and Savage vs. Akeem and the Big Boss Man. During the match, Akeem was sent outside and wiped out Elizabeth, who never got physically involved in matches. The storyline was that Hogan saw it happen but Savage, who was being beaten on in the ring, did not. Hogan grabbed Elizabeth and carried her backstage to the medical area. This part of the angle was hilariously campy and overacted, as Hogan was begging the doctor to not let Liz die. Meanwhile, the heels were double-teaming Savage. Liz finally woke up and told Hogan to help Randy. Hogan ran back down to the ring but Savage, who didn't know any of this happened, thought Hogan had abandoned him. He slapped Hogan and walked out on him. Hogan, alone, made a one-man comeback; pinned Akeem; handcuffed the Boss Man to his manager, Slick; and rushed backstage.

Macho Man Randy Savage was one of the most famous characters of the 1980s wrestling boom.

Hogan and Savage had a massive confrontation which involved Savage going berserk, screaming at Hogan that he was lusting after Elizabeth. He waffled Hogan from behind with the title belt, and as Liz bent down to check on Hogan, Savage told her that if she didn't get up he'd splatter her all over the floor as well. Elizabeth was coming off her absolute peak of popularity that summer, and Savage's line sent him over the top into becoming just about the biggest heel in wrestling history.

The Mega Powers exploded and squared off at WrestleMania V, where Hogan beat Savage to win the title. The show did the biggest wrestling gate up to that point in history, $1.6 million (keep in mind, in the entire history of WCW, even at its peak in 1997 and 1998, it never broke a $1 million gate even a single time) and 760,000 buys, the all-time record that stood until WWF's peak year of the Monday Night Wars in 2000.

Macho Man Randy Savage's WrestleMania V Promo:

"Hulk Hogan, yeah, you say you don't know where the Macho Man is coming from? Yeah, you're right, you don't know anything about the Macho Man Randy Savage and where I'm coming from. Because it's mind-boggling to you, yeah! How one man could make it to the top of the World Wrestling Federation mountain, yeah! All by myself, no Pukesters helping me to the left, and no Pukesters helping me to the right. Didn't need 'em then, don't need 'em now! And another person I don't need is Elizabeth either, yeah. Cuz I'm a champion by myself, all by myself.

"You don't know where I'm coming from, Hulk Hogan, this Sunday afternoon, but I know where you're coming from, yeah. I know everything about Hulk Hogan, yeah! I know what makes you tick, yeah. And you got the audacity, yeah, to say that in WrestleMania V, that Hulkamania is gonna survive. You don't know me, Hulk Hogan, you don't know where I'm coming from. After I beat you with that big elbow, and pin you 1-2-3, guaranteed victory! I'm going to tell you and all the Pukesters out there one last time before this Sunday afternoon: Hulkamania is dead!"

While he was involved in dozens of memorable moments both before and after, WrestleMania V was the absolute apex of Savage's career. His most famous moments outside of that include the angle where he tried to end Ricky Steamboat's career with a ring bell to the larynx on November 22, 1986 (a moment many fans of that generation remember was what first got them into pro wrestling); his famous match with Steamboat at WrestleMania III, remembered for years as the greatest match in WrestleMania history; his "retirement" following a classic match with the Ultimate Warrior at WrestleMania VII, followed by his reuniting with Elizabeth and subsequent marriage proposal (they had been married for more than seven years, and ironically divorced shortly after the storyline wedding); and, of course, the famous post-SummerSlam TV angle in 1991 where Savage was attacked by Jake the Snake and a live King cobra, which went into business for itself and gnawed on Savage's arm in one of the more famously gruesome moments in company history.

By 1993, McMahon thought Savage was getting too old and phased him out of the ring and into a commentator spot. His contract expired in October of 1994 and he chose to jump ship to WCW. Hogan—another guy McMahon felt was too old—had just signed and there was a legion of teenagers and 20-somethings who grew up in the 1980s and were ready for a trip down memory lane. They became WCW's hottest audience. Savage's feud with Ric Flair did great house show business and was the first legitimate sign, outside of Hogan's PPV numbers, that Eric Bischoff was on the right track with his acquisitions. Savage remained with the company until it closed down in 2001 but was used more and more sparingly as the years went on. He made one final return to wrestling, with TNA in 2004 and 2005, but never wanted to be the guy who fans saw as old and broken down, so he left, went into hiding, and only made the very occasional public appearance afterward.

On May 20, 2011, he was driving his 2009 Jeep Wrangler around Seminole, Florida, with his wife, Barbara. He suffered a massive heart attack, lost control of the vehicle, and crashed into a tree. He was rushed to the hospital, where he passed away shortly thereafter. He was 58 years old.

13 Subscribe to the WWE Network

I've noticed a phenomenon over the past several years during my work as host of *Wrestling Observer Live* on the Sports Byline USA Radio Network (www.sportsbyline.com): there are a lot of fans who no longer watch *RAW* or *SmackDown*, WWE's top two traditional television shows, but who happily subscribe month after month to the WWE Network.

It's hard to gauge a real number. The number of people who watch *RAW* and *SmackDown* every week is a fraction of what it was a decade ago, although TV wrestling numbers have declined at a slower rate than television viewership as a whole, which is how WWE logged record-low numbers and still signed a $2.3 billion television deal in 2018. WWE Network averages around 1.6 million subscribers, only a bit lower than the average number of people who watch *SmackDown* every week. Obviously not every television viewer has the WWE Network; it would seem that a sizeable percentage of the WWE Network's subscription base are lapsed fans who still feel enough of a connection to wrestling to pay $9.99 per month for the Network's basic package.

If for whatever reason I never needed to work again, I'd still subscribe to the WWE Network even if I never watched *RAW* and *SmackDown* again. The Network is an incredible value. As a subscriber, you get access to every new and past WWE PPV event, shows that used to cost up to $44.95 each on pay-per-view. You get various weekly television shows from brands such as NXT and NXT UK. You can sit down week-to-week and watch the entire run of *RAW* and *Nitro* during the Attitude Era. Every *RAW* ever is up there. Every *SmackDown* ever. Every NXT show, every PPV, years' worth of non-WWE archived material from dozens of territories including Jim Crockett Promotions, World Class, the AWA, and more. And unlike when people like me were kids, you don't need a closet filled floor to ceiling with old VHS tapes of shows you can't even watch because nobody has a VCR player anymore. Virtually everything you could ever want to include in an old-school tape collection is available for $9.99 on the Network, viewable on your computer, phone, iPad, Apple TV, Roku, etc., pretty much anywhere you go in the world.

What an advertisement I just wrote. I'm somewhat biased, but the two absolute best values in all of pro wrestling are subscriptions to wrestlingobserver.com and the WWE Network. If you have both, you're absolutely covered.

The WWE Network launched in 2014. Prior to that, WWE had provided a channel you could order through your cable company called WWE 24/7 Classics on Demand, which provided approximately 20 to 40 hours of largely random archived content every month. Originally, the idea was to try to get an actual television deal, where, like the NFL Network, viewers could tune into the channel via their existing cable TV packages. After years of trying and failing to secure a deal, it became clear that if the WWE Network was ever going to launch, they'd have to go a different route.

In 2014, the new WWE Network was launched through an association with MLB Advanced Media (later BamTech). For better or worse, one thing you can say about Vince McMahon is that he's largely an all-or-nothing kind of guy. Most everyone figured that the best course of action would be for WWE to offer eight PPVs per year on the Network and keep the big four—SummerSlam, Survivor Series, Royal Rumble, and WrestleMania—as pay-per-view offerings. The numbers would seem to bear that out. For example, UFC launched its own version of the WWE Network, UFC Fight Pass, and didn't put any of its PPVs on there, and while it has about a million fewer subscribers, the money it grosses on PPVs dwarfs the revenue WWE makes by putting all of their PPVs on the WWE Network for a $9.99 monthly fee. But McMahon didn't want to go halfway, and he wanted to do huge Network numbers immediately. So, he announced every PPV, including WrestleMania, would be available on the Network for one low monthly fee.

The good news is they immediately jumped from 0 to 667,000 subscribers. The bad news is they effectively killed their PPV business (although, to this day, they still do about 20,000 traditional PPV buys per month, which means there are 20,000 people who either cannot get the Network for Internet-related reasons, or are unwilling to watch wrestling on anything other than their cable-equipped television). They also saw their stock cut in half as investors saw 667,000 subscribers as a disappointment. WWE then began offering numerous free trials, and over the next few years gradually built the subscriber base up to where it likely will remain for the foreseeable future. Of course, based on the early 50 percent stock drop, McMahon is so concerned about numbers dropping that WWE continues to offer a ridiculous number of free offers. We get reports weekly from fans who quit their subscription but still had full Network access, or fans who quit and then got free one- or three-month offers, and then continued to get free offers every time they quit. Some claim to have not actually paid for the Network in years due to how many free offers they've been given. If you examine WWE's earnings report you can see that Network subscribers grow at a faster pace than its revenue increases, meaning more and more people are using free offers to watch.

Business aside, the WWE Network is a dream come true for wrestling fans. It's a virtual library of a lifetime of wrestling content, new and old, available anytime, anywhere, for practically nothing. As long as it exists it'll remain a lifeline to wrestling fans who might have given up the ghost otherwise.

Andre the Giant

There are a lot of larger-than-life myths surrounding André René Roussimoff, aka Andre the Giant, but there are also many larger-than-life truths.

Andre was not really 7-foot-4, and he didn't really have a grandfather who was 7-foot-8. He didn't really draw 93,000 fans to the Pontiac Silverdome for his WrestleMania III match with Hulk Hogan, and he wasn't discovered lumbering out of the woods to help move a giant tree which had blocked the road in front of Canadian wrestler Edouard Carpentier's car.

But he really was a giant. Although at his peak he was probably about 6-foot-9, he suffered from acromegaly, or gigantism, and thus his head, hands, and other extremities were freakishly large. With his proportions, he really was one of the strongest and most intimidating men in the world. If he liked you, he'd give you a lot in a match. If he didn't like you, he wouldn't give you anything, and until later on in life, nobody could do anything about it. His closest friends claim that the wild stories of his drinking prowess—bottle of wine after bottle of wine after bottle of wine—were absolutely not exaggerated. And while the WrestleMania III attendance is a made-up number, his most famous match with Hulk Hogan on March 29, 1987, drew WWF's largest attendance ever up to that point, the first-ever $1 million-plus gate, and their rematch on NBC set a viewership record of an astounding 33 million fans, a number that with the changes in television will never be topped.

The famous Hogan match took place at the tail end of Andre's career, although stories that he was near death and completely immobile were obviously exaggerated given he wrestled for years afterward. His began his career in the mid-1960s as Andre "The Butcher" Roussimoff, and later as Jean Ferre, Geant Ferre (both a reference to a French folk hero), and Monster Roussimoff, before finally settling on the name that brought him his enduring fame, Andre the Giant. By the mid-1970s, Andre was not only among the most famous wrestlers in the world, but also among the most famous and highly paid mainstream athletes. And he *was* an athlete; although most remember the virtually immobile Andre of the late 1980s, in his youth Andre could move around great and even threw high dropkicks and other athletic wrestling maneuvers. He got the kind of publicity no other wrestler got, appearing on *The Tonight Show*, playing Bigfoot on the *The Six Million Dollar Man*, and later, in his most famous and critically acclaimed role, taking the role of Fezzik in the cult classic, *The Princess Bride*.

In the ring he was a special attraction who would stay in territories for short periods of time before moving on to another, so as never to burn out the crowds or hurt his monstrous aura. Andre's acromegaly gave him a look and physique that enabled him to make millions and millions of dollars and live the life of a global superstar. But it also destroyed his body and led him to an early grave. Andre knew this; from the moment he became a star he lived fast, spent a lot of money, partied with friends and women, and lived life to the fullest.

The story told going into WrestleMania III was that Andre had never lost, which was the kind of storyline you could do in the mid-1980s before the Internet came along. In fact, not only was Andre not undefeated, but he'd already been body slammed by Hulk Hogan himself seven years earlier at the Showdown at Shea event. But the WWF was all about revisionist history, and the claim was that Andre had never been defeated, could not be taken off his feet, and the end of Hulkamania would be upon us after he turned on his longtime best friend Hogan to set up the match.

Hogan pinned Andre after a body slam and the Legdrop of Doom in one of the most iconic moments in wrestling history, a moment embedded in WWE's opening montages to this day. It was the last great hurrah in Andre's career, although he did continue to wrestle for the company through 1992.

Andre's father, Boris, passed away on January 15, 1993. Andre had flown home to France two days earlier to be with him. Two weeks later, on January 27, his chauffeur called to pick him up. Andre never answered the phone. He had died in his sleep of heart failure at the age of 46.

The Undertaker

The Undertaker, real name Mark Calaway, will forever be remembered as the greatest gimmick in the history of pro wrestling.

What is amazing about the character is that it's preposterous, and there is a very good chance that had it been given to anyone else, it would be completely forgotten at this point outside of readers of WrestleCrap.com. The gimmick is that he is a dead guy who can perform magic and takes the souls of wrestlers he beats, leaving them to rest in peace. Or something like that.

When you think of the hog farmers and IRS agents and Mantaurs and race car drivers and all of the other stupid gimmicks that died a quick death (so to speak), it really is incredible that a guy named "The Undertaker" became not only a success but the most successful gimmick of all, and that he was a legitimate company main-eventer for almost 30 straight years.

The Undertaker is most famous for his legendary WrestleMania streak, something that will never be equaled no matter how long there is a WWE. It was never intended to be what it was. He beat Jimmy Snuka at WrestleMania VII, his first. The next year, he beat Jake Roberts. The year after that, Giant Gonzalez. Years went by and nobody thought twice about it. At first, the only reason he won was because, well, they decided he was the guy who should win that day. It was years—1997, to be exact—before someone finally noticed that, hey, the Undertaker has never been beaten at a WrestleMania. It would be another seven years before someone explicitly challenged the Undertaker to a WrestleMania match with the sole purpose of ending the streak.

The streak is among the most controversial concepts in WWE history because of the legend of the Undertaker character. Over the years it was hotly debated whether the streak should ever end. One camp believed that the Undertaker's entire legacy should be as the man who was never beaten at a WrestleMania. Another camp—a camp, as it turns out, that Vince McMahon, the only guy who really matters, was in—was that when the time came for the Undertaker to retire, he should put someone over at WrestleMania.

And that's exactly what happened, on April 6, 2014, at WrestleMania XXX in New Orleans.

I was there.

The match was the Undertaker vs. Brock Lesnar. They built it up big on TV, but nobody believed Lesnar had any chance of

The Undertaker possessed the greatest gimmick and perhaps the most memorable entrance in wrestling.

winning. The Undertaker had beaten everyone. The feeling was, if the Undertaker's streak was going to end, it would be the culmination of a massive, historic feud, or it would be at the hands of a young superstar who needed the win to push him over the edge into Steve Austin/the Rock/John Cena territory. Not 36-year-old Brock Lesnar, a WWE and UFC megastar who absolutely didn't need the win. The Undertaker was the odds-on favorite, even with the smart money having come in (yes, you can bet on WWE outcomes, and for years the odds would swing right before the PPVs as members of the WWE staff would all of a sudden make bets since they knew the finishes).

Early on in the show, I got a text. It just said something to the effect of, "Check Taker's odds." I didn't think much of it and never texted or heard anything further.

During the match, Lesnar hit his finisher, an F-5. I thought nothing of it. The audience didn't either, as the Undertaker predictably kicking out was met with silence. The Undertaker always kicked out of everyone's finishers at WrestleMania. Brock hit another one, and the Undertaker kicked out. Thought nothing of it. Truth be told, as the match approached 25 minutes, I was bored. The match wasn't very exciting, partly because the Undertaker had gotten knocked out early and worked the rest of the match on fumes. Brock hit a third F-5. The Undertaker kicked out. Or so I thought.

But then, everyone around me was either screaming or standing in stunned silence. At first, I had no idea what was going on. I don't remember hearing a bell or anything. It took another few seconds for it to hit me. Eventually, Brock's music began to play. He had ended the streak. It was, by far, the most incredible moment I've ever experienced at a live WWE event.

Later, I watched the finish again on the WWE Network, and Lesnar had pinned him clean in the middle and the Undertaker had not kicked out. It wasn't a screw-up, it wasn't a botch. It was the plan. And in the ensuing years I've talked to other people who were there who also vividly remember the Undertaker kicking out of that third F-5. It's fascinating how the brain works. The idea of him getting beaten at WrestleMania was so inconceivable to me that my brain imagined him kicking out when he did not.

Apparently, that afternoon, McMahon saw the Undertaker at the building, observed that he wasn't moving around all that well, decided that this was probably his last WrestleMania, and made the call for the streak to end. Virtually nobody was told, including the referee, Chad Patton, who went into the ring with the belief that the Undertaker was going to win, and who was as stunned as everyone else when the Undertaker didn't kick out, and he was forced to do what he'd been trained to do—officiate the match as if it was real. He counted the pin. The Undertaker wasn't happy, but he was a company man and he did it. And Lesnar became a legend, the man who broke the streak, perhaps the most famous finish in company history behind the night that Ivan Koloff ended Bruno Sammartino's title reign on January 18, 1971.

Although Lesnar didn't need the win, McMahon tried to use the finish to build up Roman Reigns. He needed a replacement for John Cena, and Reigns was his choice. Reigns was going to beat the man who ended the streak at WrestleMania, putting him over the top as the new face of the company. But for myriad reasons, it took four years before that finally happened, and then, two months after his ultimate coronation, Reigns was diagnosed with leukemia and had to forfeit the WWE championship.

In the late 1990s, the Undertaker transitioned from a dead man to a living, breathing, "American Badass" biker character (still called "The Undertaker," however). I'm sure many people figured, well, it's the Attitude Era, it's a more gritty, realistic product, a dead man who does magic certainly has a shelf life. But the American Badass character never got over to the level that the dead man did, and in 2004 the original character returned in all its glory. His entrance, with the music and the fire and the darkness, is the most famous entrance in the history of wrestling, and he was so respected both in front of and behind the cameras that he was able to ride the gimmick successfully throughout the 2010s. His final few years in the ring were not the best, as he was racked with injuries and needed hip replacement surgery. Many fans felt he should have retired years earlier. But no matter what they thought of his work, no matter what they believed he should have done with his career, to the very end, every time that music hit, they lost their minds and became children all over again.

Triple H

On *Wrestling Observer Live* in 1999, I joked that Triple H was the smartest man in wrestling. In storyline, he'd just married Stephanie McMahon, the boss' daughter. I knew that in real life, storyline romances (and breakups) often become real. Therefore, I joked, someday he'd be running WWF.

While he's not running WWE yet, Triple H, real name Paul Levesque, is believed to be the eventual successor to Vince McMahon, having married Stephanie in real life a few years after they hooked up in storyline. He's currently in charge of the NXT brand, which, while a money-loser, has a critically acclaimed television show, and in late 2018 ran a TakeOver event on Survivor Series weekend that drew more fans than the *RAW* taping two days later, which is incredible given that NXT airs on the WWE Network and *RAW* airs on the USA Network.

Levesque was a wrestling fan for as long as he can remember, and because he loved the larger-than-life superstars he saw on TV, he got into bodybuilding in his teens. At age 19 he won the Mr. Teenage New Hampshire contest. He was working as a manager at a Gold's Gym when he met WWF wrestler Ted Arcidi, who introduced him to Killer Kowalski. Kowalski ran a wrestling school in Malden, Massachusetts. Levesque started training in 1992 and was in the ring just a few months later. Because he was tall with a good physique and great hair, he was pushed right out of the gate, and within two years he was signed to World Championship Wrestling. He started out as Terror Risin' (get it?), the name he'd used on the indies, but later that year was given the name Jean-Paul Levesque; the character was a French snob. He mostly worked mid-card tag team matches.

In 1995 he jumped ship to WWF, where he was rechristened Hunter Hearst Helmsley. This time, he was a snob from Greenwich, Connecticut, the home of the McMahons. Because of his look he was given a good push, but never seemed to get over to the level they wanted. His first major setback occurred in 1996. He'd become close with a group of wrestlers who referred to themselves as "The Kliq," consisting of Shawn Michaels, Scott Hall, and Kevin Nash. At a Madison Square Garden house show on May 19, 1996, Michaels beat Nash to retain the WWF title. Hall and Nash had signed with WCW and this was their final appearance with the company. After the match, babyface Michaels and heel Nash hugged and called Hunter (a heel) and Hall (a babyface) into the ring for what became known as the infamous "curtain call." In 2019, the idea that this would be a scandal is preposterous, but in 1996, McMahon was furious. Hall and Nash were leaving, so he couldn't punish them. Michaels was WWF champion and a very volatile personality, so he wasn't about to punish him. That left Hunter. He was scheduled to win the King of the Ring tournament that June. He didn't, and as the scapegoat he was buried for months.

He finally started to get over in the summer of 1997 when he was paired up with Michaels, Chyna, and Rick Rude as the original version of the DX stable. It was in this role that his personality finally had a chance to shine. When Michaels went down with a back injury in the spring of 1998, Hunter took over as the leader of DX, and the build toward him being a top guy began.

It was a very special time in WWF history, with Stone Cold Steve Austin and the Rock as gigantic babyface superstars. Austin's main heel foil was McMahon, the promoter. In order to make the most of the feud, McMahon, in his 50s, began working occasional wrestling matches. But as amazing as the feud was, McMahon knew it had a shelf life and that he needed to build a new monster heel to feud with the Rock and Austin. Triple H was the choice. He was scheduled to win the title from Austin at the 1999 SummerSlam, but a perfect storm of issues changed the plans. First, Austin had been hurt shortly before SummerSlam and so, out of concern for his working ability, Mankind (Mick Foley) was added to the match to make it a three-way. Second, Jesse Ventura, who had just become the governor of Minnesota, didn't want to raise the hand of a heel when the match was over. It sounds beyond ridiculous today, but it's true. And third, word had gotten out that Hunter was going to win the title, so they decided to fool everyone. Mankind pinned Austin, and then the following night on *RAW*, Hunter beat Mankind to win the title.

It was a lame beginning to a title reign and really hurt Hunter's short-term momentum. Because he wasn't over to the level they wanted him to be, he really needed to have beaten Austin. While he got great heat during interviews on TV, nobody seemed to care about him when he actually wrestled, and he struggled until finally bursting through to the top level based on an amazing feud with Foley that led to Foley's first, very short-lived retirement from wrestling. Foley deserves as much credit as anyone for the work he did getting Hunter over as a top superstar. The company did great business in 2000 with Triple H as the top heel, feuding with the Rock during a period when Austin was out of action with a serious neck injury.

He was a made man from that point forward—well, at least beginning on November 29, 1999, and the live *RAW* on which he married Stephanie. In storyline, Test (Andrew Martin) and Stephanie were at the altar on *RAW* about to be married when the officiant offered anyone an opportunity to speak now or forever hold their peace. Hunter showed up and directed everyone to the big screen, where a video played of him marrying a drugged and unconscious Stephanie at a drive-thru marriage chapel in Las Vegas. He even suggested he raped her multiple times. It was a super edgy storyline, but the following month Stephanie turned heel, revealing that she hadn't been drugged after all, but rather had planned all of it with Hunter as revenge on her father.

In real life, Hunter was dating Chyna at the time. One day, Chyna found love letters from Stephanie in Hunter's bag. She was furious and complained to Vince. Unbeknownst to her, McMahon had given Stephanie his blessing to date Hunter, and that was the beginning of the end of Chyna's run in WWF. Hunter and Stephanie's storyline marriage led to them falling in love, and on October 25, 2003, they were married in real life.

In the 2010s, Triple H wound down his wrestling career to concentrate more on his behind-the-scenes role as WWE's executive vice president of talent, live events, and creative. He took over the NXT developmental brand and built it up to the point that purely in terms of critical appeal, it was the hottest brand in the entire company. Financially, NXT has always been a money-loser, but the idea is that if it develops a superstar who becomes a main event draw on the main roster—a Roman Reigns, Braun Strowman, or Charlotte Flair, for example—that more than makes up for any annual losses. NXT TV is the most critically acclaimed of all WWE programming and the NXT TakeOver Network specials always get better reviews than the WWE PPV events that run the same weekend. Obviously, there are many factors involved and only time will tell, but it certainly does lend credence to the idea that when Hunter replaces Vince at some point in the future (contrary to popular belief, Vince McMahon will not live forever), the company is likely to end up in good hands.

17 Bret "The Hitman" Hart

The story of Bret Hart can hardly be told in capsule form. In fact, when Hart wrote his first book, the manuscript was nearing 1,000 pages before he even got to the part where he came to the WWF eight years into his career.

Hart's is a story of many ups and downs. The eighth of 12 children, Bret broke into the business working for his father Stu Hart's Stampede Wrestling in Calgary, Alberta, Canada. It was every wrestling story from that era: he started out as a referee, then one day someone didn't show up and he stepped in, and the rest is history. (Bret Hart was one of my pro wrestling idols as a child, and I broke in the same way almost exactly 20 years later.)

In August of 1984, Vince McMahon bought Stampede Wrestling largely so he could shut it down as part of his nation-wide (and continent-wide) expansion. As part of the deal, Vince promised to pay $100,000 per year to Stu and also pick up several of his stars, including Bret. He reneged on the payment deal and Stampede opened back up a few years later for what was its glory period in the mid-1980s.

Bret didn't do all that much due to the fact that, in 1984, he was considered on the smaller side. Eventually, he teamed up with his larger and more powerful brother-in-law Jim Neidhart to form the Hart Foundation tag team. It was a perfect pairing. Neidhart didn't have the working ability but he could effectively do big-man powerhouse spots, and Bret, the worker of the team, could carry the load in the ring.

The Hart Foundation was a successful tag team by WWF standards of those days, twice winning the tag team titles. But Bret's career really took off in the early 1990s after WWF was rocked

Bret Hart was one of the most decorated performers in WWE history, and also at the center of several contentious behind-the-scenes moments.

with a steroid scandal that nearly sent Vince McMahon to prison. As a result of the fallout, a number of bigger WWF stars vanished, Hulk Hogan, the Ultimate Warrior, and Sycho Sid among them. Suddenly, the title picture was dominated by smaller wrestlers (by early 1990s standards; today they'd be among the bigger guys on the card), including Ric Flair and Macho Man Randy Savage. Flair was getting ready to head back to World Championship Wrestling, so McMahon made the call. On October 12, 1992, in Saskatoon, Saskatchewan, Canada, Bret beat Flair to become the WWF world heavyweight champion.

Hart held the title until WrestleMania IX on April 4, 1993. Hulk Hogan left the show as WWF champion, but he did not beat Bret. Hart first lost the title to the much-larger Yokozuna (we're talking *much* larger—in the 500-pound range), and then afterward Yokozuna's manager Mr. Fuji challenged Hogan to an impromptu match, at which point Hogan leg dropped Yokozuna and won the championship.

Hart was under the impression that he'd win the title back from Hogan at SummerSlam, but Hogan had different ideas. He argued to McMahon that Hart was too small, so instead of laying down for him he dropped the title to Yokozuna at the King of the Ring and then left the company again, ultimately signing with World Championship Wrestling a year later.

Bret never forgot this.

For the next couple of years, Hart remained in the title picture. He won the belt back from Yokozuna at WrestleMania X the following year in a match that Lex Luger was supposed to win. Hart and Luger had tied in the Royal Rumble a few months earlier but the fans "went against script" and cheered Bret and booed Luger (this was back when McMahon would listen to the crowd and book accordingly). The Lex Express Tour that was designed to make him the next Hogan swerved off the tracks. Hart beat Yokozuna at WrestleMania to win the title in the main event, but in the opener, he lost to his brother Owen, who had turned on him, leading to a series of Bret vs. Owen matches throughout the remainder of 1994. Ultimately, the Owen feud led to Owen convincing his mother, Helen, to throw in the towel as Bret was trapped in Bob Backlund's dreaded crossface chicken wing, costing Bret the WWF title.

Backlund was merely a transitional champion to get the title on Shawn Michaels' former manager Diesel (Kevin Nash), Vince's new pick for a Hulk Hogan replacement due to his size and beautiful hair. But Diesel was a flop in the role, and almost a year later, in a no-DQ match, Bret beat him to regain the WWF title.

Bret's most famous run, because it happened during the Monday Night Wars and Attitude Era, spanned from WrestleMania XII to Survivor Series 1997. The main event of that year's WrestleMania saw Shawn Michaels beat Bret in a 60-minute Iron Man match to win the WWF title. Bret and Shawn were already having minor problems in real life. Bret felt that he was the better all-around performer, that while Shawn was pretty and flashy, he just wasn't on his level. Shawn felt the same way about Bret. Bret went home after the match (he finished out the post-WrestleMania European tour first) and stayed gone for several months contemplating his future. That summer, a bidding war broke out between WWF and WCW for his services. WCW offered him a gigantic three-year contract. WWF, whom he held more loyalty toward, offered him a 20-year deal at $1 million per year, more money overall but less per year. He decided to stay.

From the summer of 1996 on, he had two main opponents. The first was the up-and-coming Stone Cold Steve Austin. The second was Michaels. The original plans for 1996 and 1997 involved Shawn and Bret's feud leading to a rematch at WrestleMania 13, where Bret would regain the WWF title. But Michaels had political sway with McMahon, and one thing after another kept coming up. Michaels at that time had a reputation for being difficult to deal with and never dropping titles in the ring. He was supposed to lose to Vader in late 1996 but balked, citing personal problems with Vader, and Sycho Sid won the title instead. Shawn regained it in January at the Royal Rumble in his hometown of San Antonio.

The winner of the Royal Rumble historically gets the championship match at WrestleMania. The night Shawn regained the title, Bret technically won the Rumble, but the referee didn't see it and Steve Austin snuck back in and eliminated Bret. Bret was furious. The next night on *RAW* he "quit the company," only to be talked back by being offered a spot in a four-way match at the February PPV, where the winner would get the title match at WrestleMania.

But plans changed, again. Michaels, in a tear-filled, slurred-speech promo on *RAW* prior to the PPV, claimed that he'd "lost his smile" and needed to go home and get his life back in order. He was legitimately dealing with personal issues, but the timing was incredible. As a result of giving up the title, it was ruled that the winner of the four-way would now become the WWF champion. Bret won, but then lost the title the next night on *RAW* to Sid in a cage match after interference from Austin. Since Michaels was out of WrestleMania, McMahon needed a new main event, and in his mind, since they were big, the Undertaker vs. Sid would be the championship match and Bret would face Austin in a submission match with no championship at stake.

Michaels returned a few months later and the feud with Bret escalated both on TV and behind the scenes. Both would take shots at each other on live television, with Michaels being a particularly effective troll. In June, Michaels made a comment during an interview about how Bret had been seeing some "Sunny days," intimating that Bret was having an affair with Tammy "Sunny" Sytch. Bret was furious, claiming this resulted in marital issues with his wife. The two got into a huge argument backstage that broke down into a legitimate, off-TV fight, where Bret took Shawn down and yanked out a huge chunk of his hair. Shawn quit the company, claiming an unsafe working environment. (He returned a few weeks later.)

The summer of 1997 was renowned for the new Hart Foundation storyline, where Bret, a heel in the United States, created a Canadian stable with his brother Owen, his brother-in-law Davey Boy Smith, and Brian Pillman (not a Canadian but someone with close ties to the family, having trained with Stu Hart and the Hart Family in the famed Dungeon in Calgary). The storyline was one of the best in WWF history, as the Foundation would be booed vociferously in the United States but cheered wildly during WWF's frequent television tapings in Canada.

Bret ultimately found himself in the WWF title picture again, being granted a title match with the Undertaker at SummerSlam, with Michaels as the special guest referee. There were a few caveats. The first was Bret vowing that if he lost, he would never wrestle in the United States again. The second was if Michaels did not call the match fairly, he would be banned from ever wrestling in the United States again. The finish was brilliant. Hart spat in Michaels' face, and Michaels, furious, swung a chair at him in retaliation. But he missed Bret and hit the Undertaker. Bret made the cover. Shawn, to avoid being banned from wrestling in the U.S. for life, was forced to count the pin and award his arch rival Bret the WWF championship.

This all led to Survivor Series 1997, covered elsewhere in this book, where Michaels beat Bret via phantom submission to win the title in the famous Montreal Screwjob. It was the first WWE screwjob finish since the Spider Lady, aka Fabulous Moolah, legitimately pinned Wendi Richter to steal the title from her in the mid-1980s. Bret proceeded to go backstage, legitimately punch McMahon, and then leave for World Championship Wrestling.

Despite him being the hottest free agent in the entire wrestling world in November of 1997, WCW was a mess and had no idea how to capitalize on Bret's momentum. His entire WCW run was a massive disappointment. His life spiraled downward with one tragedy after another; first, the death of his brother Owen at a WWF event in May of 1999; and then suffering a massive concussion after eating a superkick from Goldberg at Starrcade that December. It led directly to the end of his in-ring career. Unable to wrestle, he was fired less than a year later.

In 2002, perhaps due in part to the series of concussions that ended his career, Hart suffered a massive stroke while riding his bike. He was confined to a wheelchair and it was a very serious situation, but he slowly and gradually recovered to the degree that he could live a normal life. WWE reached out to him on a number of occasions to return but he always declined to return, angry and bitter over the screwjob ending of his career there and the situation involving Owen's death. It wasn't until 2005 that he agreed to do some voice work for a Bret Hart DVD release, and then the following year he agreed to come back and accept an induction into the WWE Hall of Fame.

Although just about anything can happen in pro wrestling, Hart signing a one-year deal to return to WWE as a performer in 2009 was one of those rare "hell freezes over" moments. It was an intriguing period, as Hart not only did a storyline with McMahon based off the legitimate Montreal Screwjob, leading to a match where Hart beat him at WrestleMania, but he also managed to win the WWE United States championship from the Miz. Among the more amazing aspects of this already amazing story is that Hart, due to an insurance settlement with Lloyd's of London, was not allowed to take any bumps. He managed to wrestle several matches and win the U.S. title without violating those terms. While never discussed publicly, the story in wrestling was that Lloyd's was not at all happy with Bret attempting to circumvent his agreement, and it was a monetary issue that led to him no longer wrestling matches for WWE.

Bret's last WWE performer contract expired in the fall of 2010. He has since split his time between Calgary and Hawaii, making sporadic appearances as a legend for WWE. He claims all bitterness and resentment toward the company is gone, though he has not been shy about voicing his opinion when he disagrees with a decision the company has made. He is widely regarded today as one of the greatest wrestlers of all time.

18 Shawn Michaels

If you look at the names that would be in the running for the greatest in-ring wrestler of all time worldwide, names like Ric Flair, Kazuchika Okada, Kenta Kobashi, Mitsuhara Misawa, Manami Toyota, and others would spring to mind. But if we're talking strictly WWE, the name most would point to as the greatest wrestler in company history is Shawn Michaels.

Michaels had two careers, with the dividing line being 1998.

He first debuted for WWF in 1987 as part of the Rockers tag team with partner Marty Jannetty. Their first run lasted less than two weeks. Michaels and Jannetty had been teaming together since they met in the Central States region in 1985 (creatively known at the time as "Shawn Michaels and Marty Jannetty"). When they were hired by the AWA in 1986, they were put together and given the name the Midnight Rockers, a blatant rip-off of the Rock and Roll Express and Midnight Express tag teams. They had everything working against them with the name and gimmick, but they were so great in the ring that they became a very popular act. During their first few weeks with WWF, they destroyed a bar and were fired. Vince gave them a second chance a year later, and this time they made it.

Michaels and Jannetty were a famous undercard tag team during that era. They won the tag titles once from the Hart Foundation; Vince had decided to fire Jim Neidhart but then changed his mind. Since the match hadn't aired anywhere yet, they ruled that the title change didn't count because the top rope had broken during the match. Officially, the Rockers were never tag team champions.

They split in 1992 when Michaels threw Jannetty through the window of the Barber Shop during an interview segment with Brutus "The Barber" Beefcake. It was one of the most memorable angles of the era, replayed a million times on TV. Michaels broke off as a heel singles star, the Heartbreak Kid, managed by Sherri Martel.

In the fall of 1992, as a result of the WWF's steroid scandal, McMahon cracked down and instituted serious drug testing. As a result, almost overnight, everything changed. Michaels became the Intercontinental champion and Hart won the WWF title within the span of a month. Their careers would forever be intertwined.

Michaels ended up with a bodyguard, Diesel, aka Kevin Nash. Despite the fact that Michaels was the hottest wrestler in the promotion, business was down, and when business is down, Vince goes with the big guys. So, Diesel split with Michaels and became the WWF champion.

One of the defining aspects of Michaels' first run in WWF was that he almost never lost titles in the ring. He forfeited the WWF championship due to an injury that he miraculously recovered from shortly thereafter. He forfeited the Intercontinental belt and walked out after failing a drug test; he forfeited it a second time after he was beaten up outside a bar in Syracuse, New York. He vacated the tag titles because in storyline he couldn't get along with his partner. He was stripped of the tag team titles in storyline because of a disputed finish. He vacated the tag team titles a third time after a legitimate backstage fight with Bret Hart that caused him to walk out. And he vacated the European championship to Triple H in a "fake match" on *RAW*.

Michaels won his first WWF title from Hart at WrestleMania XII in an Iron Man match. Hart and Michaels already disliked each other, and over the next year and a half that would escalate into shoot comments on television, real-life backstage fights, and finally the Montreal Screwjob. Michaels left Montreal that night as champion, but his personal life was a mess. In January at the Royal Rumble, he took a backdrop over the top rope from the Undertaker and hit his lower back on the edge of a coffin, destroying his back and necessitating a four-year hiatus after dropping the title to Steve Austin at WrestleMania. During that period, he returned to WWF in various different roles, including as commissioner, but personal problems saw him sent home on a somewhat regular basis. There was a plan for him to return to the ring at WrestleMania X-Seven, but personal issues again put a stop to that.

At some point, he found religion and cleaned himself up. The match planned for WrestleMania was moved to the 2002 SummerSlam. On TV, they intimated that Shawn's back was still a disaster, that he had one bout left in him, that "he couldn't wrestle but he could fight," and he was risking serious injury by facing Triple H. He did the match, blew people away with his performance, felt good afterward, and it turned into a full-time, decade-long comeback.

While he wasn't as flashy during his second run and his athleticism was hampered by back and knee issues, he was a significantly smarter wrestler the second time around, and it could be argued that, as an all-around performer, he was much better post-2002 than he was in his athletic and physical prime. He had found God, and it made him easier to deal with as a person, although every now and then you'd see flashes of the old Shawn Michaels. But overall, the days of him losing his temper at fans and throwing tantrums in the ring were over, and those in the business who essentially hated him in the late 1990s and early 2000s came around to him. By the 2010s, he was universally considered an all-time great and a living legend.

During his second run, Michaels assumed the gimmick of Mr. WrestleMania, based on having the best match on that show almost every year. It started in 1994 with his five-star ladder match vs. Razor Ramon. In 1995 he had the best match vs. Diesel. In 1996 he had the best match vs. Bret Hart. The streak ended when he missed WrestleMania 13 due to an alleged knee injury that he returned from a couple months later by doing a backflip off the top rope. In 1998 he had the best match vs. Steve Austin despite taking a bad bump into the turnbuckle and blowing out discs in his already-injured back. He missed four years and then returned at WrestleMania XIX to have a great match vs. Chris Jericho. He had the best match at WrestleMania XX vs. Chris Benoit and Triple H. He had the best match at WrestleMania 21 vs. Kurt Angle. His streak finally ended at WrestleMania 22 vs. Vince McMahon, although he still had an extremely good match with a 60-year-old non-wrestler, which was, quite frankly, a more impressive performance than anyone else delivered on the show. The following two years he had good matches with John Cena and Ric Flair in the latter's retirement match but didn't steal the show. Then he turned it up again starting at WrestleMania XXV, where, at age 43 and 44, he won Match of the Year vs. the Undertaker two years straight in the Observer Awards (which considers every match in every promotion around the world). Michaels was, without question, the greatest big-match performer in WWE history, and is in the argument for greatest big-match performer in the history of the business.

Michaels had always told people that following his retirement match, vs. the Undertaker at WrestleMania XXVI, he was done.

He had been personally bothered by Flair coming out of retirement after losing to him at WrestleMania XXIV and wanted to stick to his word. He did admit that at some point his kids would grow up, and that there was a chance that he'd do a one-off tag team match, so they could see their father live in action. He did so at the WWE Crown Jewel event in 2018, working a tag match alongside Triple H vs. the Undertaker and Kane. Although he hadn't worked in eight years, he was still the best worker in the match (Triple H tore his pec early in the action, the Undertaker was all banged up and practically immobile, and Kane was the new mayor of Knox County, Tennessee, and hadn't worked regularly in months).

Today, Michaels works at the WWE Performance Center in Florida, helping train the next generation of wrestlers. He also works with Triple H in NXT, helping to put together storylines and matches. The belief within wrestling is that when Triple H takes over, Michaels will end up with a very well-paying job as an executive in the company, likely as Hunter's right-hand man. The founders of DX, who wanted anything in the world but to sit around in an office all day wearing suits, will ultimately end up doing just that.

19 The Montreal Screwjob

The Montreal Screwjob is one of the most famous events in wrestling history. Amazingly, had it not taken place almost exactly when it did, nothing like it could ever have happened.

As noted in the entry on *Hitman Hart: Wrestling with Shadows*, the 1999 documentary that, purely by luck, chronicled the entire event, the story is preposterous in hindsight. It's so preposterous, in fact, that even today there is a subset of wrestling fans who remain convinced that the entire thing was a work. Even by the early to-mid 2000s, the idea that the world championship of a professional wrestling organization was so valuable that a promoter would have to screw one of his most loyal longtime employees to protect it would be inconceivable. But in the fall of 1997, to the people involved, it felt almost like the life and death of pro wrestling depended upon the outcome of a single title match, and that the championship must be protected by any means necessary.

The match was Bret Hart vs. Shawn Michaels, the event Survivor Series 1997, the place—get this—Montreal. Hart was the champion, but he had agreed to sign with WCW at the behest of Vince McMahon himself. McMahon had signed Hart to a 20-year deal the prior year but immediately regretted it. He told Hart that money was tight, that he wasn't sure he'd be able to live up to his end of the bargain, and gave him the okay to negotiate with WCW in October of 1997. WCW, run by Eric Bischoff, was crushing WWF in the ratings at the time. Hart didn't really want to go but felt McMahon was giving him no choice, plus WCW was offering him an incredible deal in the range of $7.5 million over three years.

A key to the story is that as part of his deal to return in 1996, Hart was given "reasonable creative control" over all of his storylines during the final 30 days of his run, should either side choose to terminate the contract.

Shawn and Bret had hated each other for a long time, largely based on mutual jealousy. Both thought they should be the top guy. Both thought their style of wrestling was superior to the other's. Shawn hated that Bret made more money than he did. He knew which of Bret's buttons to push, and Bret took it all very personally. One day in the summer of 1997, Bret punched Shawn backstage at an event. Shawn, furious and claiming an unsafe working environment, walked out of the company. But cooler heads prevailed, and he not only returned to work, but returned to continue his feud with his hated enemy.

The summer of 1997 was among the greatest periods in company history, built around a U.S. vs. Canada feud. Michaels was a babyface in the United States and a massive heel in Canada. Hart, a Calgary native, was a heel in the U.S. but a massive babyface in Canada. And when I say massive babyface, we're not just talking pro wrestling. Hart was incredibly popular and was considered one of the most famous sports stars in all of Canada. He took this incredibly seriously, as he did his role as the WWF champion. To him, the WWF championship wasn't just a prop awarded by a promoter as a result of matches with predetermined outcomes. To him, the WWF champion was the standard-bearer of the company, the man upon whose shoulders the promotion revolved, and he took great pride in what he considered the honorable role of being champion.

Shortly before the November 1 deadline that McMahon had given Hart to negotiate with WCW, McMahon went to Bret and said company finances were turning around and that he could, in fact, afford to pay Bret what he'd promised in 1996. But every booking scenario he presented to Hart included him losing repeatedly to his hated rival Michaels and ultimately being moved down the card. Bret went back and forth inside his head and finally decided to sign with WCW. Obviously, he had to lose the title before leaving. Michaels was next in line for the championship, which he'd then hold through WrestleMania XIV before dropping it to Steve Austin. McMahon wanted Bret to lose the title directly to Michaels at Survivor Series. But Survivor Series was in Montreal, and Bret wasn't hot on the idea of losing to Michaels in Canada and letting down his most ardent fans.

McMahon approached Hart with the idea of retaining the title via DQ in Montreal, and then losing the belt to Michaels in a four-way match at the PPV in Springfield, Massachusetts, on December

7. Problem was, Hart's WCW contract kicked in December 1. Hart called Bischoff, who gave him permission to stay with WWF an extra week and then debut the next night on *Nitro*. McMahon seemed okay with the idea and even suggested that Bret beat Michaels clean in Montreal prior to him losing clean to Michaels in Springfield.

McMahon pitched the ideas to Shawn, who said he'd think about it and call him back. Shawn then called his friend Triple H, who himself was angry with Hart after an incident the previous month where he was supposed to pin Bret in a non-title match and Bret got the finish changed to a countout (since it made no sense to lose to Hunter if it wasn't setting up a title match). Triple H told Michaels it made zero sense for Shawn to lose to Bret on his way out the door. So, Shawn called Vince back and refused to put him over in Montreal.

Vince decided they had to get the belt off Bret one way or another, and to do it in Montreal. The story he and others in the company claimed was that they were concerned Bret would show up with the title the next night in Memphis (impossible because Bret was still under WWF contract), or that Bischoff would go on TV and gleefully tell the world he'd signed away the WWF champion.

That night in Montreal, Bret and McMahon met backstage and had a conversation. Unbeknownst to Vince, Bret didn't trust him and had called High Road Productions, the company behind *Hitman Hart: Wrestling with Shadows*, and asked to have a crew sent out to document the show, even though they'd wrapped production a week earlier. Bret's wife at the time, Julie, also didn't trust McMahon, and suggested he wear a wire to the meeting, which he did.

In the meeting, portions of which aired in the documentary and the full conversation of which is transcribed in the *Wrestling*

Observer Newsletter, McMahon asked Bret what he wanted to do. Bret said he wanted to leave with his head held high and suggested a schmozz finish. He also suggested that, instead of losing the title in the ring at a later date, he just show up on *RAW*, vacate the championship, and tell the fans that he was leaving. He explained that he could ask Bischoff not to make any announcement until Bret himself had a chance to do so. McMahon responded that Hart didn't need to bother asking, because everyone knew he was leaving anyway. He listened to everything Bret suggested—neither side made any actual demands—and said, "I'm all for that," and told him a DQ finish sounded good for that evening. McMahon told him to get with Pat Patterson to set up the match, since Pat was the master of finishes.

Bret and Shawn had a pretty good match that night. Near the finish, in a spot suggested by the master, Shawn put Bret in his own hold, a sharpshooter. Bret was supposed to grab Shawn's ankle, break the hold, and reverse it into a sharpshooter of his own, at which point DX would hit the ring for the DQ. But as Hart was reaching for Michaels' ankle, referee Earl Hebner, who had sworn to Bret hours earlier on the lives of his children that he wouldn't screw him, called for the bell. Michaels was ruled the winner via submission and awarded the WWF title. Hart had been screwed in his own hometown and robbed of the championship.

After heading back to the locker room, Bret confronted Shawn and asked him if he was in on it; Shawn, in tears, swore to God that he knew nothing about it. (Years later, Shawn admitted that he did know about it.) McMahon then walked in. Bret calmly asked the documentary crew to step outside. A few minutes later, McMahon, flanked by Shane McMahon, Patterson, and Gerald Brisco, stumbled out of the room. Someone told him not to look at the camera. Turns out, Bret had cold-cocked McMahon in the locker room, knocking him out. Of all the scenes in *Wrestling with*

Shadows, the image of McMahon, who prided himself on being a tough guy with "balls the size of grapefruits," stumbling out of the locker room was the thing that infuriated him more than anything else in the film.

The Montreal Screwjob led directly to McMahon reluctantly turning heel and eventually feuding with Austin in a storyline that ultimately helped turn the company into a billion-dollar multinational public corporation. For years afterward, the company would try to re-create the Survivor Series finish, and it always sucked. Bret Hart's WCW career was a disaster. Hell froze over and Bret did ultimately return to WWE, and even won the United States championship during a period where he couldn't even take any bumps as a result of a serious stroke. While he stays largely out of the public eye, Bret still makes occasional appearances for the company today.

20 The Birth of Hulkamania

The official story, particularly from the perspective of WWE, is that Hulkamania was born on January 23, 1984, when Hogan legdropped the dastardly Iron Sheik to win the WWF title. Gorilla Monsoon screamed, "Hulkamania is here!" and Hogan began cutting promos referring to his fans as "Hulkamaniacs," propelling himself into becoming the biggest wrestling star of the 1980s.

The reality is that Hogan had become a gigantic star years earlier, and not even in this country.

Hogan had a run in the then-WWWF in the late 1970s as a giant monster heel managed by "Classy" Freddie Blassie. He faced all the big stars, including a man who, years later, they'd claim was about to have his first match ever with Hogan, Andre the Giant.

Vince McMahon Sr. sent Hogan to New Japan Pro Wrestling, with whom he had a working relationship. Blassie had been a gigantic star in Japan in the 1960s, so McMahon sent the two together as a package; the idea was Blassie's presence would give Hogan instant credibility. But Hogan didn't get over as a heel. Instead, the big, blond-haired (Hogan still had hair at the time) bodybuilder became super popular with the Japanese fans, and the birth of his babyface character began.

After his New Japan run ended, Verne Gagne brought Hogan into the AWA. He also wanted to push him as a heel, but as was the case in Japan, fans took one look at the guy and cheered him wildly. Gagne had teamed Hogan up with one of his top heel managers, "Luscious" Johnny Valiant. When it became clear the fans weren't going to boo him, they shot an angle where Hogan made the save for babyface Brad Rheingans, who was being stomped on by the gigantic Jerry Blackwell. To cement his babyface turn, Hogan twice lifted up and slammed the allegedly nearly 500-pound Blackwell.

This was the real birth of Hulkamania in the United States. Hogan quickly became AWA's biggest star, leading to the hottest period of business in AWA's history. To put this into perspective, when Hogan went on tours for New Japan, AWA averaged 8,000 per show. When he returned to headline for the AWA, they averaged 16,000 per show. He was a phenomenon.

Despite being the biggest star in the company by far, Hogan never won the AWA world championship. On one of AWA's biggest shows ever, Super Sunday on April 24, 1983, Hogan beat Nick Bockwinkel with the Legdrop of Doom and was declared AWA champion, but then figurehead president Stanley Blackburn revealed that Hogan had thrown Bockwinkel over the top rope when the ref was down (illegal in the AWA), and thus the decision was being reversed. For years it has been suggested that the reason Hogan left the AWA was because Gagne never put the title on him, but he was such a huge star and massive draw that he didn't need the title. Not only that, but AWA had a working agreement with All Japan Pro Wrestling and Hogan was under contract with its biggest rival, New Japan; if Hogan had ever won the title, he'd have had to defend it in All Japan, which would have been a political disaster. Plus, often overlooked is the fact that if Hogan had beaten Bockwinkel and become the champion, he was still leaving for WWF at the end of 1983, and he'd have left as AWA champion, which in those days would have been a devastating blow to the company.

As McMahon's expansion plans began to unfold, he offered to buy out the AWA. Gagne, who was doing gigantic business, turned the offer down. McMahon concluded he didn't need the AWA if he could just sign away its biggest stars. He threw huge money at a number of them, notably Hogan, who was offered more than he made in AWA and New Japan to come in and be the face of McMahon's expansion.

The AWA, which essentially created the phenomenon that was Hulkamania, had a strong 1984 built around the return of the Crusher, the company's biggest star of the 1970s who had been pushed aside in order to make room for Hogan. But you can't run a national promotion with a 58-year-old on top, no matter how popular he might have been. With more and more of his stars jumping ship to the WWF, including Bobby Heenan, Jesse Ventura, and Gene Okerlund, AWA's business began to fall. Gagne was kept afloat by money that ESPN paid for his programming, and for a period in the mid-1980s the promotion featured some of the best young talent in the country, including Shawn Michaels and Curt Hennig. But it was slowly dying a death, and by 1991, it blinked out of existence.

Hogan returned to the WWF on December 27, 1983, beating Bill Dixon. One month later, he was the WWF champion, and the rest is history.

21 The Monday Night Wars

The Monday Night Wars began on September 4, 1995, when WCW *Nitro* debuted on TNT, head-to-head with WWF's flagship *RAW* show, and ended on March 26, 2001, when *Nitro* aired its final show following WCW's purchase by the WWF.

The Monday Night Wars also mark what many fans remember as their favorite period of wrestling history.

Looking back, the Monday Night Wars don't age well. Their success was the result of many things that you can't judge fairly with modern eyes. WWF was coming off one of its worst periods in history. Business was down following the company's sex and steroid scandals in the early 1990s, the biggest stars of the 1980s were long gone, and the company was pushing gimmicks like a fake Undertaker, Adam Bomb (get it?), Sparky Plugg, and Bastion Booger. Diesel was in the middle of the worst world championship reign in modern history.

WCW, on the other hand, was attempting to rise from its early 1990s doldrums, building around Hulk Hogan, who it paid huge money to bring in a year or so after he'd left WWF.

The announcement of *Nitro*'s debut was met with massive skepticism. A head-to-head WCW show against *RAW*, people argued, would do nothing more than split the *RAW* audience. People were wrong. *Nitro* wasn't the taped, nothing-happening *WCW Saturday Night* moved to Monday. It was a live show with main-eventers wrestling on live television, and a brand-new audience for the show sprung up immediately.

Eric Bischoff started the revolution, changing the way wrestling was promoted on Monday nights. He had Hogan wrestle for free on TV in the main event. He debuted former WWF stars in shocking surprises, like Lex Luger. He allowed cruiserweights to get in there and tear the house down, something you'd never see on *RAW*. Shockingly, he called out the competition and mentioned WWF by name, something you'd never see in WWF because it pretended no other wrestling promotion existed. *Nitro* was new and different and its audience grew. Then it exploded in the spring and summer of 1996 when Scott Hall and Kevin Nash debuted, pretending to be WWF invaders; they later joined up with Hogan, who turned heel for the first time since the birth of Hulkamania in the 1980s. From the summer of 1996 through the spring of 1998, WCW destroyed WWF in the ratings war. Not only did they win the ratings war, but at their peak they drew more money in a single year than any other wrestling company in history.

WWF struggled to gain a foothold but finally started to gain momentum in the summer and fall of 1997 behind Bret Hart and Shawn Michaels' U.S. vs. Canada feud, the rise of Stone Cold Steve Austin, and the ascendance of DX as an edgier and less-watered-down WWF version of the NWO. By the spring of 1998, business-wise the two promotions were neck and neck. The difference was on the creative side; WWF as on the way up, centered around a Vince McMahon vs. Austin feud, the rise of the Rock, and great performances by guys like the Undertaker and Mick Foley. WCW, despite a record-breaking streak of sellouts, was busy doing the same things it had been doing in 1995, pushing the same aging performers, not elevating talent, and making every booking mistake you can make without any fear of repercussions. Bischoff believed that as long as they pushed Hogan, they'd always make money.

By mid-1999, the war had drastically turned around. WWF was trouncing *Nitro* every week, and every factor of WCW's business, from ratings to PPVs to merchandise and house show numbers, was collapsing. WCW switched bookers throughout the year, finally hiring Vince Russo away from WWF in late 1999. He

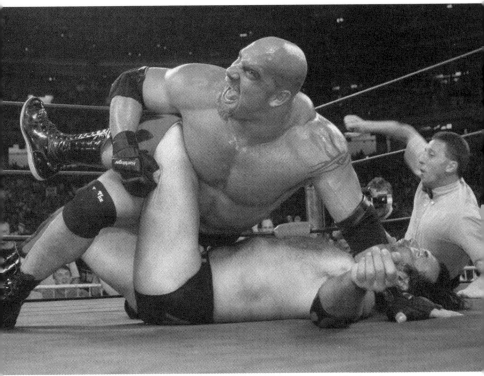

Goldberg was one of the driving forces behind WCW's success during the Monday Night Wars of the 1990s.

managed to keep ratings somewhat steady, but his insane booking decisions, including three-hour episodes of *Nitro* that managed to feature more than 70 different segments in a single show, destroyed WCW's other revenue streams. He was sent home in early 2000, returned later in the year, was sent home again, and by that time the great ship had hit the iceberg and was sinking to the bottom of the sea. WWF had grown to new heights, gone public, and made McMahon a legitimate billionaire. In March of 2001, WWF bought its competition for $2.5 million plus an agreement to buy advertising time on TNT and TBS. The Monday Night Wars were over.

The takeaways through modern eyes are that you can never rely on a pat hand for too long, and sometimes you need to steal ideas to win. Bischoff stole ideas internationally to help launch *Nitro*. WWF stole ideas from WCW and ECW to help turn things around. WCW raided WWF's talent—much like Vince McMahon did when he went national in 1984—but refused to create new headliners of its own despite having the largest and deepest roster of any promotion in history. WWF was forced to create new stars to survive, and as luck would have it happened to end up with Austin, the Rock, and McMahon all at the same time, something which, in hindsight, is like a once-in-10-lifetimes jackpot. McMahon was the greatest heel imaginable, the Rock had a level of charisma that led to him becoming the biggest movie star in the world years later, and Austin was the ideal character for the mid-1990s and the absolute perfect foil for McMahon. It was magical, so magical that fans watched the show in ridiculous numbers despite the fact that, outside of those three megastars, the shows were generally awful, with short matches, horrible finishes, and terrible comedy. WCW had the talent to put on great shows, but the booking was the worst in the history of wrestling, awful to a degree never seen before or since.

For a million reasons, it's doubtful we'll ever have another period like this in our lifetimes. Thankfully, every episode of both shows exists in perpetuity on the WWE Network. Memories are weird, and people remember terrible things as being great and awful ideas as being good. There are many lessons to be learned from the successes and failures of the Monday Night Wars. If more wrestlers, bookers, and promoters rewatched and studied those shows, the wrestling world today would probably be a much better place.

22 The Death of Owen Hart

Owen Hart died on May 23, 1999, at the WWF Over the Edge PPV, about two hours before the main event started.

But the show, WWF alerted us, must go on.

Owen Hart was the younger brother of Bret Hart and had been doing a storyline where he pretended to retire; in his place appeared a character he'd performed as years earlier, the masked Blue Blazer. In storyline, everyone knew the Blazer was Owen, but Owen insisted he was retired and that someone else must be under the Blazer's mask. On a few occasions, Owen and the Blazer showed up at the same place at the same time, but it was always evident that Owen was paying someone to pretend to be the Blazer to throw everyone off the scent.

It was a light-hearted character and storyline. At Over the Edge 1999, he was scheduled to face and defeat the Godfather to win the WWF Intercontinental title for the third time.

Then tragedy struck.

In a spoof on WCW's Sting, who had spent years repelling from the rafters as part of his entrance, the goofy superhero Blazer (he was a heel, the gimmick being that he was spoofing 1980s babyfaces like Hulk Hogan) was going to replicate Sting's entrance for his match with the Godfather. As he came within a few feet of the ring, he was going to "accidentally" trip the quick-release device and do a face-first pratfall into the ring. In order to facilitate this, instead of having a backup latch for safety purposes, he only had the one latch.

It's almost impossible to believe this was allowed to happen. But it did.

As Owen prepared to make his entrance, a video played on the TitanTron of a backstage segment. Owen, suspended 78 feet above the ring from the ceiling of Kemper Arena in Kansas City, apparently made an adjustment to get more comfortable and the quick-release latch opened. He fell. On the way down, witnesses claimed he screamed at the referee in the ring to get out of the way. He landed on the top rope near a turnbuckle, and then bounced into the air and crashed into the corner of the ring. He tried to get up but was unable to do so. He had suffered massive blunt force trauma to the chest and was bleeding internally.

The cameras never showed the fall, and many in the building were watching the big screen and didn't immediately know what had happened. Some thought a dummy had been dropped from the ceiling for comedic purposes. The WWF cut to a shot of the crowd, then to announcer Jim Ross, who told viewers at home that Owen Hart had fallen from the rafters and that it wasn't part of the entertainment, it was not part of the show. EMTs hit the ring to perform CPR. It was unsuccessful, and so he was loaded onto a gurney and rushed backstage. Vince McMahon and other WWF officials spent 15 minutes before making the decision that the show must go on.

And so, it did. Jeff Jarrett, who was close friends with Owen, had to go to the ring and wrestle a tag team match with Owen's blood splattered on the mat in the corner of the ring. Over the next few hours, more than a dozen other performers, all of whom knew and loved Owen, had to walk through that curtain and perform in that ring.

Shortly before the main event, Jim Ross spoke to the fans at home. "Ladies and gentlemen, earlier tonight here in Kansas City, tragedy befell the World Wrestling Federation, and all of us," he said. "Owen Hart was set to make an entrance from the ceiling, and he fell from the ceiling. I have the unfortunate responsibility to let everyone know that Owen Hart has died. Owen Hart has tragically died from that accident here tonight."

He was 34 years old.

The death of Owen Hart led to a lawsuit filed by his wife, Martha, the mother of his two children and his high-school sweetheart, which was eventually settled for $18 million. Martha used most of the money to launch the Owen Hart Foundation. Over the years she has vociferously fought to keep WWE from profiting on his name in any way, shooting down requests to produce documentaries, DVDs, and other merchandise. At one point WWE released an Owen Hart DVD against her wishes, and she responded with another lawsuit, claiming WWE was illegally using Owen's likeness and had not paid any royalties. The suit was settled out of court for an undisclosed amount.

The decision on whether WWF should have continued Over the Edge that night has been debated for two decades. Most fans believe the show should have ended immediately; others claim that decisions made in the heat of the moment aren't always the most logical, and that if something like that happened again, surely WWE would cancel the rest of the show. However, in September of 2012, announcer Jerry Lawler went into full cardiac arrest live on *RAW* and was rushed to the hospital, and again, the show continued. Lawler, luckily, made a full recovery.

The night after he died, WWF ran an Owen Hart tribute show in place of *RAW*. The show consisted of nothing but straight wrestling matches; no angles, no babyfaces or heels, only tributes to Owen from his friends in the company. The night ended with a silent toast by Steve Austin dedicated to Hart's memory.

Current WWE superstar Kevin Owens, real name Kevin Steen, named his son and his wrestling character after Owen, and Triple H claimed that the nickname "The Game" was to be given to Owen, and that he took it as a tribute to him after his death.

In real life, it's a cliché to say that "nobody ever said a bad word" about someone. Almost nobody ever says that about anyone in wrestling. But everyone said that about Owen Hart.

23 Chris Benoit

This is by far the hardest entry for me to write, since Chris Benoit was one of my best friends in wrestling. Then he killed his wife and child and hanged himself.

I first met Chris in the late 1990s. He was a big fan of my newsletter, *Figure Four Weekly*. He thought it was hilarious. We would talk on the phone a few times per month, often about things that were going on first in WCW, and later in WWF after he jumped ship. He would ask me what I thought about things and sometimes he would even ask me for advice, which I thought was ridiculous given he was renowned as one of the best workers on the planet. The phone call would always end with him telling me, "Take care."

He would tell me about his frustrations, but at no point, ever, did I think that he could possibly do what he ended up doing. Of everyone I knew in wrestling during that period, he seemed perhaps the nicest and definitely the most polite.

Chris was very close friends with Eddie Guerrero, and when Eddie died he was absolutely devastated. He told me that he kept a journal and that every day he would write an entry to Eddie. He said he knew Eddie couldn't read it, but it helped him to get through the trauma of his friend's death. One day he asked me for my address, and shortly thereafter he sent me a card from Eddie's funeral, a chair with Eddie's likeness on it from the PPV where

Eddie beat Brock Lesnar to win the WWE title, and a handwritten letter. I've never published this before, but this is what he wrote:

> Life is the journey we perceive it to be. I got so much of my perception from Eddie. Eddie shared so much of his life and his life's experiences with me. He was never too proud or never too ashamed to open up and share with me his experiences, at times revealing his deepest wounds. I am so blessed, so fortunate to have had Eddie's influence in my life. I pray to God that each one of my children find a friend in life, like I have in Eddie.

Chris Benoit then murdered his wife, Nancy. He bound her wrists and ankles, pinned her down with his knee in her back, and strangled her to death with a cord. The next morning, he sedated his seven-year-old son, Daniel, with Xanax and strangled him to death as well. For two days he stayed in the house with their bodies. Then, on June 24, 2007, after searching online for the best way to quickly and easily break a neck, he wrapped a towel around the lat pulldown pulley on his weight machine, tied it around his neck, and let go of the weights, breaking his neck, as he'd hoped, quickly and easily.

Nearly everybody who knew him was in complete disbelief upon hearing the news; the immediate assumption was that the Benoits must have been killed by an intruder, or that a gas leak or other accident had caused their deaths. As is usually the case when something like this happens, time passes and people learn things that they didn't know. Marital problems with Nancy dating back years. Increasingly paranoid behavior. A massive steroid problem. Heavy drinking. Painkiller abuse. And an incredibly damaged brain, the kind of brain that today would make headlines due to the degree of CTE found, surely the results of dozens of unreported concussions for a guy who made a career of diving headbutts, hard bumps, and unprotected chair shots to the head.

Benoit's idol growing up was the Dynamite Kid, whose high-risk style put him out of the business and in a wheelchair in his 30s. A 12-year-old Benoit saw Dynamite wrestle and wanted to be him. He broke in with Stampede Wrestling in Canada at the age of 18 and was throwing diving headbutts off the top rope from his very first match. He stayed with Stampede until it shut down for a second time in 1989, at which point he went to Japan, first as the masked Wild Pegasus, and later as himself. Outside of tape-traders, he first made a name for himself in ECW in the early 1990s, where Paul Heyman dubbed him "The Crippler" after he accidentally broke Sabu's neck in a match. When Eric Bischoff got control of World Championship Wrestling and talked Ted Turner into giving him a Monday night show opposite *RAW*, he scoured the world for talented cruiserweight wrestlers, one of whom was Benoit (Chris had worked for WCW briefly in the early 1990s, but they didn't do anything with him). One of his more famous WCW feuds was with the Taskmaster Kevin Sullivan, who at the time was married to the beautiful valet Woman. Sullivan put together a storyline where Woman would leave him for Benoit, and to make it believable, he booked them to travel together on the road and share hotel rooms. Woman, aka Nancy Sullivan, in a case of fantasy becoming reality, left Sullivan and married Benoit.

WCW grew into the biggest pro wrestling organization in history, and then it went off the rails due to management's desire to continue pushing the same guys while supremely talented workers like Benoit and Guerrero floundered. As the company self-destructed, Benoit, Guerrero, Dean Malenko, and Perry Saturn all jumped ship to WWF in January of 2000, a moment that was in many ways the final nail in the coffin for World Championship Wrestling. Their run was hit-and-miss early, as all four of the newly minted "Radicalz" were under six-feet tall (at the time a recipe for disaster in a McMahon-run company) and none of them were great on the mic (although Eddie eventually figured it out and flourished). Still, Benoit and Guerrero in particular were so talented and garnered so much support from fans that the company was forced to act. In 2004, Benoit won the world heavyweight title from Triple H via submission in the triple-threat main event of WrestleMania XX (Shawn Michaels was the third competitor). In what was at the time one of the more emotional moments in wrestling history, he celebrated in the ring with his best friend Eddie Guerrero, the current WWE champion. Both tearful men had spent a decade being held down due to their size and lack of promo ability, despite being two of the best in-ring wrestlers in the business. Now, here they were, standing tall as the two top champions in the biggest pro wrestling organization in the world.

And that's where the story should have had its happy ending.

But this is real life, and real life doesn't always have happy endings. Two years later, Guerrero was dead, and a year after that Benoit killed his family and himself.

It is painful to have to write that anything positive came from this period, but after Guerrero died of a heart attack at the age of 38 following a long battle with drug and alcohol addiction, the company instituted a new wellness policy that would allow it to test for steroid and drug abuse. Unfortunately, the policy was more lip service than anything else, evidenced by Benoit dying with a 59-to-1 T/E ratio (translation: he was on massive amounts of testosterone), with boxes of steroids found around his house. The Benoit murder-suicide led to a Congressional investigation by the United States House Committee on Oversight and Government Reform, and the aftermath saw WWE seriously crack down on steroid and drug abuse for the first time since the early 1990s. Obviously, as in any sport, there are dozens of ways to sneak through the cracks, and while it would be naive to claim that WWE is drug-free today, the reality is that it is significantly cleaner than it has been in decades, and the era of superstar pro wrestlers regularly passing away in their 40s has come to an end. There has not been a Chris Benoit or Eddie Guerrero since Chris Benoit and Eddie Guerrero, and hopefully there never will be again.

WrestleMania III

WrestleMania III, held in the Pontiac Silverdome on March 29, 1987, is probably considered the most legendary WrestleMania of all time, even though it wasn't the first, it wasn't the most attended, it didn't do the biggest gate, it didn't draw the most PPV buys, and it certainly didn't include the best matches.

In fact, there were only three things about the show that became famous, but they became really, really famous.

The first is the attendance. As noted elsewhere, the actual attendance for WrestleMania III was approximately 78,000. Because so many fans grew up hearing the legendary 93,173 number—and because for some weird reason when people grow up they don't want their childhood memories shattered—it is virtually impossible to convince people otherwise. The promoter of the event, Zane Bresloff, told Dave Meltzer of the Wrestling Observer in the early 1990s the actual number. Bresloff worked as a promoter for both WWF and WCW and knew everyone in pro wrestling, and he would know as well as anyone what the actual number was. But to this day, if you go on Wikipedia, the attendance is listed as 93,173.

I remember in the early 2000s when I was a wrestling columnist for *Penthouse* magazine, I wrote an article and talked about the real WrestleMania attendance. They wanted to print 93,173. They told me they'd seen that number on the Internet. I told them the promoter of the event gave us the real number based on the box office receipts he personally handled. I was told, "But the Internet says 93,173." A bunch of digital 1s and 0s in cyberspace trumped the human being in charge of the actual event.

Vince McMahon has been very open about the difference between real attendance numbers and announced numbers. He told Meltzer directly that the fake attendance numbers were for "entertainment purposes." He has admitted inflated numbers to shareholders.

The second reason WrestleMania III is famous is because of the Randy Savage vs. Ricky Steamboat match, which for years was considered the greatest WrestleMania match of all time. The two meticulously worked the match out in advance, move for move. At one point the ref drops to the mat for what seems like a 1-count, so when he counts to two everyone thinks it's a three and cheers. But the wrestlers, going by their script, do not skip a beat and continue wrestling. Steamboat won in 14:35 to win the WWF Intercontinental title.

Of course, the most famous thing about WrestleMania III was the main event, Hulk Hogan vs. Andre the Giant. The story was that this was the first match between Hogan and Andre, and that Andre hadn't been beaten in 15 years. Those stories were about as true as the 93,173 number, but at least in this case we have footage of Hogan and Andre wrestling at Shea Stadium in 1980.

The match itself was horrible. The story WWE tells is that Andre was near death and barely mobile, that it was touch-and-go whether he'd do the match, and that Hogan went in not knowing whether Andre was going to let him win. All of these stories are far more preposterous than the attendance number. Andre was hurting, certainly, but everything was decided long in advance; Andre was always going to put Hogan over, and while Andre died young he wrestled in WWF for years afterward, including against Hogan again at the following year's WrestleMania.

The big highlight of the match—the only highlight, really—was Hogan lifting Andre up, body slamming him, and then hitting his Legdrop of Doom for the pin. WWF claimed Andre had never been slammed before. He'd been slammed many times.

Not 93,173 times, but many times nonetheless.

25 The Birth of Monday Night RAW

Growing up, my favorite wrestling TV show was *Prime Time Wrestling*. Debuting on January 1, 1985, the show is best remembered for its post-1986 run when Gorilla Monsoon and Bobby Heenan teamed up in studio to present and then comment on matches filmed at various arenas around the country. Monsoon played the friendly, grandfatherly babyface, and Heenan played the petulant heel who would unabashedly cheer for all the bad guys. They had one of the better dynamics in WWF history, and it made what would otherwise have been a pretty unwatchable show watchable.

If you're a modern wrestling fan, you cannot comprehend *Prime Time Wrestling*. There was almost never anything approaching a main event with two big stars going at it. It was two hours of mostly squash matches, and every now and then two mid-level stars would face off in what were often long, boring house show–caliber matches. If a big angle happened somewhere, which in those days was a rare occurrence and not something that happened multiple times per show, it would be aired and recapped. This concept would die on television today, but in the mid-1980s this was all fans had grown to expect from a weekly WWF TV show.

To me, the show fell off a cliff in February of 1991 when they moved to a "live" format with an in-studio audience. As a fan, I presumed I was different from everyone else in that I thought Heenan was awesome. In my imagination, I thought everyone else must hate this guy. Well, the live studio audience laughed at all his jokes and it just killed the show for me. That format lasted a scant nine months before they tried something new, a panel format with roundtable discussions. It wasn't as bad as the live audience, but the magic of *Prime Time Wrestling* with Gorilla and Bobby was history.

WWF ratings would traditionally slump during the summer because, in those days, people would go outside and do fun things in the summertime. Come fall, they'd go back to school and back to watching TV more frequently. In the fall of 1991, *Prime Time Wrestling* ratings did not go back up. The show was doing terrible numbers, and so Vince McMahon came up with an idea to shake things up.

Monday Night RAW.

The first show, on January 11, 1993, was not a great one, but it was definitely different. It was a live show broadcast from the Manhattan Center in New York, and it featured an hour of in-ring action similar to a studio show you'd see in, for example, Memphis. The biggest issue in those early days was McMahon's decision to have himself, Randy Savage (who in storyline had retired), and Rob Bartlett, a local comedian who knew nothing about wrestling, do commentary. Bartlett was terrible, fans hated him, and within three months he was replaced by Bobby Heenan.

WWF had only taken out a two-month lease on the Manhattan Center, presumably in case the new show flopped. But it did not. They continued to air live for several months, then switched to a format where one show would be live and then they'd tape several weeks' worth of shows. *RAW* soon became the company's flagship show, to the point that just two years later, when WCW was preparing to launch *Nitro* head-to-head on Monday nights, virtually everyone thought doing so would be absolute suicide due to *RAW* "owning" Monday nights.

While *RAW* is hardly the longest-running weekly episodic television show in history (*WCW Saturday Night* technically still has them beat), it is still going strong over two decades later. It has seen many changes over the years, including moving from one hour to two and finally to a whopping three hours weekly in 2012, and it has jumped from USA to TNN/Spike TV and back to USA again. As the No. 1 show for the biggest wrestling promotion that ever existed, it remains the most important televised wrestling show in history.

26 Superstar Billy Graham

While he held the WWWF title for less than a year, Superstar Billy Graham was among the hottest heels of the 1970s.

Keep in mind that a 296-day title reign for a heel champion in WWWF was unheard-of prior to his win. In the 16 years between the formation of the WWWF and the day Graham won the title, the previous longest heel title run was 22 days. Even more amazingly, when you consider how reliant WWE seems to have become on heat-drawing angles, only one heel champion in the history of the main WWF/WWE championship has ever had a longer reign, and you have to go all the way to early 2013 when CM Punk broke Graham's record.

Graham was chosen to replace Bruno Sammartino, with the idea that he'd end up with a fairly lengthy title reign. The man Vince McMahon Sr. wanted as his next babyface champion was

Bob Backlund, and his feeling was that Backlund needed to be built up for some time before putting the championship on him. When Vince Sr. pitched the idea to Graham, he told him the exact day that Graham was going to lose the title to Backlund. Graham had absolutely no problem with this; at least, not at the beginning.

Superstar Billy Graham was larger than life. He was a giant bodybuilder pumped full of steroids who wore colorful, outlandish costumes and stole his promo style from Muhammad Ali. He was a sensation and captured the imagination of several young wrestlers—most notably Hulk Hogan and Jesse "The Body" Ventura—who went on to steal his schtick, and because of time and place, they became bigger stars than he ever was. It led to Vince McMahon Jr. saying that Superstar came along 20 years before his time.

He wasn't a great wrestler (to say the least), and he'd be the first guy to tell you that. But with his body and his ability on the mic, he didn't need to be. In his nine months as champion he headlined 10 Madison Square Garden shows and sold out all but one, which came close at just under 18,000 fans. In his career he sold out 19 of the 20 MSG shows he headlined, an incredible feat and a percentage nobody else in history ever came close to.

As is often the case with superstar heels, ultimately the fans fall in love with them and want them to turn babyface. Graham recognized this. In his mind, had he turned babyface instead of losing the title to Backlund, he'd have had years of big money success afterward. But McMahon Sr. had a plan, and unlike his son decades later, he wasn't open to changing his mind. Graham went so far as to fake a knee injury days before he was supposed to drop the title, but McMahon Sr. wasn't buying it, and on February 20, 1978, before the largest turnaway crowd in the history of the Philadelphia Spectrum, Backlund won the title.

Graham's life and career following his WWWF title run was a series of highs and more-frequent lows. For the first several months after Backlund beat him, he went around the territory drawing big money in rematches with Backlund, Sammartino, and others. But by the end of 1978, like all of the heels who came before him, Superstar had run his course and it was time to move on and become a headliner in another territory.

But he didn't. He wrestled sparingly around the world in 1979, then fell into a deep depression and left wrestling for several years. Rumors were that he had died, spurred on by a newspaper column written by, of all people, Gorilla Monsoon. When he returned to the WWF in 1982, he did so with a bizarre kung fu gimmick and a newly shaved head; this hardly quelled rumors that "the real Billy Graham" had died.

He continued to wrestle through the mid-1980s. During his third WWF stint in 1986 and 1987, McMahon attempted to transition him into a managerial role, and later into a commentator. He didn't do well in either position and was ultimately fired, and once again he fell into a depression.

In the 1990s, in the wake of the George Zahorian steroid trial, Hogan made his famous appearance on *The Arsenio Hall Show* and lied about his steroid history. At some point he made a comment about Graham, calling him a drug addict. Graham, who knew Hogan had lied about his own drug use, was furious. He went on the offensive and did tons of media targeting Hogan, McMahon, and the WWF. At one point he sued Zahorian and WWF, claiming they forced him to take steroids to maintain his physique. Perhaps because he'd been on steroids for a decade before going to WWF, his case went nowhere. He became so angry and bitter that he began fabricating stories regarding Hogan's steroid use and WWF's involvement in an alleged underage sex scandal. He didn't destroy any lives with his stories, but he potentially could have, and years later he wrote letters to everyone involved, apologizing to them.

In 2003, he reunited with McMahon, and a few years later they put out a DVD documentary on his life. It was the usual WWE production, telling its version of history as the winners always do, but putting Graham over in the end. While many in the business forgave him, including Hogan, others did not.

Graham has suffered from numerous health issues dating back to the 1980s, some drug-related, others injury-related from his career. He's had serious liver problems for nearly 15 years, battled Hepatitis C, and was legitimately very close to death on a few occasions. But he has survived into his mid-70s, alongside the real hero of his story, his wife, Valerie, who has remained by his side since they married in 1978.

Brock Lesnar

Brock Lesnar kind of looks like what you'd imagine a Neanderthal might look like. But looks are deceiving. He's one of the smartest businessmen in WWE history.

Lesnar was scouted directly out of college, where he was a two-time All-American and the 2000 NCAA champion in amateur wrestling in the heavyweight division. He had the look and the athletic ability, and unlike most of the guys signed to WWF developmental, he was offered a six-figure deal right out of the gate. Those factors meant he was guaranteed to be called up to the WWF main roster too early, and that's exactly what happened. He debuted on March 18, 2002, a little over a year after being signed, and was given a monster push right out of the gate. Managed by Paul Heyman, whom he'd met during his developmental time at Ohio Valley Wrestling, he ran roughshod over everyone, winning the WWE championship from the Rock at that year's SummerSlam, just 126 days after debuting on the main roster.

His first run in WWE saw him feud with such stars as the Undertaker and Kurt Angle, the latter of whom he beat at WrestleMania XIX in Seattle to win the WWE title in one of the scariest finishes in history. Lesnar had successfully pulled off a shooting star press—a gymnastics gainer, wherein you jump forward but flip backward off the top rope—during his time in OVW. It's among the most difficult moves to perform in pro wrestling, and Lesnar, at the time close to 300 pounds of solid muscle, had been told from the beginning that a guy like him shouldn't be doing that move regularly. So why not break it out at WrestleMania, in the main event, no less? Lesnar, exhausted at the end of a long, physical match, went up top, threw the shooting star, but came up short and landed right on his head. He could have died. But he's Brock Lesnar. He shook it off, jumped up, hit his F-5 finisher on Angle, and pinned him to win the title.

He spent the night in the hospital and never attempted a shooting star press again.

On February 15, 2004, at the Cow Palace in San Francisco, Lesnar dropped the WWE title to Eddie Guerrero. Guerrero had absolutely caught fire with the Hispanic audience and the decision was made that he'd be the new top star of *SmackDown*. Lesnar not only lost the title but wasn't given any indication that he was going to get it back. He decided his time in pro wrestling was over, that you only live once, and if he was ever going to give professional football—yes, the NFL—a shot, it was now or never. And so, following WrestleMania that year, he left. It seemed like a crazy idea at the time, but Lesnar was a freakish athlete. Despite having zero high-level or even mid-level football experience, he was so impressive during tryouts that he was signed to the Minnesota Vikings practice squad. He played a few preseason games but was ultimately cut at the end of August. His football career was over and his WWE career was on the rocks, so Lesnar chose to debut with New Japan Pro Wrestling.

The problem was, in order to get out of his WWE deal to try out with the NFL, the company had forced him to sign a 10-year non-compete agreement for pro wrestling anywhere in the world. He ignored it, and in his New Japan debut on October 8, 2005, he won the IWGP heavyweight belt (its version of the world title) in a three-way against Masa Chono and Kazuyuki Fujita. WWE tried to file an injunction against his continued participation in New Japan. Ultimately the situation wound up in court, and although the verdict was sealed, Lesnar continued to wrestle for New Japan and renamed his finisher "The Verdict," clearly a swipe at WWE.

Lesnar defended the title three times, once against future WWE star Shinsuke Nakamura, before ending his stint with New Japan without ever dropping the title. He wrestled one final match in Japan for Antonio Inoki's Inoki Genome Federation, billed as the IWGP champion (he wasn't, but Inoki claimed he was the rightful champion since he never lost the belt), and put over Kurt Angle, then the TNA world heavyweight champion. It was his final pro wrestling match for six years.

Lesnar made his MMA debut for the Japanese promotion K-1 Hero's on June 2, 2007, in Los Angeles. He obliterated judo star Min Soo Kim in just over a minute. Kim was hardly top-notch competition, going into the fight with a 2–5 record, but he had fought and won professionally, unlike the inexperienced Lesnar. Within four months, Lesnar had signed a deal to fight with the largest MMA promotion in the world, and a company on fire at the time, the Ultimate Fighting Championship.

Lesnar's run in UFC was incredible. Although he lost his first fight via kneebar to Frank Mir, he was winning the fight until the moment he lost. He took Mir down and was going all Donkey Kong on him, to the point where many referees would have stopped the fight, but Mir pulled a kneebar out of nowhere and got the submission. Still, it was a super impressive performance. In Lesnar's next match, he beat veteran Heath Herring, and then, in his third fight in UFC, he beat all-time legend Randy Couture to win the UFC heavyweight title. He went undefeated for two straight years and won four big-time PPV fights before finally running into Cain Velasquez and losing the title via TKO.

During that period, a lot of people made a lot of money. Lesnar got his UFC purse and also a cut of PPV revenues, making him a multi-millionaire. UFC made huge money on PPV for his fights. Interestingly, if you track PPV buys, UFC buys spiked with Lesnar on top at the same time that WWE PPV buys took a hit; when Lesnar stopped fighting for UFC, its buyrates reverted back toward normal and WWE buyrates started to increase. Long story short, even though he wasn't a pro wrestler per se, Brock Lesnar fighting caused pro wrestling fans to open up their pocketbooks and pay to see his matches. (This was my personal argument for putting Lesnar in the Wrestling Observer Hall of Fame.)

After making so much money in MMA, he parlayed that into a lucrative deal to return to WWE, and then back into another lucrative UFC contract in 2016, and then, throughout 2018, played both sides against each other in order to get lucrative deals from both organizations simultaneously. If you look at the schedule that Brock Lesnar worked in both pro wrestling and UFC from 2006 through 2018, he is almost certainly the highest-paid pro wrestler of all time when you consider the amount of money made and the number of dates worked.

He was pushed as an unstoppable monster right out of the gate upon his 2012 WWE return. Well, sort of; first, he had to lose to Triple H. The idea of Lesnar coming off a massive UFC run only to lose immediately to Hunter sounds ridiculous on the surface, until you consider that Vince McMahon probably didn't trust that he'd stick around for the long haul, given his famously temperamental mindset. In Vince's mind, Lesnar might quit at any moment, and if he beat all of his WWE stars and then quit,

Paul Heyman raises the hand of Brock Lesnar moments after Lesnar broke the Undertaker's undefeated WrestleMania streak in 2014.

what might that do to business? (The answer, historically, is nothing.) So, Vince made sure that one of his biggest stars got a huge win over the former UFC heavyweight champion, just in case something went wrong.

Once it was clear that Lesnar was happy with his current deal—and why wouldn't he be, making in the mid-seven-figure range for limited dates—Vince put into motion his long-term plan. Setting the stage for Roman Reigns to become the face of the company, Lesnar beat the Undertaker at WrestleMania XXX in 2014, ending the Dead Man's legendary streak in the most shocking upset finish since Ivan Koloff beat Bruno Sammartino in 1971. From that day forward, Lesnar was booked as an unstoppable beast, with the end-game being a WrestleMania match where Roman would beat the unbeatable Lesnar, the man who had ended the streak, and become the man himself.

For reasons discussed elsewhere, it took four years to finally pull the trigger and give Roman his big win, and by that time, WWE had, to put it gently, missed its window. Every year something came up, and every year McMahon signed Lesnar to a new seven-figure deal. It got to the point where, in 2018, Roman was supposed to beat Lesnar at WrestleMania, but once again McMahon changed his mind, put Lesnar over again, and signed him to another seven-figure deal for just *two dates*, the Greatest Royal Rumble and SummerSlam. And then, on top of that, after leaving WWE to train for another UFC run, WWE lured him back with another seven-figure deal, and by the end of the year he was WWE universal champion again.

The Brock Lesnar story could fill a book. He's a case study in deal making. He's been the biggest star in two different promotions at the same time, one real and one less real. And he's not even a die-hard fan. He spends his off days with his family on his farms, doing chores, hunting, fishing, training, and not watching TV, because he doesn't own one.

28 Attend a *RAW* or *SmackDown* Taping

Attending a *RAW* or *SmackDown* television taping and a local house show are two very different experiences.

House shows are fun events with a focus on the in-ring wrestling; a philosophy of generally having the babyfaces win unless it happens to be a heel in a championship match; virtually non-existent title changes; and, obviously, no commercial breaks.

A TV taping is different. Although title changes are usually saved for PPV events/WWE Network specials, occasionally they do happen on TV. If you're buying a house show ticket and hoping to see a title change, you may as well be playing the lottery every week too. At TV, probably once every few months, a title changes hands, so while it's not a regular occurrence, it does happen.

What you will definitely see at a TV taping is an angle, and probably several. The house shows present the matches that were built up by the angles on TV. On Monday, Roman Reigns might get beaten up by Braun Strowman, and then the upcoming house shows will feature Reigns vs. Strowman matches.

The demands of TV also mean changes to the flow of the matches themselves. For example, in several matches there will be a dive to the outside by one of the wrestlers, and then they'll go back into the ring and lay there in a chinlock or another rest hold. This is because the show is currently on a commercial break. Wrestlers come to the ring with their music playing, and then suddenly the music stops, and the lights go out for four minutes. Commercial break. Then the lights suddenly come back on and the music picks up where it left off, and you know you're live again. Sometimes a wrestler will start to come out, they'll turn off the lights and music, then they'll air a video package, then a commercial, and then another video package, and by the time they come back, the wrestler will have been awkwardly standing there in the dark for seven or eight minutes. Of course, this all comes off seamlessly when watching on TV, but when you're an audience member, it's pretty weird.

That said, I've never had a bad time at a WWE TV taping. *RAW* is three hours long, so when you watch at home it's easy to get bored or zone out and start playing on your phone or switching to another channel. At a TV taping, you're pretty much forced to watch, plus you're surrounded by other wrestling fans who are also there to have a good time. It's a much easier show to watch live than on television, and you get to see the stars, hear the music, and become a part of the show with your signs or chants. To this day, no matter what you think of the overall TV product, it's still a lot of fun to go to a TV taping.

Attend a Local House Show

When I was a kid, if WWF was coming to town, you never missed a show. I attended an event on June 8, 1990, at what was then called the Seattle Center Coliseum (later the Key Arena). I was 14 years old and had a pretty good idea that wrestling wasn't real, but I was still surprised when I saw Warlord, who was a heel, jump into a car after the show with Koko B. Ware, who was a babyface. (I'll never forget the size of the car; it was one of the smallest rental cars I'd ever seen, and Warlord was one of the largest and most muscular men I'd ever seen.) During intermission, they announced that on July 9 in Tacoma, Rick Rude would be wrestling in the main event against the new WWF champion, the Ultimate Warrior. As soon as the ring announcer said, "Ultimate Warrior," hundreds of fans jumped out of their seats and rushed to the box office to buy their tickets. Ah, the days before the Internet.

Almost exactly one month later—and today, it's amazing to see how often WWF came to the Seattle/Tacoma area in the 1980s and 1990s, considering that today they might come to a major market just once or twice a year—I witnessed a main event of the Ultimate Warrior vs. Rick Rude for the WWF title at the Tacoma Dome. This was interesting because they were scheduled to wrestle each other yet again, this time in a cage match at WWF's biggest pay-per-view of the summer. At points I thought for sure the Ultimate Warrior might lose the championship, but he did not. I went home wondering if things might be different at the pay-per-view. Imagine my surprise when I tuned into SummerSlam and found that the Ultimate Warrior and Rude wrestled *the exact same match*, move for move. That pretty much sealed the deal for me on the whole real/fake issue.

It's a different story today. I have so many friends I grew up with who never go to shows anymore. I also have friends who pay at least cursory attention to WWE who would never go to a house show unless I scored them a free ticket. And that's too bad, because I have never failed to have a good time at a WWE house show.

Back in the 1980s and early 1990s, WWF was running three shows every single day around the United States, and wrestlers would legitimately wrestle as many as 250 dates or more per year. Thus, the shows were sometimes pretty awful in terms of actual in-ring wrestling. For example, the undercard of that Tacoma Dome show I attended included Shane Douglas vs. Paul Diamond, Jim Powers vs. Buddy Rose, Barbarian vs. Jimmy Snuka, Dino Bravo vs. Tugboat, the Bushwhackers vs. Greg Valentine and the Honky Tonk Man, and Jake Roberts vs. Bad News Brown—frankly, that's a pretty horrible card. But today, with WWE's loaded roster and the pride they have in their work, you'll almost never attend a show with bad wrestling from bell to bell. Because there aren't TV time constraints, the wrestlers have more time to tell stories, interact with the crowd, and have fun. Many wrestlers prefer to work house shows over TV because they're so much more fun (some, like Batista, are very public about those feelings). Plus, with the price of a ticket being far more affordable than for a TV taping or PPV event, you can bring the whole family and enjoy a fun afternoon of pro wrestling that is about as old-school as you're going to get with the current-day, TV-oriented corporate WWE.

30 WWE Signs a $2.3 Billion Television Deal

In July of 2018, WWE announced that it had signed the most lucrative television deal in history, a five-year deal with USA and FOX totaling a staggering $2.3 billion. The irony is that ratings for *RAW* and *SmackDown* were hitting all-time lows.

How does such a thing happen?

The answer is that despite viewership for *RAW* and *SmackDown* declining year-over-year since the Monday Night Wars ended (with the decline speeding up once *RAW* moved to three hours in 2012), they have declined at a slower rate than the rest of television as a whole. Then, coincidentally, ratings just happened to tick upward during the period WWE was negotiating for a new contract. Finally, and a factor understated by many, WWE had signed one of UFC's biggest revenue generators and a mainstream United States superstar, "Rowdy" Ronda Rousey.

Right place, right time.

Conversely, UFC, which had huge business years in the mid-2010s riding a wave of success with Rousey and Conor McGregor, lost Rousey and saw its television ratings decline year-over-year during its negotiating period. As a result, while it signed a good television deal, it was disappointing considering what it was hoping to get.

Wrong place, wrong time.

The story of WWE business is rife with contradictions. In 2012, USA Network requested the company expand *RAW* to three hours. *Nitro* expanded to three hours during the Monday Night Wars, and that helped to drastically erode its audience. Three hours is just too long for a wrestling show, for both fans and the people putting the shows together. You end up with shows that drag in the third hour; you end up booking the same stars in the same matches over and over again; and you end up driving away fans who don't have 12 hours a month to devote to pro wrestling (and that's just to keep up with *RAW*—that doesn't count *SmackDown*, NXT, pay-per-view events, etc.). It makes it difficult to create new fans, because you are expected to devote at least three hours of your week to wrestling or you run the risk of missing out on a big angle. These were all the arguments people had against going to three hours in 2012. But USA Network, desperate to remain the No. 1 cable network, had nothing else that was going to draw 2 million viewers at 10:00 PM, and so *RAW* expanded.

In the end, everything people feared would happen happened. *RAW*'s audience decline since 2012 is somewhat stunning. Mathematically, one of two things are happening: either WWE is making zero new fans, or it is making new fans but losing more old fans than it is making. Either way, neither is good for the long-term popularity of WWE. The audience has fallen to the point where traditional revenue generators are way down, some in a rather startling way. Fewer people are watching shows. Fewer people are buying merchandise. Fewer people are going to live events. Amazingly, in 2018, the company lost money on house shows, something inconceivable only a few years ago.

But the audience-eroding *RAW* was still drawing more than 2 million viewers in its lowest-rated third hour, and nothing USA Network had was going to do better than that. USA couldn't afford to pay for both *RAW* and *SmackDown*, so *SmackDown* went out on the open market. FOX, seeing the value of live sports and considering WWE's product to be DVR-proof, agreed to pay the company $205 million annually, with the intention of putting *SmackDown* in a Friday night spot.

The thing is that pro wrestling is not a sport, is not promoted as a sport, and is absolutely not DVR-proof, as DVR numbers hover around 25 percent, significantly higher than for actual live sports.

But apparently nobody at FOX knew or cared about that statistic, or perhaps they thought they could push WWE toward promoting a more sports-based product when *SmackDown* jumped to FOX.

One way or another, the reality is all of WWE's traditional revenue generators could lose tremendous amounts of money and it won't really matter until at least 2024. It is impossible to predict what the television landscape will look like in the mid-2020s, but today, despite record-low television ratings, WWE for the first time in its history is on the road to exceeding $1 billion in annual revenue.

WWF Becomes WWE

First, the part of the story that most people wouldn't care about all that much. Vince McMahon Sr. and Toots Mondt founded Capitol Wrestling Corporation Ltd. in 1952. In 1963, they created the World Wide Wrestling Federation, technically a wrestling promotion under the Capitol banner. Why McMahon Sr. decided on the somewhat bizarre "World Wide" aspect of the name, as two words, is anyone's guess. In 1979, they dropped the "Wide" part, and it became known as World Wrestling Federation.

Vince McMahon Jr. founded Titan Sports, Inc. in 1980. Two years later he purchased Capitol Wrestling Corporation and thus the World Wrestling Federation from his father. In 1998, Titan Sports was renamed World Wrestling Federation, Inc., and then a year later it was renamed World Wrestling Federation Entertainment, Inc. When it first went public in 1999, its stock symbol was WWFE for that reason, although later it changed to the simpler WWE.

Now comes the part that has bothered some people for over a decade: why did the WWF become the WWE?

The answer is because Vince McMahon tried to be Vince McMahon and didn't get away with it for once.

As noted, the World Wide Wrestling Federation became the World Wrestling Federation, the WWF, in 1979. Problem was, there is another organization, the World Wildlife Fund, that was founded on April 29, 1961 (meaning it even preceded the WWWF). Long story short, in 1994 the WWF and the WWF came to an agreement where the wrestling promotion would be allowed to use the "WWF" initials inside but not outside the United States (the Fund is located in Switzerland). McMahon's company signed the agreement, and then proceeded to spend the next half decade promoting itself as WWF all over the world, blatantly violating the terms of the agreement.

Ultimately, the Fund filed suit. The wrestling promotion claimed that the suit was without merit. Justice Robin Jacob heard the case and found WWF's defense "hopeless" and "astonishingly poor." The Fund was victorious, and the wrestling promotion proceeded to change its name to WWE, at which point it ran a campaign called, no joke, "Get the F Out." At no time do I recall the company publicly admitting any wrongdoing; hence the reason so many wrestling fans believed over the years that this was all the World Wildlife Fund's fault, and led them to hate that "stupid" or "damn" panda (the Fund's logo features a panda bear).

WWE and the Fund came to another agreement in 2011 which granted the wrestling company permission to allow the old WWF logo to appear on archived footage. Prior to the agreement, the logo had to be blurred off of every show, which was an absolute nightmare, particularly with thousands and thousands of hours getting digitized in preparation for the eventual launch of the WWE Network.

Interestingly, today the World Wildlife Fund is known as the World Wide Fund for Nature everywhere except the U.S. and Canada, where it remains the World Wildlife Fund.

 WWF Goes Public

WWF went public in 1999, 36 years after the World Wide Wrestling Federation was founded by Vince McMahon's father, Vincent James McMahon. It changed the wrestling landscape forever.

The IPO speaks to the astounding success that WWF saw in just a few short years, largely as a result of Steve Austin getting hot and his monumental feud with McMahon, arguably the greatest feud in pro wrestling history. The company went from losing $6 million in 1995, by far its worst year in history, to reporting $126 million in revenue and $8 million in profits in 1998, and $251 million in net income and $56 million in profits in 1999. The stock was expected to be valued at around $15, but WWF instead valued it at $17. The day the stock began trading, it hit $35 per share before dropping down to $25.25 that first afternoon.

Vince McMahon, with his 98 percent of voting shares, became a billionaire overnight.

For over a decade some fans have blamed WWF going public for all of its ills. PG era? WWF went public. End of the Attitude Era? WWF went public. No more swearing? WWF went public. John Cena? WWF went public. Three-hour *RAW*? WWF went public. Illogical storylines and no real incentive to have anything make sense? WWF went public.

There are two realities that should be considered when talking about the company going public. The first is that most of the things fans complain about are things that would have happened whether WWF went public or not. The second is that, one way or another, the company was always going to go public, even if it didn't happen in 1999.

The Attitude Era was about time and place and competition and the age of the audience. It was always going to end someday. The PG era had little to do with the company going public, as all sorts of crazy things happened long after they went public; everything from Trish Stratus on her knees barking like a dog to Triple H pretending to have sex with a corpse to Stephanie McMahon joking about dismemberment in reference to the real-life dismemberment of Jamal Khashoggi (I am not making any of that up). The real reason the shows grew tamer was because the company started getting big-time blue-chip sponsors. For decades, despite wrestling's huge ratings, advertisers shied away due to the belief that wrestling fans were poor and uneducated. But in the 2010s, television ratings fell to a great degree and wrestling held up better than most, and sponsors started to realize that shows like *RAW* and *SmackDown* were a good value. That, more than anything else, has led to WWE's PG era.

You could perhaps argue that *RAW* moving to three hours in 2012 can be blamed on the IPO, in the sense that virtually nobody believes *RAW* is better at three hours than two. But USA Network wanted three hours and was willing to pay big money for it, and WWE owes it to its shareholders to make the most financially lucrative deals. Therefore, to the detriment of the product, it took the money.

WWE being a public company has coincided with a period where fewer people are watching than at any other time in modern WWE history (post-1995), but because they have leveraged those remaining hardcore fans in very creative ways, they are making more money than ever before. (Two ways WWE has used numbers to its advantage: making PPV shows longer, so it can brag that fans are spending more time on the Network; and touting social media numbers that have never been shown to have any bearing on revenue.) WWE's stock skyrocketed following the announcement of the new TV deal in 2018, hitting almost $100 per share before the stock market as a whole fell in combination with a rash of bad publicity concerning the decision to stage the Crown Jewel event in Saudi Arabia. Still, while the stock fell to around $65 per share, that's still about five times what it traded for over the majority of its existence, and WWE was still valued at approximately $5 billion.

The Steroid Trial

The WWF steroid trial of the early 1990s was serious enough that Vince McMahon had plans in place should he end up being sent to prison.

The story is so amazing that it sounds like a wrestling storyline. It all started in 1991, when Dr. George Zahorian was convicted of selling steroids to WWF wrestlers. Zahorian was a doctor hired by the Pennsylvania State Athletic Commission, and whenever WWF ran shows in the state he would allegedly set up shop and sell the wrestlers whatever they wanted. It seemed as though everyone was on steroids at the time. The top star, Hulk Hogan, was a monstrous 6-foot-6, 300-plus pound babyface, and so the heels, in order to appear to be a legitimate threat, had to get as big and muscular and intimidating as possible. There were a few natural wrestlers working for the company at the time, but not many.

Vince McMahon, Dr. George Zahorian, and Hulk Hogan in 1988.

WWF knew all about Zahorian; it would be hard not to seeing as to how Vince McMahon himself bought steroids from him. At one point, Pennsylvania stopped assigning doctors and so it was up to WWF to hire its own. The woman in charge of hiring local doctors, Anita Scales, knew Zahorian was trouble and wanted nothing to do with him, but according to court testimony, Linda McMahon and Pat Patterson disagreed because "the boys need their candy." As it happened, Linda just happened to be at a party and was tipped off that Zahorian was "hot." So Zahorian was never actually hired, and shortly thereafter he was busted.

Hulk Hogan, who also bought steroids from Zahorian, was subpoenaed for the trial. His lawyer, Jerry McDevitt, who later became Vince McMahon's personal lawyer, got him out of testifying. Hogan went on *The Arsenio Hall Show* and lied about his steroid use, claiming he only used steroids three times in his life to rehab injuries.

In 1993, McMahon was indicted. The main charge was that McMahon conspired to distribute steroids to his WWF wrestlers. Prior to 1991, it was illegal to distribute steroids but not illegal to purchase or use them. Since WWF had never hired Zahorian, and since Zahorian himself, under oath as a government witness, couldn't come up with any instances when he and McMahon had detailed conversations about any of this, there was no evidence that McMahon conspired to sell any steroids to the wrestlers.

The other charge was that McMahon distributed steroids to Hulk Hogan. This case was even weaker but somehow managed to go further. Hogan's steroids would be delivered to his house, the home of his friend Dan Brower, and Titan Towers. Zahorian would send a package to Vince containing both Vince's and Hogan's steroids, Vince would open the package, take his, give Hogan his, and that was that. This was what the government considered distribution. Vince was very close to going to prison over this. Amazingly, it came down to the fact that the trial was held in the Eastern District of New York and Titan Towers was located in Connecticut, outside the court's jurisdiction. As a last-ditch effort to get McMahon, the government claimed that at one point McMahon had sent the package with Hogan's steroids to Hogan's limo driver (who was supposed to testify but vanished), who was in the parking lot of the Nassau Coliseum at the time, which would be within the court's jurisdiction. But that fell apart because the Nassau Coliseum show took place before Zahorian sent the package.

McMahon was off the hook.

A lot of new information came out in the trial. Hogan admitted that, in fact, he'd used steroids forever. In interviews outside of court, he noted that when he was coming up, steroids were "legal" and that everyone used them for all sorts of reasons, including rehab, muscle growth, and endurance. He also said it was hypocritical that one day he could be doing something everyone was legally doing and then the next day be a criminal for doing it. Hogan estimated that 75 to 80 percent of the WWF wrestlers were on steroids. Jim Hellwig, the Ultimate Warrior, claimed it was 90 percent.

In the wake of the trial, WWF instituted a serious drug testing program. Everyone either shrank, quit, or was fired. The public, which for a decade had been weaned on gigantic wrestlers who looked like action figures, weren't as interested in more normal-looking guys, not to mention that among those who quit or were fired were some of the biggest stars in the company. WWF went into a down period and did not recover until the Monday Night Wars when it formally dropped drug testing and was faced with WCW—which had no drug policy—kicking its ass. WWF wouldn't start drug testing again until Eddie Guerrero died of an enlarged heart, and even that was only a half-assed attempt. A true wellness policy wasn't adopted until the Chris Benoit tragedy.

Just say no to drugs.

34 The Creation of the WWWF Title

Today's WWE title has its roots in a political battle dating back to the early 1960s.

Roderick James "Jess" McMahon formed Capital Sports Corporation with another longtime Northeast promoter, Toots Mondt, in 1952. The following year they joined the National Wrestling Alliance. Jess died a year later, and his son, Vincent James McMahon, came on board. They promoted a very powerful territory in the Northeast.

At the time, the board of directors of the NWA would choose to put the world championship on someone, and that person would tour around North America defending the title in various territories. Lou Thesz dominated the title in the mid-1950s. Thesz was largely a good draw in most territories as champion; a no-nonsense, scientific, shoot-style serious worker. But he did not draw well for McMahon in his territory.

In 1957, Thesz decided he was done as champion. The NWA board wanted to put the title on Buddy Rogers, but Thesz hated Rogers, his style, and his lack of legitimate wrestling ability. He chose instead to drop the title to the uncharismatic and poor-drawing Dick Hutton, whose best attribute—that he was a legit three-time NCAA champion and 1948 Olympian—was the one attribute that Thesz put the most stock in. Hutton flopped, and the title was put on Pat O'Connor.

On June 30, 1961, Rogers beat O'Conner at Comiskey Park in Chicago to win the NWA title, drawing 38,622 fans and $148,000, a record at the time. McMahon was pleased, as he loved booking Rogers as a champion. Rogers, whose moniker, "The Nature Boy," was eventually taken by Ric Flair, was larger-than-life and drew well. McMahon booked him so often that other promoters in the NWA had trouble getting dates for him, so one by one they began to pull out of the NWA and create their own versions of the world championship. With member territories dropping out and the NWA falling apart, the often-president and largest promoter at the time, Sam Muchnick, made the call in late 1962 that Thesz needed to win the title back from Rogers.

But McMahon didn't want Rogers dropping the title. Twice in 1962 the title change was booked, and twice, due to injuries to Rogers, it didn't take place. In those days, the champion had to put down a $25,000 bond (equivalent to about $200,000 today) to become champion. If they were asked to lose the belt and refused, their bond would be forfeited to charity. After Rogers avoided dropping the title twice, Muchnick finally told him he would either lose the title on January 24, 1963, at the Maple Leaf Gardens in Toronto, or he was forfeiting his bond. That night, as the referee was giving instructions, Thesz, still a fearsome shooter at age 46, whispered to Rogers: "We can do this the hard way, or the easy way." Rogers chose the easy way.

While having Rogers on top had caused some promoters to leave the NWA, McMahon was furious and quit the NWA when Thesz won back the title. He formed a new promotion, the World Wide Wrestling Federation, and Rogers was going to be his first champion.

This was long before the Internet, and news traveled slowly. Therefore, a number of different stories surfaced about why Rogers was champion. In some magazines, it was reported that Thesz had beaten Rogers for the title. In others, it was claimed that a tournament had been held in Rio de Janeiro (home of several imaginary tournaments), and that Rogers had won it to become the WWWF champion. On the television show that McMahon aired on WABD in New York—called, in true McMahon fashion, *Heavyweight Wrestling*—the future figurehead president of the WWWF, Willie Gilzenberg, came on television and announced that a non-title match had been held in Canada, Rogers had won, and therefore he was presenting him with this, the WWWF belt, and also a trophy for Rogers celebrating his long, allegedly uninterrupted, winning streak.

Despite all the rigmarole involving the NWA, the title, dates on the champion, and McMahon's desire for Rogers to be his champion, in less than six months he dropped the title to Bruno Sammartino. Rogers claimed he had heart issues; others, including Sammartino, doubted this. But something was physically wrong with Rogers, as he went from working long matches to very short matches, and was forced to take a lot of time off. The match with Sammartino was only 48 seconds long. Afterward, he wrestled in either tags or very short singles matches sporadically, before leaving wrestling altogether for several years.

35 Bob Backlund

Bob Backlund was the World Wide Wrestling Federation champion and top clean-cut company babyface in the years preceding the birth of Hulkamania in early 1984. Interestingly enough, after a lengthy semi-retirement, he returned to the company in the mid-1990s as a heel and briefly held the WWF title again as the bridge between the Bret Hart and Diesel title reigns.

Backlund won the title from Superstar Billy Graham on February 20, 1978, a date that Vince McMahon Sr. had chosen almost a year in advance. Graham had been the exception to the rule that heels in the WWF were only transitional champions. From the time he won the title through the end of 1983, Graham faced a wide variety of opponents not only from the WWWF but also from other territories, including champion vs. champion matches with the likes of Harley Race and Ric Flair from the NWA, and Nick Bockwinkel from the AWA. Although WWE's official title history lists Backlund as champion during this entire period, he dropped the title to Antonio Inoki in Tokushima Japan in November of 1979 (which led to Inoki refusing the title and Backlund regaining it after a match with Bobby Duncum), and kind-of sort-of dropped the title to Greg Valentine in New York in October of 1981 (the referee had been knocked out and accidentally awarded the title to Valentine, at which point the title was considered vacant only in New York, and Backlund went on to beat Valentine in a rematch to the end the controversy).

By the early 1980s fans were growing weary of Backlund's technical wrestler act, and Vince McMahon Jr., who had purchased the company from his father, wanted to put the title on a gigantic muscular superstar who had made it big already in Verne Gagne's AWA—Hulk Hogan. McMahon wanted Backlund to turn heel and drop the title to Hogan, but Backlund refused, so on December 26, 1983, Backlund lost the title to the Iron Sheik after his manager, Arnold Skaaland, threw in the towel as Backlund was trapped in the feared Camel Clutch.

By midway through 1984, Backlund was gone from the WWF. It was eight years before he returned. Since his entire championship run had preceded Vince's national expansion, Hulkamania, and the rise of WrestleMania, most new fans had little idea who he was. For the first few years he largely wrestled as the same character from the late 1970s and early 1980s, which didn't get him over with the early 1990s crowd.

His second big run began in late July of 1994 when he wrestled Bret Hart in what was billed as a friendly scientific match. Backlund thought he won but was mistaken, and Hart capitalized on this and beat him. Backlund went crazy after the match, snapping and putting Bret in the crossface chicken wing. This was the beginning of his first official heel turn in the WWF. He began to dress in suits and bowties, snapped regularly, attacked the innocent, and acted erratically both on and off television (stories of the crazy things he'd do with fans in public, including demanding they recite the U.S. presidents in order before giving them an autograph, are many). He ranted and raved that he'd never really lost the WWF title because he never submitted to the Iron Sheik and was never pinned, and he should still be WWF champion today. This led to his famous match with Bret Hart at Survivor Series 1994, a submission match for the WWF title.

At the time, Bret was feuding with his brother Owen, who had turned on him in a fit of jealous rage. Owen had beaten him at WrestleMania X in the opener, prior to Bret winning the WWF title in the main event, and they'd feuded throughout the summer. Owen, therefore, was Backlund's second in the match, and Bret's second was his brother-in-law Davey Boy Smith.

Bret had the match seemingly won with his sharpshooter submission, but Owen hit the ring to break it up. Smith went after him but got laid out on the outside. This distracted Bret, allowing Backlund to put him in the famed chicken wing. Bret was stuck in the hold for eight minutes, refusing to quit. Owen, who hated his brother, was pleading with his parents to stop the match. Their father, the legendary Stu Hart, refused, figuring Owen was just trying to screw his brother out of the title (Stu was a wise man). But their mother, Helen, could not take seeing her son in such pain, so she grabbed the towel from Owen, threw it into the ring, and Bob Backlund won the WWF championship the same way he lost it, this time at the age of 45.

Backlund claims that McMahon told him that he would have a long heel run; whether McMahon changed his mind or just lied to get him to do what he asked, the reality was much different. Three days later, in Madison Square Garden, Diesel hit Backlund with his powerbomb finisher and won the WWF title in just eight seconds.

Backlund remained with the company for a while afterward, including putting Hart over a second time in an "I Quit" match at WrestleMania, but the Madison Square Garden show marked the end of his main event run in the WWF. He has appeared sporadically on and off for the company ever since, even as late as 2017 when he managed Darren Young on *RAW* for a short period of time. His book, *Backlund: From All-American Boy to Professional Wrestling's World Champion* released in 2015, is one of the better wrestling autobiographies.

36 Bobby "The Brain" Heenan

Bobby Heenan is arguably the greatest manager who ever lived, and one of wrestling's all-around best performers.

Younger fans probably only have a faint memory of Heenan since his last national run ended prior to the death of WCW, and by that point he was largely sailing his way through commentary, sometimes appearing to be drunk. His final years saw him stricken with throat cancer, a disease that necessitated the removal of his jaw, and so he was rarely seen in public outside of occasional appearances at fan fests. Even to the very end, when he could no longer speak, he kept his incredible wit and sense of humor.

That wit and sense of humor was what made him one of the great talkers in wrestling history. He could cut an incredible promo as a manager, and when in his younger years he was an incredible commentator. Fans who grew up on the WWF of the 1980s probably best remember him as co-host alongside Gorilla Monsoon on the old *Prime Time Wrestling* TV show. The show itself was often terrible, featuring almost exclusively boring house show matches—fans who grew up on *RAW* would be astounded at what pre-1991 WWF television fans watched on a weekly basis—but the interplay of Heenan and Monsoon, who in real life loved each other but on television played good-natured adversaries, was incredible. Gorilla played the straight-man babyface and Heenan played the smart-ass heel who would invariably get foiled in whatever wacky scheme he came up with whenever the show traveled outside its studio setting. Part of the fun of the show was how much you loved Heenan even though you were supposed to hate him. As a young teenager, I thought the show fell off a cliff when it moved to being presented before a live studio audience and you could see and hear everyone constantly laughing at Heenan's jokes.

Besides being a great manager and commentator, Heenan was also an exceptionally talented pro wrestler, although he never had much of a career due to his limited size and physique. His favorite wrestlers were also great workers: Curt Hennig, Ric Flair, and Ray Stevens, the latter of whom were two of the greatest in the ring of all time. Heenan's bumping ability, even into his older years, was incredible, but unfortunately the damage caught up with him, which was what led him to retire from managing in the early 1990s. His feeling was that he didn't want to just stand out there at ringside; if he couldn't get in there and bump around and sell for the babyfaces, there was no use in him being out there.

Most WWF fans never saw it, but among his greatest runs was as a manager for Nick Bockwinkel in the AWA in the late 1970s and early 1980s. The role of a manager is normally to do all the talking for whoever he is managing, since historically that wrestler usually isn't a great talker. But the pairing of Heenan and Bockwinkel put together two of the great talkers in wrestling history; the most analogous modern pairing would probably be Paul Heyman and CM Punk.

Heenan, who had been a wrestling fan since age 10, got his start in the business in 1965. His first major success came as a manager for Blackjack Lanza in Sam Muchnick's St. Louis territory. Muchnick hated the idea of managers, and in his entire run as one of the great promoters in wrestling history he only allowed one man to be a main event manager on his show: Bobby Heenan. Although tales of the insanity of pro wrestling in the mid-20th century are often exaggerated, Heenan was such a heat magnet during this period that he was once shot at by a fan in Chicago.

The Lanza pairing was what made him a star. The AWA period in the late 1970s and early 1980s was probably his biggest creative success. The WWF run in the 1980s and early 1990s was his most

Bobby "The Brain" Heenan at the announce table alongside Vince McMahon.

famous period, as he'd manage one monster after another in a quest to dethrone Hulk Hogan and relieve him of his WWF championship. Perhaps his two most famous programs were the mid-1980s Andre the Giant vs. Hogan feud that led to WrestleMania III, and his role as the manager for "The Real World's Champion" Ric Flair when Flair jumped from Jim Crockett Promotions to the WWF in 1991. He had planned to retire after his WWF run, but

WCW contacted him and offered him an incredible deal to come in and do commentary. He remained one of the voices of *Nitro* and later *Thunder* until Vince Russo came aboard in October of 1999; Heenan was eventually replaced by Mark Madden.

Bobby Heenan passed away on September 17, 2017, at the age of 72.

Eric Bischoff

Eric Bischoff's legacy is that he was one of the greatest promoters in the history of wrestling—for about two years.

Bischoff was the man who convinced Ted Turner in 1995 that if WCW wanted to compete with WWF, they needed two hours live on Monday nights. Turner gave it, and an almost unlimited checkbook, to him, and for two years WCW kicked WWF's ass. But then it all came crashing down to the point where, six years after he was given those two hours, WCW, at one point the largest wrestling company in the history of the planet Earth, was out of business.

Bischoff initially got into wrestling in the late 1980s, working in sales for the AWA. As was the case with hundreds of pro wrestlers, one day someone didn't show up, and since he was there and wearing a suit, he was asked to fill in as an announcer. The rest is history. After his AWA run he tried out as an announcer for the WWF but wasn't hired. He then went to work for WCW where, over the next few tumultuous years, he was the last person standing in a seemingly monthly revolving door of different leaders.

Bischoff had been in wrestling for barely five years before he was running the second-biggest wrestling company in the United

States, which is virtually inconceivable today. But he had fresh ideas. He knew the company needed to spend money to bring in better talent, and he saw money in guys like Hulk Hogan, who had spent a year wrestling in Japan because the WWF at the time felt he was too old to be its top star (among other issues). He signed Hogan, who helped turn company business around. He talked Turner into launching *Nitro*. The show was expected to die going head-to-head with *RAW*, but they ended up neck and neck, and a year later *Nitro* surpassed *RAW* and went on to defeat it for 84 straight weeks.

Bischoff's reinvention of WCW was similar to Vince's destruction of the territories in the early 1980s, but Bischoff's feat was more impressive. Vince outspent everyone and stole all of their top stars, including the hottest star in American, Hogan. Bischoff built up WCW with guys who were former WWF wrestlers, but not top stars. Hogan had been gone from WWF for over a year. Randy Savage was well past his prime. Lex Luger was supposed to be the next Hogan, but plans changed; he wasn't even under contract when he jumped, which tells you where Vince thought he was in the hierarchy. Kevin Nash had been WWF champion, but he was the worst-drawing long-term WWF champion up to that point in history. Scott Hall had been the Intercontinental champion. And most everyone else Bischoff brought in that got over big, including Rey Mysterio, Chris Benoit, and Eddie Guerrero, were guys Vince never even gave the time of day to because he thought they were too small physically.

But what built it up is what tore it down. Bischoff ran with his workhorses—chiefly, Hulk Hogan—too long. In Bischoff's mind, Hogan would draw forever—as in, literally, for as long as he lived. Obviously, that wasn't the case, but Hogan and Bischoff were close friends and Hogan had done so much for the company that Bischoff couldn't fathom a time when fans wouldn't pay to see him. But it happened. And because so many talented guys had been held down and thus slotted as mid-carders or worse in WCW, when the stars stopped drawing, there was nobody ready to replace them. The closest they had was Goldberg, an honest-to-God, WCW-created superstar drawing card, but they beat him way too early. Their other great hope, Sting, who was hardly a fresh new star given he'd been a staple of Turner programming since 1988, helped draw their biggest PPV buy rate of all time when he took on Hogan, but the match itself killed Sting and the follow-up buried him six feet under.

By the middle of 1999, the wheels were off the wagon and Bischoff was removed from power. His replacement, Vince Russo, initially slowed the ratings decline with his crash TV format, but even that ran its course. Worse, his booking devastated all of the other actual income generators, including house show attendance and, worse, pay-per-view buys. In 2000, Russo and Bischoff, who didn't get along, were brought back as a supposed booking dream team; all you need to know about that is the company lost approximately $62 million that year and went out of business in March of 2001.

Bischoff later went to work as an on-screen character for WWE. Whatever you want to say about his business acumen, he was an excellent on-screen character, usually playing a heel. That was part of the problem in WCW, as he inserted himself into the NWO storyline and began to play the role of both an on-screen performer and real-life WCW president; you could see on TV that as soon as he became a character, the storylines and consistency began to badly suffer.

After his WWE on-screen role had run its course, he tried to run head-to-head with McMahon again in 2010. He signed a deal with TNA (Total Nonstop Action) and decided that he was going to re-create the Monday Night Wars. Suffice it to say, the wrestling landscape had changed in the intervening years. Nonetheless, Bischoff convinced TNA and Spike TV to move the *Impact* television show to Monday night against *RAW*. The first night they were beaten by 3 million viewers, but there was enough interest in the experiment that *Impact* drew a 1.5 rating and 2.2 million viewers, the best it would ever do, and a Hogan appearance drew them a 3 million quarter-hour.

It was a one-week blip. Week Two saw their rating cut nearly in half, drawing a 0.98. From there they ranged from a high of 0.95 to a low of 0.50, and by May it was clear the experiment was a failure, and they moved back to Thursday nights. Bischoff was sent home the following year and ultimately filed a lawsuit against the company.

Bischoff has largely been absent from the wrestling scene since, although he has made sporadic appearances for WWE and has done podcasts talking about his time in the business.

38 Captain Lou Albano

Younger fans probably remember Captain Lou Albano as a fat guy with rubber bands in his beard who did goofy things on WWF's old studio shows, and as Cyndi Lauper's dad in a 1980s music video. But he helped change WWF history.

Captain Lou started out as a wrestler but he wasn't a great one. Back then, if you weren't a great wrestler, you didn't have a very long career unless you had exceptional size or charisma or drawing power. He was one of the first guys in WWWF history to transition from a wrestler to a manager, largely at the behest of Bruno Sammartino, who told Vince McMahon Sr. that this guy wasn't very good in the ring, but boy, could he talk.

And could he ever. Wrestlers and fans of the era claimed that nobody could draw heat like Captain Lou Albano. His first major charge was Crusher Verdu. Albano talked him up so big that in his first major match with Sammartino on June 15, 1970—and keep in mind the popularity of Sammartino during the 1960s—they drew the first Madison Square Garden sellout in five years. The more Albano ranted and raved—and not always in the most polite manner, as he was prone to using racial slurs or any other comments he could to draw heat—the more sellouts kept coming.

He became so successful as a manager that he was chosen to manage Ivan Koloff in Koloff's quest to eventually unseat Sammartino as the World Wide Wrestling Federation champion. Albano parlayed that into a career full of promos talking about how he was the man who had led Koloff to the top, and it gave him a credibility that allowed his wrestlers to draw with all of the babyface champions throughout the 1970s, including Pedro Morales, Sammartino again, and finally Bob Backlund. His success also led to the flood of managers in the early 1970s WWWF, including the Grand Wizard and the legendary "Classy" Freddie Blassie.

Albano's biggest accomplishment historically was in setting up the WWF/Lauper pairing and the subsequent "Rock 'n' Wrestling Connection" that led to two monster cable ratings and the first WrestleMania. Albano met Lauper on a flight to Puerto Rico, they hit it off, and she hired him to star as her father in the music video for "Girls Just Want to Have Fun." The song was a hit and was played ad nauseum on the new MTV channel, and Albano, with his larger-than-life personality and facial expressions, stole the show in the video. Lauper then did an angle on WWF programming where Albano was trying to take credit for her success and she politely tried to explain that he had nothing to do with it, and he turned heel on her. This led to a special on MTV where Lauper seconded Wendi Richter in a match against the Fabulous Moolah, managed by Albano. Moolah was billed as the undefeated

Captain Lou Albano with Cyndi Lauper in 1984. (Getty Images)

women's champion for 28 years, and Richter beat her to win the title. The show drew a huge 9.0 rating on MTV, and footage of Richter and Lauper dancing to "Girls Just Want to Have Fun" played everywhere in all sorts of outlets that would never before have anything to do with wrestling. While the show didn't sell out Madison Square Garden—drawing, in fact, a much lower-than-usual crowd—the media in New York jumped on it and concluded that wrestling was super popular.

Later, Albano and Lauper did an angle where Albano apologized to her, but as it was happening he was attacked by the dastardly Rowdy Roddy Piper. Mr. T, at the time a superstar actor on the hit show *The A-Team* and a gigantic pop culture icon, made the save, setting up a tag match of Hulk Hogan and Mr. T vs. Piper and Paul Orndorff as the main event of the very first WrestleMania.

The success of Lauper in the WWF opened up many doors for the company, everything from Mr. T agreeing to get involved, to publicity on the hot new MTV, to NBC agreeing to give it network time for *The Main Event* and later *Saturday Night's Main Event*. All of this because of a chance meeting between Lauper and Albano, with Albano becoming the intermediary between her manager, David Wolff, and Vince McMahon.

Many longtime fans felt Albano never got the credit he deserved for changing WWE history, and while sadly it took his death for that to happen, his passing on October 14, 2009, received a massive amount of publicity all over the world, more than for any but the most famous pro wrestlers, and led to an increased awareness of his role. In 2012 he was enshrined in the Wrestling Observer Hall of Fame.

39 Watch the First and Last *Nitro*

If you're a WWE fan you should head to the WWE Network and watch the first and last episodes of *Nitro*. They are truly bookends in history.

It's not about the quality of the shows themselves, although big things happened on both. It's more about watching two pivotal moments in wrestling history that occurred, astoundingly, only six years apart.

If you lived through the Monday Night Wars as it was happening, it seemed like a lifetime of action. In hindsight, it's astounding how quickly it goes by. Like a child's first few years, you blink and it's over. But so much happened between those two shows, between September 4, 1995, and March 26, 2001, that books have and will be written about it.

The first *Nitro*, from the Mall of America, featured three matches: Jushin Liger vs. Brian Pillman, which kicked off the golden era of cruiserweight wrestling in the United States; Ric Flair vs. Sting, a rematch of one of the greatest rivalries in WCW/NWA history; and Hulk Hogan vs. Big Bubba Rogers (the former Big Boss Man, who feuded with Hogan in the WWF in the 1980s). The show also featured the shocking debut of Lex Luger, who had been working without a contract with the WWF and had appeared at a WWF house show the night before. The war was on.

Both WWF and WCW were struggling heading into *Nitro*'s debut. WWF was trying to push a "new generation" of stars (younger and smaller after the steroid trial essentially knocked the older, bigger stars out of the company), such as Bret Hart and Shawn Michaels. The company had tried pushing Luger toward the title, but fans gravitated toward Bret, the same Bret who ended the one-year failure of a title reign by Diesel a year earlier.

WCW's business had picked up a year earlier with the debut of Hogan and a hot house show feud between Ric Flair and Randy Savage. *Nitro* gave them a renewed burst of life, and by the spring of 1996, when Razor Ramon and Diesel jumped to WCW under their real names of Scott Hall and Kevin Nash, pushed as invaders from WWF, the company was gaining momentum. That summer, Hogan joined them as the third man, the NWO was born, and WCW was off to the races.

WWF, meanwhile, was gaining momentum on the strength of Steve Austin and the Austin vs. Vince McMahon feud. By 1999, WWF was handily kicking WCW's ass. WCW removed from power Eric Bischoff, the man who created *Nitro* and the Monday Night Wars, and hired WWF writer Vince Russo. Russo, without McMahon to edit his ideas, sank WCW even further. By 2000 the company managed to lose over $60 million in a single year, astounding when you consider that just a few years earlier it had grossed $125 million, the most for any wrestling company in history.

The short story of the death of WCW was that Ted Turner lost power and was ousted in the Time Warner/AOL merger, and the new man in charge, Jamie Kellner, hated wrestling. That said, if WCW was grossing $125 million per year in 2001, it likely wouldn't have died. But it was bleeding money, there was no light at the end of the tunnel, and so the show was canceled. WWF bought the remnants for less than $3 million and an agreement to buy ad time on TBS and TNT.

On that final *Nitro*, Vince McMahon opened the show doing a simulcast from *RAW*. He bragged about buying the company, and in revenge for being held up for six figures in 1999, fired Jeff Jarrett live on air. The show, from Panama City, Florida, featured, poetically, the final Ric Flair vs. Sting match under the NWA/WCW umbrella, which, of course, Sting won. And then, just as the show was about to end, WWF shot its big angle—Vince's son, Shane, appeared and revealed that he had bought WCW, and he was going to war with his own father.

Great story on paper. But real life turned out quite different.

# Chris Jericho

Chris Jericho is a pro wrestler and a rock star, and like other rock stars he has gained the ability to stay relevant by attempting to change everything about himself on a regular basis.

He's been the wacky guy with the top knot that jumped over from WCW. He's been the suit-wearing monotone heel who did everything in his power to not get cheered in an era where it was cool to cheer the bad guys. He's been a crazy, swearing psychopath, he's gotten over something as banal as "the list," he's been the "first-ever" undisputed champion, and everything in between, often in his early years having to fight harder than he should have for everything he got.

Born the son of hockey star Ted Irvine, Jericho broke into the business after training at the Hart Brothers School of Wrestling, which by 1990 was a far cry from the famous Dungeon of the Stampede Glory years. Only one other guy from that class ever made it in wrestling, but it happened to be Lance Storm. He and Jericho started out together before going their separate ways around the world, reuniting again a few years later for Jim Cornette's Smoky Mountain Wrestling.

Jericho had success in various promotions, including WAR and ECW, before finally becoming a star in WCW in the mid-1990s. It was an interesting situation. He was obviously very talented, a good-looking guy who could work in the ring and cut promos, but he was also small and so was typecast largely—but not exclusively—as a cruiserweight. While he wasn't a Hulk Hogan or Goldberg, he was among the more pushed guys on the undercard, constantly holding one title or another, whether it be the cruiserweight title or television title (he had five championship runs during that period). He was involved in meaningful feuds back when the company took its cruiserweight division more seriously, and he was a memorable character.

Problem was, he wanted to be Hogan or Goldberg.

In fact, he didn't even need to be Goldberg, but he felt at the very least he should be able to work a program with Goldberg. By 1998, three years into his run, the company was on its way down and Jericho was frustrated. He'd built up a storyline on television where he'd constantly call out Goldberg, knowing full well that ultimately Goldberg was just going to Jackhammer and pin him.

But as it turned out, Goldberg had no interest in doing a program with him at all. Jericho saw the writing on the wall and wanted out. Unfortunately, WWF had never really shown any interest in acquiring his services. He'd begrudgingly agreed to re-sign with WCW in 1999, but the company was in such disarray that it took months to send him a new contract. In the meantime he just happened to be contacted by WWF, flown to Vince McMahon's house for an all-day meeting, and agreed to make the jump.

The company had promised him big things, and his debut in late 1999 saw him go head-to-head on the microphone with the best promo guy in all of wrestling and one of WWF's biggest stars, the Rock. But it all fell off a cliff from that point forward as he was almost immediately moved down the card, with criticism internally of both his work and his promo ability. He took the role Jeff Jarrett had when he jumped to WCW around the same time, feuding with Chyna over the Intercontinental title. Later, he feuded with Chris Benoit and Kurt Angle, essentially putting him in the same spot he was in when he was frustrated in WCW: an upper mid-carder having great matches, but nowhere near the main events.

He finally got his shot at the main event in the winter of 2001 when he became the so-called first-ever undisputed world heavyweight champion. He beat the Rock and Stone Cold Steve Austin on the same night at the Vengeance PPV to win the former's world championship and the latter's WWF championship. While it sounds like a career-making win on paper, there is a difference between being the champion and being the top guy. The Rock and Steve Austin, who were at the tail end of their WWF careers, were top guys, as was Triple H. Jericho was the allegedly historic dual-champion, but he was pushed as a setup guy to lose the titles to Triple H at WrestleMania, which is exactly what happened.

By the mid-2000s, Jericho was burnt out on wrestling. He left the company in August of 2005 after his contract expired, and while everyone expected he would return quickly, he instead threw himself into touring with his band, Fozzy, and pursuing other interests. It was years before he returned for what became a much more successful second act.

Jericho's feud with Shawn Michaels was among the best-booked programs in company history. Because Jericho and Michaels had so much input into the booking, it was far more layered than your usual storyline. Michaels beat Batista in a PPV match after selling a leg injury, but then hitting his superkick to win. Jericho, who was slowly morphing into a soulless heel based on the character Anton Chigurh from the film *No Country for Old Men*, claimed that Michaels, a babyface, had faked the leg injury and cheated to beat Batista. The key is that Jericho was right, but the fans didn't want to believe he was right, and the more he insisted he was right the more the fans began to turn on him. In the end, it turned out that he was right; Michaels faked the injury, but the way they booked the storyline left Michaels the babyface and turned Jericho into a massive heel. It was a turn because the fans had grown to hate Jericho, and he had a logical reason for hating them back, since they supported the cheating Michaels and didn't believe Jericho when he was right all along.

The feud had so many great moments, including an incident where Jericho threw Michaels headfirst through his JeriTron monitor during a segment on his Highlight Reel talk show, busting up Michaels' eye (Michaels had eye problems going in, and has continued to suffer from them ever since), and another where Jericho threw a punch at Michaels, who ducked, and Jericho punched Shawn's wife, Rebecca, right in the face, accidentally busting her open for real. There was such a mix of fantasy and reality that the fans lived and died with the program, and it won Jericho Wrestler of the Year in the 2008 Wrestling Observer Newsletter Awards. He also won Best on Interviews, and Shawn and Jericho together won Best Feud that year and Match of the Year.

He had many memorable WWE moments over the next decade, but his Fozzy touring schedule became such that his hiatuses became much more frequent. Still, he had memorable programs with CM Punk over the world title, with Big Show and Kevin Owens in both tag teams and as rivals, managed to get over seemingly little things like a list of wrestlers who had gotten on his bad side ("You just made the list!"), was involved in critically acclaimed *RAW* segments (the Festival of Friendship), and found himself involved in several historical moments (including costing Kevin Owens his match with Goldberg to set up the Goldberg vs. Brock Lesnar WrestleMania main event).

The year 2017 was a turning point in his career. From the day he signed with WWF, through all of his long-term and short-term contracts and times away from the company, he'd never even considered going anywhere else. Many companies had made offers and he'd turned them all down. He'd always said that if he was going to wrestle, he'd only wrestle for the WWE, the biggest promotion in the world. But in the fall of 2017, New Japan commentator and longtime friend Don Callis suggested to Jericho that he do a match with Kenny Omega on the January 4, 2018, New Japan Tokyo Dome show, their version of WrestleMania. In Jericho's mind, nobody would expect it, and it was a match on the biggest show of the year for the second-biggest promotion in the world, against one of its biggest stars. He wasn't under WWE contract but he told McMahon about it out of courtesy, and there didn't seem like there would be any issues, so he did it. It was both a business success in terms of opening up the doors of America to New Japan (New Japan World, its version of the WWE Network, saw a huge increase in subscribers because of the feud), and artistically, as the performance of Jericho and Omega both in building up and pulling off the match was among the best in pro wrestling worldwide that year.

By the end of 2018, Jericho was fully in bed with New Japan, winning its IWGP Intercontinental title, working occasional big shows, and even involving himself in non-WWE and non-New Japan events to push his feuds, most notably the All In show in September, promoted by the former Cody Rhodes and the Young Bucks. In 2019, Jericho announced he had signed with Rhodes' new promotion, AEW, "for the long haul."

Daniel Bryan

Daniel Bryan's career vividly illustrates the difference between WWF in the Attitude Era and WWE following the death of Chris Benoit.

The 1990s were the absolute wild west of pro wrestling. Mick Foley got thrown off the top of the Hell in a Cell cage and onto the announcers' table, nearly killing himself; returned to continue the match, then fell through the top of the cage to the mat below in an accident that nearly killed him a second time; and then, after all that, appeared on *RAW* the next night hardly selling anything. Kurt Angle got knocked out early in a match with Triple H, couldn't remember anything, and came back to wrestle the entire match. Steve Austin got dropped on his head by Owen Hart and was partially paralyzed, but finished the match anyway. The Rock absolutely destroyed Foley with over a dozen vicious, unprotected chair shots to the head at a Royal Rumble.

In 2016, following a concussion suffered during a live event, Daniel Bryan told a WWE doctor that he'd suffered a couple of seizures years earlier. WWE promptly retired him.

Bryan Danielson started wrestling in 1999 after training at Shawn Michaels' Texas Wrestling Academy. He trained directly under Michaels, who would later give up control of his school. Bryan told me that much of the training consisted of him and Brian Kendrick beating the hell out of each other while Michaels laughed. Whatever Michaels' training consisted of, he turned out a great first class of wrestlers, and Danielson and Kendrick very quickly became names on the indy scene following the 2001 King of Indies tournament that inadvertently launched Ring of Honor.

Danielson worked briefly for WWF in the early 2000s, but at the time he was deemed too small and generic and was quickly back out on the indy scene. By the mid-2000s, he was one of the top stars for Ring of Honor and widely regarded as one of the best wrestlers in the entire world. In 2009 he was signed by WWE again, and after a year in "developmental" he was brought up as part of NXT, which at the time was more of a worked version of *Tough Enough* or *Diva Search*. The wrestlers were paired with a "pro"—Bryan's pro being, of all people, the Miz, who he could have worked circles around blindfolded—and fans voted on who should be eliminated from the competition. In order to apparently prove that "the best in the world" wasn't as good as anyone in WWE, Bryan lost nearly all of his matches and was eventually the first person eliminated.

Following the show, WWE brought up several of the wrestlers, including, as he was now called, Daniel Bryan, to the main roster as part of a heel group called the Nexus. On May 31, 2010, on a *RAW* show where the Nexus was supposed to beat up and destroy John Cena, Bryan took ring announcer Justin Roberts and "strangled" him with his own necktie. It was an awesome, unplanned moment, at least on television. Sponsors complained behind the scenes, and Bryan Danielson was fired.

It is believed that WWE's plan was to fire him, let the heat die down, and then rehire him. Whether he suspected that or not, Bryan went full-bore out onto the indy scene, working all over the

Daniel Bryan has proven to be one of WWE's most unlikely champions.

country for various major promotions. In his mind, he might not ever go back to WWE. But in the middle of negotiations with New Japan, he was offered a new WWE deal three months later and returned at SummerSlam.

The rise of Daniel Bryan to world champion is one of those stories that WWE would like to take credit for, but they fought it tooth and nail and only acquiesced to the fans when they had no other choice. It all started at WrestleMania XXVIII in 2012. Bryan went into the match as the world champion, having won the title with a Money in the Bank cash-in the prior December. He was never supposed to win the title that day. The company had been burying him for months and he wasn't even booked on the show, but someone came up with the last-minute comedy idea of him cashing in on champion Mark Henry. He'd win the title, and then they'd do a three-way program with Big Show, and Bryan would sneak his way to victories as the giants, Henry and Show, kept costing each other wins. In WWE's mind, Sheamus was the future star, and so in a match that fans were very much looking forward to at WrestleMania, Sheamus gave him a Brogue kick and won the title in 18 seconds. A sizable portion of the fans was furious. Not only did they turn on Sheamus, but they let it be known through their chants and reactions to Bryan that they were not happy with this decision, and they wanted Bryan to get the respect and the push they felt he rightly deserved.

The so-called Yes Movement—WWE fans' attempt to get Bryan pushed as a top star—took its name from a catchphrase that Bryan stole from UFC fighter Diego Sanchez, who would unironically march to the ring for his fights chanting, "YES! YES! YES!" Bryan thought it was so awesomely and unintentionally heelish that he stole it, which is funny considering it ultimately became the ultimate babyface chant, one that extended outside of WWE. Once, on a *RAW* show in his "hometown" of Seattle, Washington (he's actually from Aberdeen), he was one of a dozen or so wrestlers standing in the ring during a segment dedicated to Cena and Randy Orton, setting up what was supposed to be a legendary WWE title vs. world title unification match. The fans began to chant for Bryan and then they wouldn't stop, hijacking the show for several minutes. The Movement culminated at WrestleMania XXX, where Bryan walked out as both the WWE champion and world champion in a match he was never supposed to be involved in.

As noted later in this book, the plan was supposed to be Batista vs. Orton for the title, but the fans hated the alleged babyface Batista and wanted nothing to do with the match. Triple H's opponent was supposed to be CM Punk, but Punk quit. With nothing resembling a main event that fans would care about, WWE finally gave in and announced that Bryan would face Triple H in the opener, and if he won, he'd be added to the main event. He beat Hunter and went on to win the three-way main event to become the new WWE champion.

While WWE acquiesced to the fans with a happy ending to WrestleMania XXX, the company had no intentions of going with Bryan as a top guy, as evidenced by his post-WrestleMania feud with Kane. But it was all for naught anyway; shortly after his crowning achievement Bryan suffered a serious neck injury that required surgery and was forced to give up his title 64 days after he won it. He returned six months later but was never put into a position near where he'd been at WrestleMania XXX, focusing instead on the Intercontinental title.

It was one of the best and worst years of Bryan's life. His WrestleMania pinnacle, which was followed just days later by his marriage to Brie Bella (they had been put together in storyline, but as often happens in wrestling, storyline became reality, they fell in love, and eventually married and had a child), was then followed by the unexpected death of his father at the age of 57, and then very shortly thereafter the death of Connor "The Crusher" Michalek, a very charismatic child he'd grown particularly close to via the Make-A-Wish foundation.

Bryan was injured on March 31, 2015, in a match with Sheamus at the *SmackDown* taping. He probably suffered a concussion but still worked the next seven straight days, although he did barely anything in any of his matches. He was finally sent home from the European tour he'd been working and didn't wrestle again for two years afterward.

Bryan had suffered 10 documented concussions during this career, and probably more that had been undocumented during his indy career. At one point during an examination with WWE's concussion doctor, Joseph Maroon, he admitted to post-concussion seizures in his past, and Maroon told him he should never wrestle again. Bryan himself was cleared by a number of doctors who determined that he was fine to wrestle and had above-average cognitive abilities. But Maroon held firm and WWE, for fear of legal action in the future, would not allow him to wrestle without clearance. Bryan was insistent that he was fine and asked for his WWE release to wrestle elsewhere around the world but was denied.

The turning point came when he underwent tests with Evoke Neuroscience in New York. Evoke had created a new testing procedure that examined all portions of the brain for potential damage, first experimented with on soldiers and at that time gaining traction in the mixed martial arts world. Less than a week later, the results came in: he had a chronic lesion in his brain, which had almost certainly caused his post-concussion seizures.

And that was it. He willingly decided that there was a problem with his brain and that the best course of action for himself and his family was to retire. Vince McMahon called him shortly before *RAW* returned to Seattle on February 8, 2016, and encouraged him to do a retirement speech. While Bryan wasn't ready to do it, he did, delivering a near-30-minute from-the-heart speech to his hometown fans. It was one of the most memorable *RAW*s of all time.

Many of the doctors who had examined him felt he'd made the decision to retire too early. But it was too late. Completely depressed, he then vanished. He loved wrestling so much that in his mind, sticking around WWE and not being able to wrestle was going to be too hard to deal with, and so his decision was to walk away and try to start a new life doing something else.

In June, he was talked into coming back to do commentary for the Cruiserweight Classic alongside Mauro Ranallo. He had a really good time and concluded that maybe he could find happiness in a non-wrestling role in WWE. In July he was made the new general manager of *SmackDown*, which he was less thrilled with because it meant he'd be back on the road weekly and he'd have to watch all of these men and women getting into the ring doing what he was no longer able to do. There were some particularly rough patches, including a period where he had an incredible verbal feud with the Miz on both *SmackDown* and WWE Network's *Talking Smack* which had fans clamoring for a match, but it was a match the company could not deliver due to his injury.

During this period, he continued to visit doctors who continued to give him a clean bill of health. He also discovered hyperbaric oxygen therapy. After dozens of sessions, tests showed his cognitive abilities were improving. He continued visiting doctors. Because he was working as *SmackDown* GM, he was working off dates on his contract. By 2018, or 2019 at the latest (WWE had claimed it had put a legal one-year freeze on his contract due to injury, but we never found out whether that would have held up in court), he'd be free to leave the company and wrestle elsewhere if he felt it was in his family's best interests. Both Bryan and his wife, as a result of one promising test result after another, reversed their position on his future; he had every intention to wrestle one way or another, wherever that might be, the first moment he was able.

Bryan finally went to Dr. Maroon and hit him up with one final offer. He asked to be sent to the very best brain specialists in the entire country, and if even one of them said he shouldn't wrestle again, he'd accept that he'd never have another match for WWE. Maroon sent him to Dr. Robert Cantu, Dr. Jeffrey Kutcher, and Dr. Javier Cardenas. All three cleared him. Maroon examined him one final time, and after three years of relative inaction, Bryan was cleared to return to a WWE ring.

At WrestleMania 34, Bryan and Shane McMahon beat Kevin Owens and Sami Zayn. In-ring, because of the match structure, it was a big letdown, but that was irrelevant in the larger picture.

Daniel Bryan was back to resume his Hall of Fame career, and before 2018 ended, he was the WWE champion again.

42 Eddie Guerrero

Eddie Guerrero was one of the greatest wrestlers in the world who for years couldn't figure out the personality side of things, and then when he did, unfortunately, his body had already begun to turn on him. Ultimately, his demons caught up with him and he died before his time.

Guerrero was one of six children fathered by legendary Mexican superstar Salvador "Gory" Guerrero. Almost from the time Eddie could crawl he was practicing pro wrestling. The Guerreros had a reputation of being great athletes but also painfully shy, something Eddie struggled with through the late 1990s and early 2000s. He was a great amateur, but shortly after his high-school graduation he was working shows for the family in both his hometown of El Paso, Texas, and Mexico.

His first gimmick was Mascara Magica, or "Magic Mask," for CMLL in Mexico City. He became good friends with Konnan, a top star at the time, who suggested to him an angle where he would voluntarily unmask and announce that he was the son of Gory Guerrero and that it was ridiculous for him to be wearing a mask. Eddie was against the idea but did it anyway, and it got over big. He was paired with Hijo del Santo as Los Nuevos Parejas Atomicos, the New Atomic Pair, a takeoff on a hugely famous team from the 1950s which consisted of Gory and the biggest star in the history of Lucha Libre, the original El Santo. As was the case with the original duo, Eddie and Hijo del Santo eventually split with Eddie switching his allegiance to a newcomer in the promotion, an American, Art Barr.

Barr had worked in both Portland and WCW but had seen his American career grind to a halt after being accused of rape. He came to Mexico on the advice of Konnan and was paired up with Guerrero. They were the perfect combo as Eddie was the far superior worker, but Barr had about 50 times the charisma and turned into an incredible heel. In their most famous match, on November 6, 1994, at the Los Angeles Memorial Sports Arena before 12,000 insane fans, Eddie and Barr lost to Hijo del Santo and Octagon in a double mask vs. double hair match. Eddie and Art were shaved bald. The match is considered an all-time classic in Lucha Libre and one of the greatest tag team matches of the 1990s.

Paul Heyman was interested in bringing them both to ECW. Unfortunately, three weeks later, at the age of 28, Barr went to sleep with his son Dexter in his arms and never woke up. Eddie was obviously devastated. As a tribute, he took Barr's frog splash and made it famous in America, ultimately winning the WWE championship with it a decade later.

Although ECW is remembered by many as the hardcore promotion, the reality is that Paul Heyman wanted to get over anything that would get over, and what Eddie Guerrero and Dean Malenko and Chris Benoit did best was have incredible wrestling matches, and so that's what he promoted. The three of them were renowned as among the greatest workers in the world, and when Eric Bischoff talked Ted Turner into creating *Nitro* and scoured the world for the best talent, he signed all three of them.

None of them were used to their full potential, particularly Guerrero and Benoit. For years they were involved in mid-card feuds, usually for the cruiserweight, television, or U.S. titles, occasionally getting the opportunity to work with the bigger names, but largely being slotted in the same spot doing the same thing week after week, month after month, and year after year. Guerrero's most famous WCW match was probably a title vs. mask match with Rey Mysterio at Halloween Havoc 1997, a match Mysterio was booked to lose, but at the last minute Bischoff changed his mind and Rey won the match and the cruiserweight title. It might be the shortest five-star match in history.

On December 31, 1998, Guerrero's life changed forever. The wrestling world in the 1980s and particularly the 1990s was rife with alcohol, steroids, and pain pills, and Guerrero was an addict. After a night of drinking and taking pills he crashed his car and was so badly injured that his family was first told he wouldn't survive longer than 48 hours. Later, doctors said he'd live but would have to relearn to walk. Instead, exactly five months later, he not only returned to WCW but was soon working at the level he'd been at before the accident.

Unfortunately, in order to work at that level, his drug and alcohol usage increased, and on top of that, in order to try to be competitive and get better opportunities, the 5-foot-6½ Guerrero upped his steroid use. By the time he, Malenko, Benoit, and Perry Saturn debuted with the WWF as the Radicalz in early 2000, he was gigantic, far too heavy for his frame. But the reality is that the WWF probably would not have hired him at his natural weight. At his absolute biggest and most muscular, he was still perhaps the smallest person the WWF had ever booked as its heavyweight champion.

Guerrero showed flashes of charisma in WCW, but it wasn't until he was paired up with Chyna as his love interest on WWE television that things suddenly clicked for him. Unfortunately, at the same time his pain pill usage had increased to the point where Benoit and Malenko went to management behind his back and explained that they were concerned about his safety. He was forced into rehab by the company. He was released, almost immediately got another DUI, and was fired. Then his wife left him. As a result of tax issues, he was broke and now unemployed.

But he didn't give up. He immediately hit the indy scene, did whatever he could to clean himself up the best he could, and within six months WWF hired him back for the biggest run of his career. He'd finally figured out the charisma part of the business, which he essentially had to because his body was falling apart after the years of in-ring abuse and drug issues. Within a year he was a massive babyface superstar, drawing gigantic ratings among the Hispanic audience. I'll never forget the moment when he came to the ring through the crowd and the fans reacted to him like he was Stone Cold Steve Austin. The company recognized it as well and made the decision to have him beat Brock Lesnar and become the new face of the *SmackDown* brand, which he did on February 15, 2004, at the No Way Out PPV in San Francisco. On the *RAW* side, the company decided to take a chance on Chris Benoit, and so, in one of the most incredible moments in company history, Benoit won the world title at WrestleMania XX via submission on Triple H. The show ended with Benoit and Guerrero, friends dating back to the early 1990s in New Japan, who had been told for years that they were too small to ever headline a major U.S. promotion—especially WWE—standing together in the middle of the ring as WWE's two champions.

Although wrestling is predetermined, for many performers, especially the super-driven ones like Eddie Guerrero, the pressure of having to be the face of the company can be too much to bear. The stress was too much for Guerrero and he went into a personal tailspin; the company was forced to take the title off of him and give it to John Bradshaw Layfield. With the pressure off, things turned around again. He remained a massive ratings draw. He began working his way out of his tax problems. He got back together with his wife. He was involved in good matches and interesting storylines, including one where he revealed that he was the father of Rey Mysterio's son Dominic.

On November 8, 2005, Eddie wrestled Mr. Kennedy at a *SmackDown* taping in Indianapolis. He got waffled with a steel chair and probably suffered a concussion. It was serious enough that people later theorized that his death was the result of a brain aneurysm (it wasn't). That same night, Batista, the world heavyweight champion, tore his lat. The plan was to switch the title the following Tuesday at *SmackDown*. Following Guerrero's death, several WWE sources claimed that he was scheduled to win the title, while others have denied it. One way or another, the match never happened. Guerrero was found dead in his hotel room on November 13 in Minneapolis, slumped over the sink with his toothbrush lying beside him. The belief was that he had a massive heart attack and died almost instantly. His nephew Chavo found him, tried to revive him with CPR, but he was gone. The coroner told his wife he died of heart failure. He was 38.

Guerrero's death struck a massive blow to the industry because he was so beloved. It also led to Vince McMahon announcing the first new WWE drug-testing policy in a decade one week later. The reality was, while the effort was real it wasn't all that real, and it took Chris Benoit murdering his family and killing himself in a house filled with steroids for WWE to clamp down and institute a more serious policy that did result in positive changes to the industry. Unfortunately, it came far too late to help save Guerrero.

43 Roman Reigns

Roman Reigns was the hand-picked successor to John Cena as the face of WWE in the 2010s. Due to circumstance, he was hated by the fans for four straight years. The harder WWE tried, the harder fans pushed back. What finally turned the crowd was, unfortunately, real life, as he announced in October of 2018 that he was taking an indefinite hiatus from the company to battle a recurrence of leukemia.

Reigns, real name Leati Joseph Anoa'i, is the son of Sika, best known as one half of the Wild Samoans tag team. He was a college football star at Georgia Tech, and was briefly signed to both the Minnesota Vikings and Jacksonville Jaguars before playing one full season for the CLF's Edmonton Eskimos.

Reigns is a product of the WWE's developmental system, as he started in WWE from scratch in 2010 in what was called at the time Florida Championship Wrestling. For two years he worked as Roman Leakee before changing his name to Roman Reigns in 2012, shortly before his promotion to the main roster.

He was paired with Seth Rollins and Dean Ambrose as a heel trio name the Shield. They went seven months unbeaten (outside of one DQ loss) before Rollins finally was submitted by Daniel Bryan on *SmackDown*. Reigns himself went almost a full year without doing a job, finally getting pinned on the September 23 *RAW* in a ridiculous 11 vs. three handicap elimination match. During the 2014 Royal Rumble he entered at No. 15 and set an elimination record taking out 12 different wrestlers. He was cheered wildly.

The Shield broke up on June 2, 2014, when Rollins turned on the team and joined the Authority. While the storyline was that Rollins was the hand-picked guy, behind the scenes that status

Roman Reigns was Vince McMahon's choice to succeed John Cena as the face of the WWE.

belonged to Reigns. The idea was that he would win the Royal Rumble and go on to WrestleMania and defeat Brock Lesnar—the man who had ended the Undertaker's undefeated streak at the 2014 show—and thereby cement himself as the new face of the company.

The problem was that the fans had gotten behind Daniel Bryan, forcing the company to put him in the main event of WrestleMania and giving him the title. But Bryan was forced to relinquish the belt due to injury shortly thereafter; upon his return, fans were clamoring for him to return to the top spot, but the company had other plans. The prior year, fans had wanted Bryan to win the Royal Rumble, a match he was never advertised for, and because he didn't appear the fans took it out on Rey Mysterio, who entered at No. 30 and did nothing wrong except not be Daniel Bryan. In the 2015 Rumble, Bryan was unceremoniously eliminated by Bray Wyatt and the fans were absolutely furious. They turned on the company, they turned on the match, and most of all they turned on Roman Reigns, who had won the match.

This was the beginning of a three-year-long battle. Despite being pushed as the top babyface, Roman was booed at every turn in practically every town on every televised show (interestingly enough, he was almost always cheered at house shows). He was booed so badly that Vince McMahon decided 2015 wasn't the year to crown him champion after all, so in the Lesnar vs. Reigns WrestleMania match he instead had Rollins do a surprise cash-in of his Money in the Bank briefcase and steal the title.

And still Roman was hated, week after week, month after month. Even though this all began because of Bryan, even when Bryan was forced into retirement due to concussion-related issues, the fans still hated Reigns. He became a symbol of everything that they hated about WWE, and he'd done nothing to deserve it.

In the company's eyes, Cena had been booed as top babyface for years and it didn't make a lick of difference to business. During his entire run Cena was by far the biggest star in the company; he sold the most merchandise; he was pretty much the only person who could move house show numbers; and his big WrestleMania matches, particularly with the Rock in 2012 and 2013, did gigantic business. While Reigns didn't do the business Cena did, he was the top merchandise seller, and although he was getting the "wrong" reaction, he was still getting a bigger reaction than anyone else in the company. So, they kept pushing him.

Rollins went down with an injury later in 2015 and Reigns won a tournament to win the WWE title for the first time, beating former Shield member Dean Ambrose in the finals at Survivor Series. He lost the belt immediately to Sheamus, who cashed in his

Money in the Bank briefcase. The idea was this would make Reigns a sympathetic character who the fans would cheer. Didn't work. The only time he was cheered on TV in a year was in regaining the title from Sheamus on the January 4, 2016, *RAW*, and that was only because he punched out Vince McMahon.

The next idea was to have him defend his title in the Royal Rumble, something that had never happened before, after being forced to enter at No. 1. The idea again was that he'd become a sympathetic character as a result. This also failed. Part of it was because he was "injured" early on, having been put through a table by the League of Nations, and carted backstage, only to return much, much later. To fans, it was less an injury angle and more a chance for Roman to sit out most of the match. Triple H, the eventual winner who was supposed to get massive heat eliminating Reigns, instead got a monster babyface pop. Reigns went on to beat Hunter to win the title a third time at WrestleMania. The idea was he'd get cheered by accidentally putting Stephanie McMahon through a table. He put her through a table. He was still booed.

WrestleMania 33 ended up being all about Lesnar and Goldberg based on Goldberg getting over huge for what was supposed to be a one-and-done appearance at Survivor Series. Reigns faced the Undertaker. The idea was he'd beat the Undertaker at WrestleMania 33, becoming only the second man, along with Lesnar, ever to do so. This would build toward the 2018 WrestleMania where the two men who beat the Undertaker at WrestleMania would square off, and Reigns would beat the man who ended the streak and finally be crowned the face of the company. Reigns appeared on *RAW* the night after beating the Undertaker and received one of the loudest and longest negative reactions in company history, a full 10 minutes of nonstop vociferous booing.

We'll skip over countless ideas that were tried to get Reigns cheered, including, if you can believe this, one where Roman would beat Daniel Bryan and Bryan would endorse him after the match, an idea which, you'll be stunned to learn, was a colossal swing and miss. Perhaps the company's final attempt was to reunite the Shield. This failed. Well, not exactly; the Shield was cheered when they came out, but the fans took every opportunity to boo Roman specifically. The Shield reunion fell apart before it could even begin when Ambrose suffered a triceps injury and was out of action for nine months.

Reigns won an Elimination Chamber match in February of 2018 to become the top contender to Lesnar's title at WrestleMania 34. At the time, Lesnar was negotiating to fight again for UFC. WrestleMania was the final date on his contract. It seemed certain that this time, finally, Roman was going to beat him and win the title. McMahon came up with a new plan to get him cheered. The storyline became that Lesnar hated WWE, hated the fans, was lazy, never wanted to wrestle, and was just collecting a paycheck. Roman, on the other hand, was there every week, never missed a show, busted his ass, and was the man who would rescue the WWE championship that Lesnar was holding hostage. Didn't work. Instead, the fans went from hating Reigns and loving Lesnar to hating both of them. As WrestleMania drew near, McMahon determined—can you imagine?—that Roman might, in fact, be booed in the main event. So, he changed the plan to Lesnar beating Reigns again, clean in the middle of the ring, with an F-5. The fans turned on the match, booing both guys out of the building and paying zero attention to the action, concentrating on wacky chants and throwing beach balls throughout the building. It was a sadly hilarious embarrassment.

Another day, another attempted storyline: the next idea was that Reigns was being held down by the company, forced to lose over and over despite the fact that he "deserved" to be champion. This also failed. He lost again via screwjob finish in a cage match at the Greatest Royal Rumble show in Saudi Arabia on April 27.

Both guys were still hated. They continued the storyline of Lesnar holding the belt hostage through SummerSlam, where Reigns finally beat him clean to win the title. By this point, they had long since passed the peak of effectiveness, the title change was terribly anti-climactic, and Reigns had lost tremendous steam ever since he was beaten at WrestleMania for the umpteenth time.

He continued to be terribly hated all the way up until October 22, 2018. On that day he came out on *RAW* and was massively booed by the crowd. He then explained that he had been lying to the fans, that his name was not Roman Reigns, but rather Joe Anoa'i, and that he had been living with leukemia for 11 years.

The crowd went absolutely silent.

He said he had been diagnosed 11 years earlier, that it had gone into remission at the time, and that he wasn't going to lie, it was the hardest fight of his life. But he beat it, WWE was the only place that would take a chance on him, and for that he was forever grateful. He said this was not a retirement speech, and that after he kicked leukemia's ass he would return with a purpose, to show his family and the world that when life threw him a curveball, he'd swing for the fences every time. "You'll see me very, very soon," he said. "Thank you very much. God bless you, and I love you."

And just like that, the fans who had hated him for so long, many of whom had probably forgotten why they even hated him in the first place, let it all go. Sadly, it took a medical crisis for it to happen, but Roman Reigns finally walked out of the ring the most beloved wrestler on the roster.

The following February, Reigns returned to *RAW* and told the fans his leukemia was in remission. Reigns then defeated Drew McIntyre at WrestleMania 35 in his first singles match since returning, less than six months after his initial announcement.

44 The WCW Invasion

As I wrote in *The Death of WCW*, the WCW "Invasion" was the worst invasion in the history of warfare.

The Monday Night Wars ended on March 26, 2001, when, on the final *Nitro*, Shane McMahon announced that he'd purchased the company out from underneath his father. Of course, in real life, WWF had purchased the company for virtually nothing. They had grandiose plans. Believe it or not, Vince's original idea was to move *RAW* from Monday nights to Thursdays on UPN, and give *Nitro* the Monday night time slot. The storyline was going to be that his wife, Linda, was going to catch him with his pants down attempting to seduce Torrie Wilson, file for divorce, and get the Monday night time slot in the proceedings. She'd hand it over to Shane, who would team up with Stephanie to "run" *Nitro*, feuding with Vince who would "run" *RAW* on Thursday. In reality, of course, Vince would run everything, much like he does today with the *RAW* and *SmackDown* brands. They even began renting out buildings for Monday night shows, billed as "Shane McMahon's WCW." This was the real deal.

Then Tacoma happened.

The show took place on July 2, 2001. Even though I live in Bothell, Washington, just 40 minutes from Tacoma, I wasn't there that night. The idea was that the first hour and 40 minutes would be *RAW*, then the final 20 minutes would be given to WCW. What that meant was they transformed everything during a commercial break, from the ring apron to the canvas to the announcers to the music to the TV bumpers. In the ring, they had Booker T defend the WCW title against Buff Bagwell. Bagwell was terribly out of shape, the match was a disaster, the fans hated everything about it, and they booed WCW out of the building.

My friend Craig Proper messaged me from the building: "They killed this town," he wrote.

McMahon was furious. Even though it was one match in one town on one day, to him, all of his grandiose plans went right out the window. WCW as a separate brand was a dead idea; instead, WCW would "invade."

Problem was, in order for an invasion angle to work, WWF needed the biggest WCW stars, and WCW needed to win the early battles.

Neither happened.

Kevin Dunn, McMahon's longtime television producer and right-hand man, convinced him that they'd built WWF up for far too long to have some outsiders from a dead promotion come in and beat their superstars. What would fans think? Why should WWF stars be treated as inferior? Especially since the WWF stars that they'd signed from WCW, 24 in all, ranged from upper mid-carders like Lance Storm down to guys like Elix Skipper and Shannon Moore? WCW's biggest stars, like Ric Flair, Hulk Hogan, Sting, and Goldberg, were under long-term, big-money Time Warner deals, and WWF refused to buy them out.

Two things to keep in mind. One, WWF grossed $456 million that year, and despite losing over $140 million on the XFL, the company was still swimming in cash. Second, WWF eventually brought in all those high-priced talents anyway, long after their value would have been at its highest.

The two biggest invasion stars ended up being Diamond Dallas Page and Booker T, who were eager to work for WWF. Page was absolutely brutalized in booking during a feud with the Undertaker, made out to look like a complete geek. Booker ultimately became a bona fide star and future multi-time world champion.

The summer built to the famous Invasion PPV on July 22, 2001. The storyline was that WWF would fight against "The Alliance," a group of WCW and ECW stars. In the late 1990s, the idea of a WWF vs. WCW PPV was the stuff of fantasy. Imagine, at the peak of the Monday Night Wars, Hulk Hogan, Scott Hall, Kevin Nash, Sting, and Goldberg squaring off against the Rock, Steve Austin, Shawn Michaels, Mick Foley, and the Undertaker, for example. It would have destroyed all previous PPV records. In July of 2001, WCW was dead, and WWF was presenting a "WWF vs. WCW" Invasion PPV. And what was the main event? The WWF team of Steve Austin, the Undertaker, Chris Jericho, Kane, and Kurt Angle vs. the Alliance team of DDP, Booker T, D-Von and Bubba Ray Dudley, and Rhyno. The Alliance won after Steve Austin turned on his team, giving Angle the Stunner to lead to the pin.

Despite the astoundingly lame lineup given the possibilities, the show drew a massive 770,000 buys on PPV. You can imagine what business would have been like had they put together the fantasy lineup listed above (which they could have, since everyone listed was available at the time if WWF had been willing to pay for them).

From July through November, the WWF side beat the WCW side week after week, month after month. The Alliance would get a win here or there, but the angle was clearly designed to convince fans that WWF was the dominant promotion in this war. It all built to the 2001 Survivor Series and a Winner Take All match between WWF and "WCW." The match saw the WWF team of the Rock, Chris Jericho, the Undertaker, Kane, and the Big Show beat the Alliance team of Steve Austin, Kurt Angle, Booker T, Rob Van Dam, and Shane McMahon. The show, the finale of the alleged dream storyline fans had been fantasizing about since 1995, drew 10,142 fans and a little over half a million dollars.

The day after Survivor Series, Ric Flair debuted. Over the next few years, WWE would sign Eric Bischoff, Goldberg, Kevin Nash, Scott Hall, Hulk Hogan, and Rey Mysterio, among others. They all became stars and made some money for WWE, but ultimately, they all would have meant so much more during the Invasion than they did in 2002 and 2003. The Invasion remains, all these years later, the biggest flop of an angle in wrestling history.

45 The WWE Wellness Policy

WWE's Wellness Policy, launched in the wake of the death of Eddie Guerrero and the Chris Benoit murder/suicide, is available to the public on the company's corporate site.

The drug-testing policy is far from perfect. There are loopholes in it that allow the talent to get chemical help to look more like action figures. But the policy is such that the drug culture of the 1980s, 1990s, and early 2000s has largely dried up in pro wrestling, and thus the under-40 deaths that plagued wrestling for decades are now a thing of the past.

The drug policy is not designed to completely eliminate performance-enhancing drug use in the company, nor is it likely the company could do so if it tried. The idea that everyone in sports is drug-free is ridiculous, as the more money you possess the more you can get away with, thanks to designer steroids and access to the best doctors. What it is designed to do is put an end to the days where everyone was taking everything under the sun and dying young. As a whole, WWE is healthier today than it has ever been.

A few notes. The policy obviously bans steroids, steroid precursors, and human growth hormone. However, a normal person has a 1:1 testosterone-to-epitestosterone ratio. WWE's policy allows a performer to have a 4:1 T/E ratio and still be considered clean. What does this mean? Well, the human body creates an equivalent amount of testosterone and epitestosterone. If you naturally have a low level of testosterone in your body, your ratio is 1:1; if you naturally have a high level of testosterone, your ratio is 1:1. However, if you inject steroids (testosterone), your T/E ratio will be skewed. Chris Benoit, whose house was filled with steroids when he and his family were found dead, had a 59:1 T/E ratio. In other words, with 4:1 allowed, if a talent has access to the right doctor who can figure out exact dosages, the talent can take a low level of testosterone and remain below the 4:1 threshold. On top of that, while growth hormone is banned, there is no real-world reliable test for GH. GH and testosterone react synergistically. Therefore, if a talent has the money and inclination, he or she can find a doctor to keep them below 4:1 and also take growth hormone, develop an exceptional physique, and never fail a test. You're not going to have anyone who looks like the Ultimate Warrior, but you can have a bunch of performers with physiques that couldn't be achieved naturally.

Another loophole is that executives, part-time talent, and those who are able to command special contracts are not subject to the Wellness Policy and can pretty much take whatever they want.

While rare, the company also allows TUEs, or therapeutic use exemptions. If you are an older wrestler who used steroids for years, your body likely shut down its natural ability to make testosterone. A doctor will then prescribe it to you, and if cleared by WWE, you can take your therapeutic testosterone without fear of reprisal. Although it's supposed to be "therapeutic," some wrestlers got gigantic utilizing TUEs.

Wrestlers who fail a drug test are suspended for 30 days on the first offense, 60 days on the second, and terminated on the third. After termination, they are allowed to return to the company in a year if they pass a drug test, and they remain with two strikes on their record. WWE also offers a "redemption program," meaning if you remain clean for 18 months under the program they'll remove your second strike, leaving you with only one.

Marijuana is banned, but if you fail you aren't given a strike but rather a $2,500 fine. Most wrestlers who smoke consider it the "pot tax."

Unlike in UFC, the drug testers don't require your whereabouts at all times and will not come to your home at all hours of the day. Testing almost always happens at WWE PPVs, *RAW*, or *SmackDown*. It's another loophole that allows the use of fast-acting street drugs, like cocaine, which are in and out of the system in a matter of days, provided talent times it to coincide with time away from TV (Wednesday or Thursday, for example).

It's not perfect. But the WWE Wellness Policy has absolutely had a positive effect on the company.

46 CM Punk

The story of CM Punk is the story of a guy who was his own best friend and worst enemy.

Punk was a guy with a very high opinion of himself, which rubbed many people the wrong way but also drove him to achieve far more than he ever should have given the time period in which he managed to become a star.

He also had a reputation for being a moody, sometimes difficult-to-deal-with individual, which in the end helped cost him his career in pro wrestling, and also took a bite out of what should have been a more comfortable retirement.

CM Punk had a volatile run in the WWE before walking away from wrestling in 2014.

Phil Brooks began his career in 1999, and over the next six years rose to prominence on the independent scene. He became one of the most popular non-WWE stars in the country, headlining shows first for IWA Mid-South and later for Ring of Honor, where he became the company's world champion. Depending upon whose opinion you were listening to, he was either one of the best wrestlers in the world or a terribly overrated indy darling.

In 2005, after a short and uneventful run in TNA, he signed with WWE and was assigned to its developmental territory, Ohio

Valley Wrestling. Less than a year later, he was moved up to the main roster as part of the new ECW brand. He was pushed as an upper mid-carder for the first year, sometimes entering into the title picture but always coming up short. (Here's a piece of trivia: the weekend that Chris Benoit killed his family and then himself, he was scheduled to wrestle Punk at the WWE Vengeance PPV for the vacant ECW title. Benoit, who had already killed Nancy and Daniel, called the office and claimed that Daniel had been vomiting, and that he and Nancy were at the hospital with him. He claimed he was still going to make his flight to the show. He then killed himself. When he didn't arrive, John Morrison was put in his place and beat Punk for the title.)

Punk finally won the ECW title on September 1, 2007, and held it until he dropped it to Chavo Guerrero the following January. A few months later he won the Money in the Bank ladder match at WrestleMania and went on to cash it in against Edge in June, winning the WWE world heavyweight championship for the first time. He was forced to vacate the title in September after Randy Orton punted him in the head, leaving him with a storyline concussion. History then repeated itself. Punk won the Money in the Bank ladder match a second time at the following year's WrestleMania, the first person in history to win it twice, and cashed in on Jeff Hardy, almost exactly one year from his cash-in on Edge, to win the world title. He lost the title to the Undertaker in October in a Hell in a Cell match.

He was involved in various storylines over the next several years, including stints as a Messianic character for the Straight Edge Society and the leader of the New Nexus. But his career skyrocketed following a June 2011 storyline where he claimed that his contract was getting ready to expire, that he was going to leave WWE, and that he was going to do it as the WWE champion.

On June 27, 2011, in the most famous moment of his wrestling career, Punk cut what became known as the "pipebomb promo" live on *RAW* as John Cena lay prone in the ring:

John Cena, while you lay there, hopefully as uncomfortable as you possibly can be, I want you to listen to me. I want you to digest this, because before I leave in three weeks with your WWE championship, I have a lot of things I want to get off my chest. I don't hate you, John. I don't even dislike you. I do like you. I like you a hell of a lot more than I like most people in the back. I hate this idea that you're the best, because you're not. I'm the best. I'm the best in the world. There's one thing you're better at than I am, and that's kissing Vince McMahon's ass. You're as good at kissing Vince's ass as Hulk Hogan was. I don't know if you're as good as Dwayne [the Rock], though, he's a pretty good ass-kisser, always was and still is. Oops, I'm breaking the fourth wall.

I am the best wrestler in the world. I've been the best ever since day one when I walked into this company, and I've been vilified and hated since that day because Paul Heyman saw something in me that nobody else wanted to admit. That's right, I'm a Paul Heyman guy. You know who else was a Paul Heyman guy? Brock Lesnar, and he split, just like I'm splitting, but the biggest difference between me and Brock is I'm going to leave with the WWE championship. I've grabbed so many of Vincent K. McMahon's imaginary brass rings that it's finally dawned on me that they're just that—they're completely imaginary. The only thing that's real is me, and the fact that day in and day out, for almost six years, I've proved to everybody in the world that I am the best on this microphone, in that ring, and even on commentary. Nobody can touch me.

And yet, no matter how many times I prove it, I'm not on your lovely little collector cups, I'm not on the cover of the program, I'm barely promoted, I don't get to be in movies, I'm certainly not on any crappy show on the USA Network, I'm not on the poster of WrestleMania, I'm not on the signature that's produced at the start of the show. I'm not on Conan O'Brien, I'm not on Jimmy Fallon, but the fact of the matter is I should be, and trust me, this isn't sour grapes, but the fact that Dwayne is in the main event of WrestleMania next year and I'm not makes me sick.

Oh, hey, let me get something straight, those of you who are cheering me right now, you are just as big a part of me leaving as anything else, because you're the ones sipping out of those collector cups right now, you're the ones that buy those programs that my face isn't on the cover of, and then at 5:00 in the morning at the airport, you try to shove it in my face so you can get an autograph and try to sell it on eBay because you're too lazy to get a real job. I'm leaving with the WWE championship on July 17, and hell, who knows, maybe I'll go defend it in New Japan Pro Wrestling, maybe I'll go back to Ring of Honor. Hey, Colt Cabana, how you doing?

The reason I'm leaving is you people, because after I'm gone you're still going to pour money into this company. I'm just a spoke on the wheel. The wheel's going to keep turning. And I understand that, that Vince McMahon's gonna make money despite himself, he's a millionaire who should be a billionaire. You know why he's not a billionaire? It's because he surrounds himself with glad-handing nonsensical douchebag yes-men like John Lauranitis, who's gonna tell him everything that he wants to hear. And I'd like to think that maybe this company will be better after Vince McMahon's dead, but the fact is it's gonna get taken over by his idiotic daughter and his doofus son-in-law and the rest of his stupid family.

Let me tell you a personal story about Vince McMahon, alright? You know we do this whole bully campaign?

And at that point they cut his mic.

The idea was that fans were supposed to believe he was "shooting," or going against the script. He wasn't. But everything he said was believable enough that he was immediately the hottest star in wrestling, and sure enough, on July 17, the final day he was under contract to WWE, he beat John Cena in the main event of Money in the Bank to win the WWE championship.

Believe it or not, the idea was that the fans would boo Punk for all of the terrible things he was saying in his promo about WWE, McMahon, the Rock, and Cena. Instead, unsurprisingly to anyone outside the WWE bubble, the exact opposite happened, and he became a massive babyface, almost a folk hero. He had gone out there and said all the things disgruntled WWE fans had been saying themselves for years. The pop he got when he beat Cena for the title at Money in the Bank was monstrous. WWE appeared to be sitting on top of a gold mine. But it was not to be.

In real life, Punk re-signed his contract before Money in the Bank and wasn't going anywhere. But the fans didn't need to know that. There were so many things WWE could have done with the storyline, including opening up working agreements with other companies, perhaps even Ring of Honor, where Punk could go, seemingly as an outsider, having "stolen" the WWE title. The further they'd have gone with it, and the longer he was gone, the bigger a star he'd have been upon his return. But there was no patience for that sort of thing, or there was concern about what fans might do if they truly believed Punk had quit and taken the WWE title with him. So, within two weeks he was back on TV. WWE promoted a WWE title tournament to crown a new champion in his supposed absence, and Rey Mysterio won. John Cena beat him for the title later in the night. Punk then returned to TV, claiming to be the rightful champion, and a match was set up to determine an undisputed WWE champion at SummerSlam between himself and Cena. Punk won the match, but then, in a cruel twist given how many times Punk had done it to others in the past, Alberto Del Rio cashed in the Money in the Bank contract and beat Punk for the title.

The Summer of Punk was over.

Punk's final major run began when he beat Del Rio for the title at Survivor Series. What appeared to be just another WWE title run turned into what was later promoted as the longest reign of any WWE champion in "the modern era," whatever that was (presumably post-1995, as nobody will ever approach the time as champion that Bruno Sammartino amassed, or Hulk Hogan in his first run). Paired up with Paul Heyman as a modern-day version of the Nick Bockwinkel/Bobby Heenan duo from the AWA in the 1970s, Punk's 434-day run as champion was by far the highlight of his WWE career both from a match-quality and star-power standpoint. Still, he was never pushed as the singular face of the company—that role remaining with Cena—and because Cena and the Rock headlined WrestleMania XXVII, he was kept out of the spot he'd wanted since day one, and the prize he valued above anything else—the main event slot at WrestleMania.

He lost the title to the Rock at the 2013 Royal Rumble, which set up the Rock vs. Cena II for that year's WrestleMania. Punk wanted the match with the Rock at WrestleMania so badly and was disillusioned with the call to take the title off of him. He was getting more and more upset with the company over the course of the next 365 days, and it all came to a head one year later at the 2014 Royal Rumble.

Long story short, Punk suffered a concussion during the match and quit the company before *RAW* the following day. It was his final day in pro wrestling. A year later he broke his silence in a podcast with longtime friend Colt Cabana, where he tore apart the company and also one of the company's doctors, Chris Amann. Amann was very upset about what was said about him in that interview, and Cabana was asked to take the podcast down. Punk allegedly told Cabana not to take it down, and that if anything happened he had his back. Well, something happened. Amann filed a lawsuit. This led to a lengthy court battle that ran up bills for Punk and Cabana into the six figures and dragged on for two grueling years. In the end, Punk and Cabana won, but none of their legal bills were recouped. Cabana then filed suit against Punk, claiming that Punk had promised to pay his legal bills but then reneged on his offer. One of the longest friendships in pro wrestling dating back almost two decades was over.

With no desire to ever return to wrestling, Punk then embarked on a second career, a bucket-list dream of fighting for the UFC. At the time, he was 36 years old. He had no amateur wrestling or any real-sports experience outside a few years of occasional jiu-jitsu private lessons with Rener Gracie. It's a cliché, but the odds were stacked against him. One of his biggest complaints in his final years in WWE was that the Rock just waltzed in and headlined WrestleMania two years in a row, based solely on his name and drawing power, taking a spot away from someone who had busted his ass as a regular for an entire year prior to the big show. Well, CM Punk, with no experience whatsoever, was immediately signed to UFC based solely on his name and drawing power, and his first fight was on the lucrative main card of a UFC pay-per-view event, taking a spot away from any given UFC regular who had busted his ass on the undercard.

After two years of training, the chickens came home to roost as Punk was utterly destroyed in his first fight by Mickey Gall in just 2:14 of the first round at UFC 203 on September 10, 2016. Despite a terrible showing, he was given a second fight based on the fact that the PPV did better than expected due to WWE fans tuning in to see how Punk would fare in a real fight. The WWE bump was not there for the second show, where he was beaten by Mike Jackson at UFC 225 on June 9, 2018, in his hometown of Chicago. While he lost, he wasn't finished in the fight, which was at least a moral victory of sorts.

For years fans have wondered if Punk will ever return to WWE. Based on history, the odds seem to be in favor of that happening, since practically everyone who has ever been on bad terms with the company, from Bruno Sammartino to Bret Hart, has eventually come back. The difference here is that Punk is an exceedingly stubborn person, and he himself has told people that he would consider returning a massive personal life failure on his part. He also told people that even before a two-year lawsuit—which he felt was probably in some way financed by WWE—drained him of hundreds of thousands of dollars. You can never say never in wrestling, but Punk may end up one of those rare people who left the company on bad terms and never came back.

 **Batista**

Although he doesn't get the credit because he wasn't as big a star as the Rock or as renowned an MMA fighter as Brock Lesnar, Dave Bautista, aka Big Dave Batista, is one of the only individuals in WWE history to become a WWE main-eventer, a mainstream film actor, and an undefeated MMA fighter.

He also happens to be one of the only people who ever publicly said that he didn't like how he was trained in Ohio Valley Wrestling.

Before NXT, OVW in Louisville, Kentucky, was WWE's main developmental territory. Run by Danny Davis, Jim Cornette, and Rip Rogers, OVW turned out a who's who of the greatest stars of the 21st century, including John Cena, Brock Lesnar, Randy Orton, the Miz, John Morrison, and dozens of others. Nearly everyone who went through OVW praised the training they received there. Not Batista. He felt that the gimmick they gave him, Leviathan, was too much of a one-dimensional Goldberg-like monster, and that training didn't help him prepare for WWE where he'd ultimately have to sell, work long matches, and become more of a well-rounded performer.

Of course, no amount of training would have prepared him for the brilliant role they came up with for him when he debuted on *SmackDown* in 2002—Deacon Batista. Yes, a deacon, an ordained minister of an order ranking below that of priest. He was Deacon Dave under Reverend D-Von, formerly of the Dudley Boyz. It was a terrible gimmick. Thankfully, about six months later he was moved to *RAW* and quickly put into a main event stable, Evolution, alongside Ric Flair, Triple H, and Randy Orton.

For two years, Batista was a cog in the wheel of Evolution, but it was obvious that at some point he was going to do a big babyface turn and become a singles superstar. The build for the turn began in the fall of 2004, and it was one of those storylines where it was patently obvious that the fans wanted him to be a good guy, but instead of just pulling the trigger out of nowhere like they've done countless times throughout history, they exhibited patience. In an interview years later, Triple H said that Vince McMahon did, in fact, want to rush the turn, and Hunter had to convince him to let them build it up into a WrestleMania main event.

And that's exactly what happened. Batista had won the 2005 Royal Rumble, and as a result had the opportunity to challenge for either the WWE title or the world heavyweight title at WrestleMania. JBL was the WWE champion and was scheduled to face John Cena, and Triple H was the world heavyweight champion. The story was that Triple H, allegedly Dave's friend, was doing everything in his power to convince Dave not to challenge for his title. He tried to convince him to challenge JBL and make the WrestleMania match with Cena a three-way, and when Dave wouldn't go for it Triple H tried to concoct various schemes, including one where he would have Dave run over by a limo allegedly driven by JBL. None of this worked, and by the time Batista turned the fans were salivating to see him take out Triple H, which he did with a powerbomb through a table. Their WrestleMania match for the WWE world heavyweight title wasn't just the culmination of one of the best storylines WWE ever followed through with, but it paid off at the gate and on PPV, doing at the time a record-breaking 1.09 million buys, the most-purchased non-boxing PPV event in history.

While he remained in WWE and was a main event star through 2010, the Triple H program was by far the highlight of Batista's career. He left in mid-2010, disgruntled with the direction of the company.

His return in 2013 was in many ways a turning point in WWE history. The plan was simple: he'd return as a babyface, win the 2014 Royal Rumble, and go on to beat Randy Orton at WrestleMania for the WWE title. Simple. Or so it seemed.

The fans in Pittsburgh, site of that year's Rumble, loved Daniel Bryan. They wanted him to be pushed harder, they wanted him to win the Rumble, and they wanted him to win the title at WrestleMania. The problem was, he wasn't even entered in the Royal Rumble. He was in a match against Bray Wyatt. Now, to be fair, in the past wrestlers who worked a singles match on the Rumble card had also appeared in the Rumble itself, so it wasn't a massive stretch to think Bryan would reappear. But he was never advertised to be in it and the company had never planned for him to be in it. Nevertheless, throughout the Rumble itself, the fans eagerly anticipated Bryan's entrance. It finally came down to the last entrant, the big No. 30, and everyone thought it would be Daniel Bryan. The clock counted down, the fans began a "YES! YES! YES!" chant, the buzzer sounded, and out came—Rey Mysterio. The fans were furious. Rey, a career babyface, was booed out of the building. The fans completely turned on the match, started cheering heel Roman Reigns (remarkable, given Reigns' career from that point forward), and when Batista won the Rumble by eliminating Roman, they left in a fury.

So much for Batista as a babyface.

On top of that, CM Punk, who was scheduled to face Triple H at WrestleMania, quit the day after the Rumble. For the next two months, the fans booed Orton, the heel; they booed Batista, the babyface; they chanted for Daniel Bryan; and WrestleMania was looking to be a gigantic disaster. And so, in a rare moment for the 21st century Vince McMahon, he finally acquiesced. The plans were changed, and Bryan got the WrestleMania moment the fans wanted. The storyline was that if he could beat Triple H in the opener, Batista vs. Orton would become a three-way in the main event. Bryan beat Hunter, and he went on to win the three-way and become the WWE champion. It was one of the great moments in WWE history, and despite what WWE will claim today, it was never the plan.

Batista was left out in the cold. He only lasted about two more months before getting completely fed up with the creative direction of the company—again—and quitting.

Between his first and second WWE stints, Batista decided to try MMA. He'd been training various martial arts for years and had achieved a blue belt under Cesar Gracie. In the grand scheme of things, however, he had very little combat training experience and was 43 years old. Fighting seemed like a terrible idea. But it seemed to be something on his personal bucket list, so he trained his ass off, went through a legitimate MMA camp, and on October 6, 2012, in

Providence, Rhode Island, Dave Bautista beat Vince Lucero in 4:05 of the first round on a show promoted by Classic Entertainment and Sports MMA. Lucero was hardly a world-class opponent and he had a losing record, but he'd fought more than 40 times and was coming off two straight wins, so it was a real victory for Batista.

Batista had done some film work dating back to the mid-2000s and picked it up again after leaving WWE the second time. His big breakout role was in 2014's *Guardians of the Galaxy*, where he played Drax the Destroyer. His career took off at that point and was followed by dozens of additional roles in everything from *Kickboxer: Vengeance* to *Avengers: Infinity War*.

In 2019, Batista returned for his farewell match against Triple H at WrestleMania 35. The day after his loss, he announced his retirement from the ring.

48 Degeneration X

One of the most popular acts in WWE history is best known for its music and comedic talent, which is interesting because it was a legitimately edgy act when it first debuted in the fall of 1997.

The original DX consisted of Shawn Michaels, Triple H, and Chyna. At the time, Hunter was a solid wrestler struggling to make it to the level both he and the company wanted him to reach. Chyna was his valet, a big, strong, tall, mute female bodybuilder. Michaels was the hottest heel in the business based on a feud with both Bret Hart (prior to Bret turning heel) and the Undertaker. In real life, Triple H and Michaels were close friends not only with each other, but with Scott Hall and Kevin Nash, who were running

The founding members of Degeneration X, Triple H and Shawn Michaels.
(Getty Images)

roughshod in WCW alongside Hulk Hogan as the New World Order.

While there were similarities between DX and the NWO, DX wasn't a clone. The NWO were heels, but Hall and Nash had no problem doing things that got them over as babyfaces to a large portion of the audience. DX was more a traditional heel faction, with Shawn in particular going out of his way to be as annoying as possible. They were trying to portray themselves as juvenile delinquents, the annoying kids at school who did whatever they wanted and were never punished for it, the kind of kids people hate.

Never mind that Shawn was 32 and Hunter was 28.

Technically the original DX had four members, the final being Rick Rude, who was there to play the male bodyguard role opposite Chyna. He left the company shortly after the Montreal Screwjob, in November of 1997, and his run with the group was so brief that most people don't consider him a founding member.

DX ran roughshod through WWF as a strong heel faction all the way through WrestleMania XIV, when Steve Austin beat Michaels to win the WWF title. Shawn had been dealing with back and knee issues for at least most of the past year, and his back problems were worsened during a match at the Royal Rumble when the Undertaker backdropped him over the top rope and he smashed his back on the edge of a casket sitting at ringside. He took what was scheduled to be a hiatus after WrestleMania, but his back injury, combined with personal problems, led to him retiring from the ring for four years.

In his absence, Triple H took over as the head of DX, and alongside Chyna they added new members X-Pac and the New Age Outlaws. Personally, I always thought the original 1997 DX was the strongest, but for many fans, largely because the company exploded in popularity in 1998, the glory run of the faction was the post-Michaels version.

The post-Michaels version, however, is a much harder story to tell, since it existed concurrently with Vince Russo's tenure as head writer. DX added members. They turned babyface. They turned heel. Members left. They randomly returned for no reason. They broke up. They got back together. They broke up. They randomly appeared together again. But fans during this period, a large number of which were starting to get into wrestling for the first time, weren't so much into the storylines or internal logic and consistency. Monday night was wrestling night and they were merely along for the ride.

Among the more memorable moments for the new DX was an incident on April 27, 1998, when *RAW* and *Nitro* were both running live events within 20 miles of each other, *RAW* in Hampton and *Nitro* in Norfolk, Virginia. DX "invaded" *Nitro*, showing up at the building with bullhorns as the WCW fans cheered wildly. They pretended they were trying to get inside the building and chanted for Ted Turner and Eric Bischoff to let their friends, Hall and Nash, go free. Watching back with modern eyes, it's almost painfully lame, but in the spring of 1998, it was an iconic moment. It also led to a lawsuit as WWF, among other things, used computer graphics to replace a sold-out sign on the Norfolk Scope with a sign that claimed tickets were still available (insinuating that *Nitro* was having trouble selling tickets, which was the furthest thing from the truth).

DX fizzled out as a regular act by early 2000, although for the next 18 years we'd see some sort of reunion every few years or so. By the time Hunter and Shawn were in their mid-40s, DX reunions were mostly comedy spots where they would joke about their age, the fact that they were trying to pull this off in the post-Attitude era, and essentially push that they were largely out there for a nostalgia pop and to sell their merchandise.

Probably the most historically notable DX reunion took place in 2018, largely because it involved Michaels coming out of retirement after eight years to team with Triple H to take on the Undertaker and Kane in the main event of the WWE Crown Jewel show in Saudi Arabia. Shawn, despite his long hiatus and protestations that he was done as an in-ring performer, was the best worker in the match; amazingly, the second-best worker was Triple H despite the fact that he tore his right pec off the bone about five minutes into the match and went on to work another 20-plus. In the end, Hunter pinned Kane after Michaels hit a superkick.

The most popular version of DX, plus Michaels but sans Rude, were inducted into the WWE Hall of Fame in 2019. With their iconic music by Christopher Warren, crotch chops, and "Suck it!" catchphrase, not to mention strong merchandise numbers, they will likely continue to be wheeled out every few years until Michaels and Triple H can no longer physically appear on television. At which point, hey, they've got kids.

Brian Pillman

Brian Pillman died alone in a hotel room on October 5, 1997, at the age of 35.

Pillman's life, particularly the last five years or so, was like a meteor that flashed across the sky of the wrestling world. While he never made it to the very top of WWF or WCW, he was on the precipice of doing so when he died, long after his immense athletic gifts had been taken from him. Every time you see an angle on television post-1997 that blurs the lines between fantasy and reality—for good or bad, mind you—you can thank Brian Pillman for it.

Pillman was also proof that if you want something bad enough and are willing to do whatever it takes to make it happen, you can achieve almost anything, all the way down to opening up a *Penthouse* magazine one day; becoming completely enamored with that month's Pet, Melanie; telling people she was the woman he was going to marry; and then marrying her.

Pillman was born with throat polyps and underwent more than 30 surgeries during his life, the result of which was his uniquely raspy voice. He was always undersized, at least for that era, and had to fight for everything that he wanted. He was a star football player in high school and later made the Cincinnati Bengals in 1984. In 1985, he was traded to the Buffalo Bills, but steroids were found in his locker and he was cut from the team. He briefly played for the

CFL's Calgary Stampeders but broke his ankle, and that was it for his football career.

Kim Wood, the strength and conditioning coach for the Bengals, who became a lifelong mentor for Pillman, happened to be a longtime hardcore wrestling fan. He told Pillman that since he was already in Calgary he should try out pro wrestling with the Hart family. He debuted on November 5, 1986, in the main event of a show at the Calgary Stampede Pavilion, where he was pushed as a local football hero in a multi-man match that his team won. He was off to the races.

He was signed by WCW in 1989 where he began what would be a tumultuous seven-year run. Steroids or not, in that era he was always going to be undersized. After a rocky start he developed the reputation as a good worker who could have great matches but wasn't going to be a main-eventer. He teamed up with Tom Zenk as "Flyin'" Brian Pillman and later became the company's light heavyweight champion. He always wanted more. In 1992, he signed a new three-year deal at $225,000 annually. This was during the period where WCW had a new person in charge on seemingly a weekly basis. Soon after signing, Bill Watts came aboard, couldn't believe what a guy Pillman's size was making, and told him that they needed to renegotiate his deal. Pillman refused. Watts told him he either renegotiated or he'd lose every single week on TV. Pillman said he'd be fine being the highest-paid jobber in the world. Watts, also stubborn, was determined to follow through, but he ran into the issue of being a guy in charge who was jobbing out a guy who was making $225,000 per year, and eventually both sides worked out their issues. Watts dropped the light heavyweight division and in 1993 Pillman teamed with the man who would become the centerpiece of the WWF just a few years later, the at-the-time "Stunning" Steve Austin. The "Hollywood Blonds" (Austin had hair at the time) were an awesome tag team, but they took the heat for a low Clash of the Champions rating and were broken up. With no tag team and no light heavyweight division, Pillman was back in no-man's land. He ended up heading to ECW as part of a talent exchange with WCW for most of 1994.

His most famous run began with his return to WCW in 1995. His three-year deal was soon coming to an end. He wanted to be a top guy and make more money. He and Woods sat down and came up with the idea of "The Loose Cannon" Brian Pillman. In wrestling, the best characters are the ones closest to the people playing them, and Pillman was, as much as anyone in wrestling, a loose cannon. He began to act out-of-control both inside and outside the ring, and he didn't let on that what he was doing was part of a new character he'd developed. People thought he was losing his mind. Among the people who did know were Eric Bischoff, at the time the man in charge of WCW, and Kevin Sullivan, the booker. Pillman's supposed insanity led to a very famous match with Sullivan at SuperBrawl VI on February 11, 1996. The two had earlier been involved in what to fans was a weird confrontation on TV, where it looked like they weren't cooperating with each other in a match. Of course, this was all part of their story. At SuperBrawl, in a "respect match," they once again worked the match to seem like it was real, brawling and going for each other's eyes, and in the end Pillman stood up and said, "I respect you, booker man!" and walked out of the ring. Insider fans thought they'd just seen a legitimate shoot on live TV. It wasn't just some of the fans; virtually all of the wrestlers—with the notable exception of the Disco Inferno, who saw through the ruse—thought Pillman and Sullivan had just had a real fight on live PPV.

Keep in mind, as compelling as this was, there is no evidence it was making any money whatsoever. But it had everyone talking, and the people in the office seemed to love the idea that they were fooling everyone.

In one of the craziest stories in wrestling history, Pillman approached Bischoff and Sullivan with an idea. Let's go all the way with this, he said. He convinced them to fire him—for real—to "prove" to everyone that this was all legitimate and not just a storyline. So, the paperwork was drawn up and sent to him, giving him his release.

He immediately began negotiating with the WWF.

In the end, the only person who made any money off the entire Loose Cannon run in WCW was Brian Pillman. It drew no money but it made him the talk of the business, and both McMahon and Bischoff offered him deals in the $400,000 range.

In the middle of negotiations, he was involved in a terrible Humvee accident which nearly killed him; only Brian Pillman could find a way to flip a Hummer. He needed multiple surgeries, including to an ankle which was completely destroyed, and there was no guarantee he'd ever be able to wrestle again. He thought for sure he was doomed, but McMahon and Bischoff kept their offers on the table. In the end, he signed with WWF for a number of reasons, mainly that WWF was offering him a guaranteed deal and WCW would not, and given his physical state, he needed the guarantee.

The two most famous moments of Pillman's WWF run both involved Austin, his former Hollywood Blonds partner. The first involved an angle, shortly after he had to get surgery to re-break and reset his broken ankle after it failed to heal properly, where Austin broke into Pillman's house and Pillman, to defend his family, pulled out a gun. The satellite transmission supposedly went down and as the TV turned to snow you could hear shots fired. Of course, in storyline, Pillman missed, but it was an extremely controversial angle at the time. WWF took him off TV and he laid low for several months afterward.

His other famous WWF moment saw him and the Hart Foundation (Pillman, Bret and Owen Hart, Davey Boy Smith, and Jim Neidhart) face Steve Austin, the Legion of Doom, Ken Shamrock, and Goldust in the main event of one of the WWF's most critically acclaimed PPV events ever, In Your House 16: Canadian Stampede. What he considered his in-ring career highlight took place just three months before his death in the place where his own wrestling career began 11 years earlier.

Pillman was found dead in the Budgetel Hotel in Bloomingdale, Minnesota, the morning of the WWF Badd Blood show. While a number of muscle relaxers and pain pills were found in his room, all had been prescribed and none of the bottles were empty. His death was officially attributed to a heart attack. Those close to the family believe he actually died of arteriosclerotic heart disease, which took his father's life when Brian was just three years old. His lifestyle, which involved a lot of partying and steroid use, were likely contributing factors. WWF announced his death at the beginning of that evening's PPV, and then ran the show as scheduled, with Shawn Michaels beating the Undertaker in the first-ever Hell in a Cell match as the main event.

The following night, *RAW* ran a very controversial Brian Pillman Tribute Show, which included Vince McMahon interviewing Melanie Pillman live on the air via satellite from her home, asking her questions such as, what would she do now that Brian was dead? It was widely regarded as one of the most tasteless and exploitative *RAW*s in history. In later years, Les Thatcher helped arrange Brian Pillman Memorial Shows, with the proceeds going to Pillman's family. Four shows were run through 2001.

50 Watch Every WrestleMania

While it certainly takes longer than watching every Royal Rumble, every WWE fan should eventually watch all of the WrestleManias in order.

To modern fans, WrestleMania is the biggest annual event in pro wrestling, the granddaddy of them all, the one show that you still find a way to watch even if you don't religiously watch wrestling week to week.

It wasn't always like that.

The first WrestleMania was a big and heavily promoted event, based around Hulk Hogan, Cyndi Lauper, Roddy Piper, Mr. T, and MTV. WrestleMania III at the Pontiac Silverdome, featuring Hogan vs. Andre the Giant, was an iconic event. WrestleMania VI, featuring Hogan vs. the Ultimate Warrior, was the young Attitude Era fans' favorite show. WrestleMania X was considered at the time the greatest WrestleMania ever. WrestleMania XIV, where Shawn Michaels dropped the WWF title to Steve Austin, helped kick off WWF's hottest period in history. WrestleMania X-Seven, with the Rock vs. Austin, brought the company to new heights, and was considered the new greatest WrestleMania ever, at least until Steve Austin turned heel. From that point forward, with a few exceptions including the 2004–06 period when the company was in the doldrums, WrestleMania became a stadium event, with every show drawing 50,000-plus fans and being pushed as the most must-see event of WWE's calendar year.

A couple things you should know about WrestleMania. First, pay no attention to the attendances listed on Wikipedia. WWE regularly makes up attendance numbers, usually inflated about 10,000 above the real number, rationalizing that the announced attendance is part of the show. Since WWE has gone public, you can do the math when going through the earnings reports and calculate what the real attendances are, or you can read that week's *Wrestling Observer Newsletter*, where Dave Meltzer gets the actual attendances from the box office or the local police. WrestleMania 32 in Arlington, Texas, is the legitimate most-attended show in WWE history, drawing just over 93,000 paid. The company claimed 101,763, although in an earnings call Vince McMahon himself admitted that number was inflated. WrestleMania III, the most disputed attendance in all of WWE history, drew about 78,000 paid, less than the SummerSlam 1992 event, which drew a legitimate 79,127. To this day, fans who refuse to believe that the story they were told in their childhood was a lie—including Wikipedia editors—still list WrestleMania III as drawing WWF's claimed 93,173.

Second, particularly in recent years, WrestleMania is the show where all of the legends of the past return. Be prepared to see guys like the Rock headlining in 2012 and 2013, long after he left wrestling to become one of the biggest A-list stars in Hollywood. Despite the discontent from wrestlers who feel it's unfair for part-timers to work the WrestleMania main event, the reality is that WrestleMania is all about business and drawing the most money possible, and if that means bringing in special attractions and pushing them above the regulars, so be it. Obviously, the business is much bigger today, but if you compare WrestleManias headlined by guys like the Rock to shows headlined by the two guys involved in the company's most-pushed feuds—Hulk Hogan vs. Sgt. Slaughter at WrestleMania VII, for example, a show that drew so poorly based on attempting to capitalize on the Gulf War that they had to move it to a smaller building—you'll see that nostalgia and big stars do trump WWE's regular storylines. And as a publicly traded company, business will always come first.

Watching every WrestleMania, like watching every Royal Rumble, is a trip down memory lane. Some shows are terribly boring. Some of the early shows are so bad it almost seems inconceivable that WrestleMania could have been, at any point in time, such a nothing-happening event. Some of them are true spectacles, among the greatest shows in company history. You'll see the biggest stars on the biggest stage; you'll see people you forgot had ever even wrestled for the company; you'll see good matches, bad matches, great angles, terrible angles, and sometimes some really horrible skits and attempts at comedy. You will, in a nutshell, see WWE for everything that it is and always has been.

51 Jim Ross

Jim Ross is arguably the best and most famous wrestling announcer in history.

From the day Ross began working in the business for NWA Tri-State in 1974, he's worn many hats. For Tri-State he worked as a broadcaster and a referee. In Mid-South he worked as a broadcaster and vice president of marketing. And in his most high-profile run in WWF, he worked as a broadcaster and head of talent relations, an unforgiving job where he had to play bad cop to Vince McMahon's good cop.

Ross spent 13 years working for NWA Tri-State (which rebranded itself as Mid-South Wrestling and then the Universal Wrestling Federation), during which time he developed his play-by-play style. He came up working in a territory that was very different from the 1980s WWF, which was built around superheroes and comic book characters. Mid-South was a tough and gritty promotion, filled with badasses who worked a tough style of wrestling on television designed to be episodic as opposed to just a hodgepodge of prelim matches. As a result, Ross called the action like he was calling a legitimate sport, and he carried that with him throughout his entire career, even after going to work for the WWF.

In the mid-1980s, Mid-South rebranded as the UWF in an attempt to go national. They, like many others, failed, largely due to the high cost of purchasing TV time and an oil market crash in 1986 that devastated the region. The territory was purchased by Jim Crockett Promotions, which proceeded to run the second-most ill-fated invasion angle of all time. Ross became the third announcer for JCP alongside David Crockett (who was incredibly passionate but not very good at his job) and Tony Schiavone (who was excellent for most of his career before giving up all hope when the rest of us did at the end of WCW). He stayed with the promotion through the early 1990s when he ran headlong into Eric Bischoff, who was rising through the ranks at World Championship Wrestling, and who Ross was ultimately unable to work under.

Ross' WWF run began on April 4, 1993, when he came out at WrestleMania IX dressed in a toga (the show was at Caesars Palace in Las Vegas, but still, what a debut). Despite the fact that he was without question the best play-by-play man the company ever had, he had the strangest relationship with Vince McMahon. McMahon fired and rehired him multiple times. He put him in angles and storylines that seemed designed to humiliate him, and he seemed to regularly look for ways to get rid of him. But Ross was the Ric Flair of announcers, in that, for years, every time they tried to get rid of him his replacement would fail, and they'd go back to him, over and over again.

His first contract expired on February 11, 1994, and it was not renewed. Two weeks later he suffered his first attack of Bell's palsy, an affliction that paralyzes facial muscles. Later that year,

McMahon was indicted in the steroid trial and Ross was re-hired to take his place on *RAW*. For two years he blew everyone else away at his job. Then, in the fall of 1996, McMahon wrote an angle where Ross would turn heel—yes, a heel play-by-play man—which included a storyline where Ross would bring "Razor Ramon and Diesel" back to WWF in the wake of them jumping ship to WCW. It turned out he was introducing a fake Razor Ramon and a fake Diesel. The angle died a death and it was quickly dropped.

Ross was removed from television after another attack of Bell's palsy following his mother's death in 1998. Michael Cole, who was being groomed to be his replacement, took over. When Ross returned, McMahon tried the heel announcer gimmick again, this time having Ross act like a crazy man, including building his own announcing booth at ringside. The problem was, Cole sucked as a replacement and everyone knew it, so they cheered Ross like crazy and ultimately Ross returned as head play-by-play man. Ross and analyst Jerry Lawler became an iconic duo during the Attitude Era.

On October 10, 2005, Ross departed the company again, although this time it was to deal with a serious issue with his colon that threatened his life. He was able to recover, which he attributed in part to the support of his wife, Jan, whom he'd met on a flight in 1991. She was a flight attendant and he was traveling with Ric Flair, and she paid more attention to him than Flair, so he knew she was a winner. Two years later they were married. They stuck together through thick and thin, including all of his bouts with Bell's palsy and his subsequent issues with depression. Tragically, she died on March 22, 2017. She was riding her scooter to the gym, which was a few blocks from their home, and a 17-year-old who was texting hit her from behind. She suffered massive injuries including multiple skull fractures and was pulled off life support two days later.

Ross remained the voice of *RAW* through 2008 when WWE drafted him to the *SmackDown* brand, having Cole replace him on

RAW. Despite a decade of experience, Cole still couldn't fill Ross' shoes. A year later, Todd Grisham, who was even worse than Cole, was given Ross' role as lead play-by-play man on *SmackDown*, with Ross being moved to the color position. This was the beginning of the end of his full-time role as a commentator for the company. On October 20, he suffered his third Bell's palsy attack, and his days as a regular on WWE television were over. He continued working for the company through August of 2013, when, following a very weird and controversial WWE 2K14 panel that he hosted, he announced his retirement on WWE.com. There were allegations that he was drunk during the panel, which he denied, noting that the real reason for his firing was because a sponsor had been insulted by something and requested Ross be released. Vince McMahon claimed Ross asked for his release to spend more time with his family. Whatever the truth, that was the end of Ross' WWE career after 21 years.

He did return to the company for a year in 2017, where he called a few matches on the main roster and the WWE Mae Young Classic on the WWE Network. What was fascinating about this return is that he had gotten a job in 2015 calling New Japan Pro Wrestling for AXS TV, meaning, for a one-year period, he was doing commentary for the two largest pro wrestling organizations in the world at the same time, something previously inconceivable. WWE even allowed him to re-sign with AXS TV in 2017. By 2018, WWE had smartened up to the underground success of New Japan among hardcore fans and put the kibosh on him re-signing for 2019, at which point his job went to Kevin Kelly and Cyrus, the English language commentators for New Japan World.

Ross has and continues to keep busy with various outside endeavors, including a very popular podcast, one-man shows throughout the world, voiceover work for video games, and more.

52 Jerry "The King" Lawler

The highlights of Jerry "The King" Lawler's wrestling career, and what made him a Hall of Famer, all happened outside of WWE, but it was his WWE run that made him the most famous.

While he did wrestle for several years in WWE and did have a well-known feud with Bret Hart in the mid-1990s, the vast majority of his post-1997 run was as a commentator, most famously alongside Jim Ross during WWF's hottest period. Lawler, among the most quick-witted personalities in wrestling history, was an awesome color commentator, adding levity to broadcasts where Ross built a legendary Hall of Fame career as a play-by-play man.

Aside from a brief period in the early 2000s when he quit the company to protest the firing of his girlfriend at the time, Stacy "Miss Kitty" Carter, Lawler has remained with the company ever since. While he mostly worked as a commentator, he would return to the ring for matches every few years, all the way up until he died during *RAW* and came back to life.

The date was September 12, 2012; the location, the Bell Centre in Montreal. Lawler, who had wrestled independently nonstop through most of his WWE career (his announcing contract allowed him to take indy dates) was doing a tag team match on *RAW* where he teamed with Randy Orton to face CM Punk and Dolph Ziggler. Lawler wrestled the match, returned to the announce table afterward, seemed totally fine, and then shortly thereafter suffered a massive heart attack. WWE's medical staff reacted immediately and he was quickly transported backstage. Michael Cole, his broadcast partner on and off for over a decade, alerted fans to his condition throughout the show. He was without a heartbeat for anywhere from 10 to 15 minutes, but they were finally able to revive him. In a minor miracle, given how long he was out, he suffered no brain damage, returned home a mere seven days later, and was back working for WWE two months later.

Doctors said that having the heart attack on *RAW* with so much medical personnel around was probably the best thing possible outside of having a heart attack inside a hospital. Lawler claimed that there was nothing wrong with his heart, and that he believed the reason it happened was because Ziggler had dropped a series of elbows on his chest during the match which had interrupted his heart rhythm. Of course, Lawler was never much of a gym rat, rarely trained, and had a horrible diet, but he was convinced it was a freak accident and was back wrestling as soon as he got clearance.

Lawler's biggest success in pro wrestling came in the Memphis territory, where he began in 1970. His first successful run came as a heel feuding with the territory's top babyface star, Jackie Fargo, who Lawler would eventually supplant in becoming the biggest babyface in Memphis history. Although he's remembered as the King of Memphis, he drew best as a heel in the early 1970s.

Lawler's most famous rivals were Bill Dundee, with whom he feuded for what felt like eternity, and manager Jimmy Hart, whose First Family attempted to destroy Lawler for five straight years before Hart finally left for the WWF in the mid-1980s.

On a national basis, Lawler's most famous rival was Andy Kaufman. Kaufman, best known for his role as Latka Gravis on the hit 1970s show *Taxi*, was one of those celebrities who loved and was obsessed with pro wrestling. He wanted to be a wrestler but was too skinny, and so he did a gimmick where he played an over-the-top male chauvinist who wrestled women on TV (including once on *Saturday Night Live* with the first WWWF champion, Buddy Rogers, whom he idolized, as his manager). He billed himself as the World Intergender Champion. He tried to get into the WWF but Vince McMahon Sr. had zero interest in anything that he felt made a mockery of wrestling. But Memphis was different, the perfect place for this kind of storyline, in fact, so Bill Apter of *Pro Wrestling Illustrated* put Kaufman in touch with Lawler, and they were off to the races.

Kaufman came into the territory and wrestled women until finally, after he kicked one of them after a match, Lawler showed up to put a stop to this nonsense. This led to a match—more an exhibition, really, as Lawler did a "real" title match earlier in the show—on April 5, 1982. Lawler beat Kaufman, then gave him a piledriver and left him for dead. Kaufman sold it huge and was taken to the hospital and fitted with a neck brace that he proceeded to wear everywhere. The angle got a ton of mainstream attention, which Kaufman loved, and many newspapers reported that he'd been legitimately injured in a pro wrestling match. He continued to return for a few months.

And then, in July of 1982, both men appeared on *Late Night with David Letterman*. Lawler claimed he was there to apologize. Of course, he and Kaufman got into an argument and Lawler slapped him. They went to commercial and came back and Kaufman started cutting a promo on Lawler that had to be censored. He then threw a drink at Lawler and Lawler chased him off the set. The next day, Letterman revealed to the world that the entire thing had been set up, but for whatever reason people believed that what they'd seen was a shoot for decades after.

Lawler and Kaufman continued to feud. The pinnacle of the angle began in December of that year. Lawler destroyed Jimmy Hart in a cage; two weeks later, Lawler and Nick Bockwinkel fought for the AWA world heavyweight title and did a disputed finish that resulted in the title being held up. The rematch took place on January 10, 1983. Hart returned to ringside, wrapped up like a mummy to sell the beating Lawler had given him. He hit the ring during the match, distracted Lawler, and Bockwinkel pinned him to become AWA champion. Hart then removed his bandages to reveal that he was not Jimmy Hart after all—he was Andy Kaufman, and he had cost Lawler the title.

While Lawler and Kaufman continued to feud, the reality is that Kaufman was a great character but not one who sold tickets over the long haul. The more he appeared, the more business declined; just over a year after he debuted, he was drawing around one-third of what he'd drawn at the start.

Kaufman died of cancer on May 16, 1984. Lawler, in all the national media, felt he needed to maintain kayfabe, so he couldn't reveal to the world how devastated he really was.

It is possible that Lawler is the most decorated pro wrestler in history if you add up all of his various title reigns. He won, at minimum, 227 championships during his career, and the real number is possibly much higher. Of course, winning titles in Memphis is much different than, for example, the nearly two dozen NWA-, WCW-, and WWF-recognized world championships won by Ric Flair during his career, but one way or another, Lawler was the biggest star ever in a very prolific territory and a sure-fire Hall of Famer inside and outside the ring.

53 Jimmy "Superfly" Snuka

Jimmy Snuka could have been Hulk Hogan but personal issues destroyed his career. He was the biggest star in the WWF prior to Hogan being raided from the AWA and pushed to the moon.

Jimmy Snuka was born James Wiley Smith. A native of Fiji, his family moved to Hawaii and he took the name of his mother's husband, James Reiher, who was not his biological father. He was beaten regularly. Later, because he was so adept at the game of snooker, his wrestling name became Jimmy Snuka.

Snuka could not read or write and didn't say much, so he was always paired with a manager. He became a star in the Pacific Northwest in the 1970s, first as a babyface and later as a heel. His persona was that of a real-life Tarzan (his childhood idol), with his long hair, leopard-print gear, dark tan, and crazy eyes.

In one of the most famous moments of the 1980s, he was wrestling Don Muraco in a cage match at Madison Square Garden on October 17, 1983. Snuka lost the match but dragged Muraco back into the cage afterward. Snuka, whose Superfly Splash was one of the most amazing sights in wrestling in those days, climbed to the top of the cage and crushed Muraco with the big splash. Dozens and dozens of wrestlers have done far bigger moves off far higher cages ever since, but because it has been replayed countless times over the years—including as part of WWE's opening montage for all its TV shows—his is the most legendary of all.

A number of kids were there in the building that night who would go on to become pro wrestlers, including Mick Foley, Tommy Dreamer, and Bubba Ray Dudley. Foley, 14 years later, would go on to perform the second-most-famous cage spot of all time.

Snuka started his WWF career as a heel. During his feud with WWF champion Bob Backlund, however, fans began to cheer for Snuka and boo Backlund. Nowadays, that seems par for the course. In those days, it was unheard-of. So, they went with it, shooting an angle where Snuka's manager, Lou Albano, was revealed to have been cheating him on his payouts. He turned babyface and was a sensation. McMahon strongly considered making him WWF champion, but there was concern that something would go wrong.

Which it did.

Snuka's legacy will forever be tied to the death of Nancy Argentino. Months earlier, Snuka and Argentino, his 23-year-old mistress, had gotten into a fight at a hotel. He reportedly dragged her to his room by the hair and refused to open the door for the police. They eventually broke down the door. Snuka, who'd had major drug issues since the beginning of his career, went crazy, attacking eight officers and two police dogs while completely naked.

On May 10, 1983, Snuka called the Allentown, Pennsylvania, police and said his girlfriend was in bad shape. She was rushed to the hospital and died shortly thereafter. The coroner's report listed the cause of death as "undetermined craniocerebral injuries"— head and brain trauma. Police said the injuries were consistent with domestic abuse. She had cuts and bruises all over her body. The forensic pathologist and coroner both believed she'd been murdered.

Two weeks later the case was dropped. No charges were filed. Local residents believed for years afterward that there had been a cover-up. Argentino's family was devastated. Two years later they filed a wrongful death lawsuit against Snuka and won. They were awarded a $500,000 default judgment. They never saw a dime. Snuka claimed he was destitute.

Meanwhile, he was wrestling all over the world and had just been featured as a cornerman in the main event of WrestleMania, the biggest wrestling show of all time up to that point. He was fired from WWF in 1985 after a pair of incidents during overseas tours (one involving women and another involving drugs, his two vices) and immediately went to work for New Japan and then the AWA. He returned to the WWF on April 2, 1989, at WrestleMania V, largely to put over younger talent, and stayed through 1993. At the time, he was 50 years old. He spent two years in ECW, back when it was Eastern Championship Wrestling, and then wound down his full-time career. He would continue to take independent dates through 2015.

On June 28, 2013, Lehigh County district attorney Jim Martin announced Argentino's murder was going to be revisited, 30 years after she died. The following year the case was handed over to the grand jury, and on September 1, 2015, Snuka, 72, sitting in a wheelchair and connected to a feeding tube, surrendered himself to police and was charged with third-degree murder and involuntary manslaughter. He pleaded not guilty two months later.

On December 2, 2016, Snuka was moved into hospice care. His family claimed he was suffering from serious dementia and stomach cancer. On January 3, 2017, Judge Kelly Banach dismissed all charges, ruling Snuka not mentally fit to stand trial. Twelve days later, he died.

54 Shane and Stephanie McMahon

Stephanie McMahon is the daughter of Vince and Linda McMahon, and the sister of Shane McMahon. She, along with her husband Paul Levesque (Triple H), appear next in line behind Vince McMahon to take over World Wrestling Entertainment, Inc.

The story of Shane and Stephanie's relationship to the business has always been complicated. In the late 1990s, it was presumed that Shane would be his father's successor. He had started working for the company as a referee at the age of 19, then transitioned into more of a backstage role, including helping to launch WWF.com in 1997. Vince never intended to be Steve Austin's main rival, but luck and circumstance led to it happening. Shane was a TV character very early on in the feud, and by mid-1998 he was being pushed on television as his father's successor. He played a huge television role, both as an authority figure and in the ring, throughout the late 1990s and early 2000s.

Stephanie debuted as a character right around the same time. She was 22 years old, but they pushed her as a naive teenager, wide-eyed and innocent. She was in an on-screen romantic relationship with wrestler Test, a storyline that ended with Triple H allegedly drugging her and marrying her at a drive-thru chapel in Las Vegas. The following month it was revealed that the newly married Stephanie and Hunter had been in cahoots, and the McMahon-Helmsley Era began. With McMahon and Shane out

Shane and Stephanie McMahon at a Monday Night RAW *show in 2009.*
(Getty Images)

of the picture due to storyline injuries, Hunter and Steph took over as the heel authority figures, running roughshod. (Here's a piece of trivia: Hunter and Steph married in storyline in November of 1999. Although most fans have forgotten, they got divorced in storyline in January of 2002. In October of 2003, Stephanie and Hunter got married in real life. Although they were never remarried in storyline, the real-life marriage that everybody knew about just eventually bled over onto television, and ultimately it was just accepted that they were married again.)

It's never been made clear what led to Stephanie usurping her brother for eventual control of the company. It's clear from early 2000 storylines that Shane at that point was still the chosen one. Stephanie was a storyline character who left the company in 2003 to start a family. Shane, on the other hand, was planned to be the face of WCW back when the original plan was for it to remain its own separate touring organization. Shane had also suggested other acquisitions, including of ECW in 2000 and the PRIDE Fighting Championships in 2006, but Vince always shot the ideas down.

Ultimately, on October 16, 2009, in a move that shocked everyone, Shane publicly resigned from the company at the age of 39. The belief is that he was upset with Vince for never getting behind his acquisition ideas, and that he'd figured out that Hunter and Steph were going to end up running the company when all was said and done, and not himself. Many in the company were devastated, as his reputation was that of the "nice McMahon." Realistically, given the way Vince has run the company since day one, the "nice McMahon" isn't necessarily the one he'd want running the company after he was gone. Stephanie's reputation had always been that she was the more aggressive business person, perhaps more cutthroat, perhaps less starry-eyed.

Shane worked on business projects in China; he served as CEO of both China Broadband and You On Demand in 2010, though he stepped down as CEO of the latter in 2013. On February 22,

2016, in a huge surprise and to a ridiculously massive ovation, he returned to WWE television as an on-screen character. While he carries no official role backstage, he has remained a popular TV character ever since.

Stephanie is currently the chief brand officer for WWE, with Levesque holding the title of executive vice president of talent, live events, and creative. Hunter works side by side with McMahon booking *RAW* and *SmackDown* and runs NXT on his own. Stephanie has no hand in creative and is more a global brand ambassador. Both appear regularly as television characters as well, and Hunter still works occasional matches on big shows.

59 Watch *Hitman Hart: Wrestling with Shadows*

Hitman Hart: Wrestling with Shadows is one of the most intriguing documentaries ever produced on pro wrestling, because it covers one of the biggest events in WWF history and also paints a picture of a transitional period in the business.

The documentary, produced, written, and directed by Paul Jay, was originally envisioned to be a look at the final few months of Bret Hart's WWF career before he headed off to World Championship Wrestling. Unbeknownst to everyone involved, the story would end with the infamous Montreal Screwjob, covered elsewhere. Because Jay and his cameras were granted full backstage access, he captured footage of both the discussion Bret and Vince McMahon had prior to the match—where McMahon agreed to do a DQ finish—and footage of Vince stumbling out of a locker room after Bret knocked him out following the main event.

It was certainly fortuitous that Jay managed to capture all of these events on film, but the documentary is an excellent inside look at the business even without it. It covers Bret's life during a pivotal time, following McMahon telling him that he couldn't afford the 20-year deal he'd promised him a year earlier, and giving Bret permission to sign a deal with WCW that Bret really didn't want to sign. It followed Bret from the Calgary Stampede PPV in July 1997 through Survivor Series in Montreal, including highlights of the peak of the U.S. vs. Canada feud, one of the great storylines in WWE history. We are offered glimpses backstage, at the time revolutionary, and get to know what the wrestlers were like when they weren't being wrestlers. The fearsome Vader, real name Leon White, calmly explained that he'd just gotten his real estate license and was making plans that would take him through the rest of his life. Sunny, who Bret insists was only a friend, is shown playing around backstage with Bret's son. A flippant comment by Shawn Michaels on live TV regarding Bret and Sunny's relationship was one of the powder keg moments in the real-life Hart vs. Michaels feud. We are also given a tour of the world-famous Hart House, including shots of Bret's father, Stu, stretching trainees in the infamous downstairs "dungeon."

It's a wrestling documentary but it was produced by a non-wrestling company, High Road Productions, in association with the National Film Board of Canada. As a result, it's compelling to both fans and non-fans, as it's more the story of a compelling personality who happens to work in a weird industry. *Entertainment Weekly* gave it an "A" rating at the time; it won several film festival awards; and Jordan Bernt Peterson, a clinical psychologist and professor of psychology at the University of Toronto, called it "one of the best documentaries about anything, ever."

The key to the documentary is that it captures a time in wrestling that was coming to an end. In Bret Hart's mind, the world championship was an institution to be respected even if the outcomes of the matches were predetermined. Being the champion meant you were the top guy in the promotion, the anchor, the biggest draw and the person the promotion revolved around. In Vince McMahon's mind, if Eric Bischoff announced that he'd signed the WWF champion, his promotion was sunk, and therefore it was imperative that Bret lose that championship by any means necessary. By the end of the 1990s and certainly by the early 2000s, the world title was seen by fans as a prop to be passed around for storyline purposes. Today, fans see it as a participation trophy that practically everyone deserves at one point or another. Bret and Vince's struggle over the fate of the championship, seemingly a life-or-death battle in *Wrestling with Shadows*, is almost silly to watch through modern eyes.

If you've never seen it, watch it. In 2018, Paul Jay made it available for free on YouTube.

56 Kurt Angle

There is a good chance that Kurt Angle is the most naturally gifted athlete to ever wrestle for WWE.

Everyone knows the story he tells about winning an Olympic medal with a "broken freakin' neck." The real story is even more impressive. He broke his neck in the 1996 U.S. Olympic Trials. He was facing Jason Loukides, and in attempting to avoid losing points on a takedown he tried basing on his head. He suffered two cracked vertebrae, two bulging discs, two herniated discs, and four pulled muscles in his neck. Two minutes later he was back on the mat, took down Loukides, and won the match. Six hours later, he wrestled Kerry McCoy and won a decision, also, obviously, with a broken neck. Keep in mind, when he first broke his neck he was warm and full of adrenaline. Six hours later, prior to the McCoy match, he was in intense pain. Doctors told him to take six months off and miss the Olympics, or he risked paralysis or worse. He finally found a doctor willing to regularly inject high-powered painkillers into his neck, and competed in the Olympics

Kurt Angle won gold at the 1996 Olympics before joining the WWE in 1998.

as a severely undersized heavyweight (Angle refused to cut weight and would often go into matches giving up 40 pounds to his opponent). He beat Abbas Jadidi of Iran via decision in the finals to become the 1996 Olympic heavyweight freestyle gold medalist.

Angle was never a pro wrestling fan growing up. He didn't even really know what it was. WWF offered him $250,000 right out of the Olympics and he turned it down. He attended an ECW show as a guest of Paul Heyman and was appalled at an angle involving Raven and a mock crucifixion (Angle was a Christian) and wanted nothing to do with the business. He wanted to be a sportscaster. He tried and failed.

In 1998, with no other high-paying career options on the table, he went back to WWF. The company had signed Mark Henry to a 20-year-deal coming off the same 1996 Olympics, and while Henry became a memorable character on TV playing the role of Sexual Chocolate, to say his Olympic fame did not pay off in WWF is putting it lightly. So, WWF told Angle the best it could offer was a tryout. He blew people away and was immediately signed. People who were there at the time said he was already a pretty good worker within weeks, and others said he picked it up faster than anyone they'd ever seen who wasn't a fan as a kid. After a year working around Memphis he was brought up to the main roster. He was a very good worker and talker from the day he debuted. They gave him a heel goody-goody character who would promote his three I's—"Intensity, Integrity, and Intelligence"—and preach about what a great role model he was as the only Olympic gold medalist, the only "real athlete," in WWF history.

He got over huge. Within a year he'd won the WWF championship. Within four years of his debut he'd won five versions of the world title, headlined 13 PPVs, was largely considered one of the best workers in the entire world, and was one of the favorite opponents of all the top stars, including the Rock, Steve Austin, and Ric Flair. By the time he left the company in 2006 he was already a legend in the business and a Hall of Famer, with some of the biggest names in history having stated that he was the best worker they'd ever been in the ring with.

But the pain of his broken neck never left him, and worse, he worked such a hard style that he was crippled with pain and suffered nerve damage and atrophy, among other things. He'd first gotten hooked on pain pills while attempting to win the 1996 Olympics, and by 2006 his problems were so bad that the company released him, concerned that he was inevitably going to overdose, and the last thing anyone wanted was an Olympic gold medalist dying on its watch.

In a very controversial move, he was immediately hired by TNA and pushed to the moon. He had two matches with Samoa Joe that broke TNA's records, hitting 60,000 PPV buys for both, a number never seen prior and a number the company never came close to again. In WWE, he had proved to be so great at comedy that the writers loved writing it for him, but it put a ceiling on his money-drawing potential. TNA, on the other hand, pushed him as a badass shoot fighter who could destroy anyone in the ring. Although he's most famous for his early 2000s run in WWE, he spent the majority of his career in TNA.

But he was a mess. Between 2007 and 2013, Angle was arrested on five different occasions (that we know of, as the history of wrestling is filled with unreported legal incidents due to the fame of the individuals involved and a tendency by law enforcement officials to sometimes let famous people off the hook) for DUIs and DWIs. According to Angle, after the 2013 arrest he knew he needed to make a change or he'd probably die, so he went cold turkey on everything, locked himself in his house for two weeks while he underwent withdrawal, and claims he's been clean ever since.

Angle was inducted into the WWE Hall of Fame in 2017 and returned to TV in April as the new general manager of *RAW*. After a series of farewell matches on *RAW*, Angle lost his retirement match to Baron Corbin at WrestleMania 35. He intends to stay involved in the business, but no matter what his future brings, he'll forever be remembered as one of the greatest workers and characters to ever step foot inside a WWE ring.

57 Mean Gene Okerlund

Mean Gene Okerlund was one of the greatest interviewers in the history of pro wrestling.

Okerlund was a disc jockey who moved to Minneapolis in the 1970s and began working for Verne Gagne's AWA. The ring announcer and interviewer at the time, Marty O'Neill, was getting older. Okerlund would fill in for him from time to time, and by the end of the decade he'd taken over his role permanently.

While he's best remembered for his work during the two boom periods—WWF in the 1980s and WCW during the Monday Night Wars—to many older fans his best work was in the AWA. Part of that was because he had the chance to work with some of the greatest promos in wrestling history, guys like Superstar Billy Graham, Bobby Heenan, Nick Bockwinkel, and Jesse Ventura (Ventura was the man who gave him the nickname "Mean" Gene).

In 1983, Vince McMahon was expanding nationally and appeared to take a certain glee in kneecapping Gagne's AWA. He took loads of his biggest stars, including Hulk Hogan, and Hogan, in being raided, requested McMahon bring in Okerlund as well. Okerlund became not only one of the most famous wrestling television characters of the 1980s, but also a workhorse. In those days, WWF ran a ridiculous number of house shows, close to 1,000 per year utilizing several different crews of wrestlers, and in order to build them up they'd have the wrestlers record localized promos. In other words, the wrestlers would talk about how they were coming to, say, Seattle, and they were going to face so-and-so on the card. Then they'd cut another promo about how they were coming to Portland, and so on and so forth. While each wrestler had to cut dozens of promos, Gene was the guy who had to hold the mic for *all* of them, and with retakes and such he was the man behind tens of thousands of promos, God only knows how many, during the decade.

Gene was special because, unlike the robots today who stare blankly at the camera, ask a scripted question in a wooden manner, and then stare into space for 10 seconds before the camera cuts away, Gene was a human being. He asked great questions, he was quick-witted, he'd remember lines guys had forgotten, and if the guy couldn't cut a promo, he could cut the promo for him, or at least led him through it. He was a master of his craft.

McMahon began to phase him out in 1993 and Okerlund jumped ship to WCW. He was hit-and-miss during this period. Sometimes he was great, sometimes he tried to make it too much about himself, and sometimes he kind of helped make a mockery of everything, although to be fair, at least he was lending some comic relief as the ship sank. He remained with the company until it went out of business, at which point he returned to WWF, where he made sporadic appearances until he passed away in January of 2019.

There was nobody like Mean Gene Okerlund, and because of how he was brought up in the business and the experience he developed in two unique eras, there never will be again.

Mick Foley

Mick Foley was born in Bloomington, Indiana, on June 7, 1965, about 30 years too early.

Given his wrestling ability and superior promo skills, Foley would almost surely be a main-eventer if he debuted today. But because of the physical specimens who surrounded him when he broke in, his talents weren't quite enough to get him over, and so he was forced to take risks which did make him famous but which ultimately shortened his career.

Foley is most famous for his two bumps off the Hell in a Cell cage at the King of the Ring pay-per-view on June 28, 1998. Today, while wrestlers do take bumps off the top of the Cell, they gimmick the announce table, putting a giant crash pad underneath it; it's still dangerous, but it's a performed stunt more than anything else. There is also a concussion protocol in place, and a match will be stopped if someone is clearly knocked out.

None of this was the case in 1998. Watching shows from that era today, you almost think they were trying to get someone killed, or at the very least were unconcerned if it happened. It was the Wild West, and while nobody died in the ring during that era (outside of Owen Hart in a freak accident), the culture itself cost countless lives.

Foley took the first bump off the cage shortly after the match began. He and the Undertaker started the contest by climbing up on top of the cage, and after a short brawl, the Undertaker tossed him off. The announce table Foley landed on was not gimmicked. He crashed through the table from a legitimate height of 15 to 18 feet, smashing onto the cement and nearly killing himself.

Earlier that afternoon, Vince McMahon had asked Foley if he'd gone on top of the cage yet to gauge his comfort level. Foley assured him that he had. He was lying. He later admitted that if he had gone up there before the match, he never would have taken the bump.

He dislocated his shoulder and likely suffered a concussion. Several people, including McMahon, Terry Funk, and WWF's doctor at the time, Francois Petit, hit ringside to check on him. Foley was a mess. They loaded him onto a stretcher and were carting him backstage when he leapt off and started lurching back toward the ring. He managed to get up on the cage a second time. The Undertaker, who was working with a broken foot, managed to follow him up.

The second spot was worse than the first. The Undertaker was going to choke slam Foley through the top of the Cell. The Cell had been gimmicked with the idea that the ceiling would sink down after the choke slam, and when the panel finally broke, Foley would have a manageable fall to the mat. But it didn't work out that way. The panel swung open and Foley went through it like a hot knife through butter, smashing onto the canvas. The first bump off the cage he knew was coming. This one he did not. Worse, WWF hadn't yet redesigned its rings to allow for more give, so while the mat wasn't quite as hard as solid rock, it was pretty damn solid. Several people—including commentators Jim Ross and Jerry Lawler, the Undertaker, and Funk—legitimately thought Foley was dead. Foley was knocked out and almost certainly suffered another concussion. To somehow make matters worse, a chair had fallen through the cage and landed on his face, dislocating his jaw and sending a tooth up his nose.

Incredibly, they did not stop the match. Foley recovered enough to finish the rest of his planned spots, which included the Undertaker choke slamming him onto a scattering of thumbtacks and then Tombstoning him for the pin.

McMahon later thanked Foley for his commitment but told him he never wanted to see anything like that again.

After nearly killing himself at King of the Ring, Foley got over a move called the Socko Claw, a nerve hold which involved him putting a sock with a happy face drawn on it on his hand and stuffing it in his opponent's mouth. Despite all he had done in the ring, he got more over than he'd ever been in his career because of a sock. But by that point, his body was ruined. Foley realized it was time to hang up the boots (for the first time, at least). He retired on February 27, 2000, following a Hell in a Cell match with Triple H; the stipulation was that if Foley didn't win, he'd retire. He took another bump through the top of the Cell, but they'd heavily gimmicked the ring so that he was able to land onto a crash pad this time. Hunter then Pedigreed him to end his career.

For two months.

Yes, at WrestleMania that year Foley came out of retirement to wrestle in a four-way main event. McMahon begged him to do the show and Foley spent 20 minutes begging him to get someone else, but McMahon insisted. Foley was upset in the sense that he didn't want to go back on his word, especially after only two months, but he also realized that it was going to be the biggest one-night payoff of his entire life. So, he put over Triple H in the four-way, and then he really did retire for several years.

Over the next decade he wrestled sporadically for WWE and later TNA. At one point WWE made him an announcer, a job he loved at first but grew to hate due to Vince constantly screaming in his ear over the headsets. Despite his injuries, he was still able to have classic matches with the likes of Randy Orton and Ric Flair. He continued to wrestle through 2012 when, prior to a SummerSlam match with Dean Ambrose, doctors refused to clear him to wrestle. He retired for real after that.

Foley's legacy is as a guy who overcame all the odds, became a massive superstar, and for better or worse helped to change the business. A generation of fat guys tried to become stars by hitting each other with stuff and falling off high places, not understanding that while Foley was best known for his hardcore matches, he was first and foremost a very good worker and incredible talker. He also opened the door to authors everywhere thanks to the success of his first book, *Have a Nice Day*, which topped the *New York Times* bestseller List. He still makes sporadic non-wrestling appearances for WWE today. While his body pays for his wrestling style daily, various surgeries have allowed him to remain mobile, probably more so than people feared he'd be at this stage. He remains a fan after all of these years, and you can probably count on one or two hands the number of people throughout history who have loved pro wrestling more than he has.

59 NXT

NXT is WWE's current "developmental" brand. In recent years it has become a critical success, promoting NXT TakeOver events on WWE PPV weekends, often outperforming the main shows.

Ohio Valley Wrestling, based out of Louisville, Kentucky, was WWF's first developmental territory, beginning in 1999. Prior to the mid-1980s, wrestlers traditionally worked in different territories around the world, traveling from one place to another if they wore out their welcome, or if a better offer came their way. Hulk Hogan, for example, traveled from the CWA in Memphis to Georgia Championship Wrestling to the WWWF to Japan to the AWA and then back to the WWF for his monster run in the 1980s. There was no Internet and word traveled slowly, largely through wrestling magazines.

By 1999 the territories were dead, and the wrestling business had consolidated down to WWF, WCW, and ECW, the latter of which was in a perpetual state of financial distress. Sure, WWF could raid WCW and vice versa, but there was no longer an endless stream of territories from which to acquire fresh talent. So, through the suggestion of Jim Cornette, OVW became the company's official developmental system.

Run by Danny Davis, Jim Cornette, and Rip Rogers, OVW in the late 1990s and early 2000s turned out a string of the greatest stars of the decade—John Cena, Randy Orton, Batista, Brock Lesnar, Bobby Lashley, John Morrison, the Miz, and dozens of others. It wasn't always smooth sailing. OVW had weekly TV shows and the people in charge had a very old-school attitude, booking long, intricate, logical storylines. WWE would decide to bring people up on a whim, which many times destroyed OVW storylines and forced Cornette to try to make sense of the changes.

WWE eventually switched its allegiance away from OVW in the mid-2000s, and after a short-lived stint backing Deep South Wrestling, Florida Championship Wrestling became the company's new developmental home base. To this day, in terms of pure developmental and creating stars from scratch, nobody has ever equaled what Cornette, Davis, and Rogers did in OVW. But Florida was a more logical base than Louisville, since so much talent lived there, and Cornette and WWE had many problems and blow-ups over the years.

NXT was originally a reality show, kind of a modern version of the old *Tough Enough* TV show. It featured FCW stars (rookies) pairing up with main roster stars (pros), with the rookies trying to win a spot on the main roster. The first two seasons of *NXT* replaced the ECW television show and aired on Syfy but was replaced once *SmackDown* moved from UPN to Syfy. The remaining seasons aired on WWE.com, since the WWE Network did not launch until 2014. The following four seasons followed the same format as the first, although without a TV outlet, only the hardest of the hardcore WWE audience could tell you anything about them.

The fifth season of *NXT* was bizarre. The longest season prior was the first, at 15 episodes. Season Five hit 15, then 16, then 17, then 20, then 30, then 40, then 50. By the end, the season consisted of 67 episodes, and, more bizarrely, it morphed in midseason from a reality show to a new brand with matches and storylines. The season ended out of nowhere, and from that point forward, NXT became the name of the brand as opposed to the name of the show, championships were introduced, and NXT became the NXT we know today on the WWE Network.

As part of the evolution of WWE's developmental approach, Florida Championship Wrestling was dropped in 2013 with the creation of the 26,000-square-foot WWE Performance Center, a world-class pro wrestling training facility featuring seven rings, one of which was padded to teach high-flying moves, a strength and conditioning gym, and full television production center. Virtually everyone who signs with WWE spends time in the Performance Center before being moved to NXT television or the main roster.

The modern NXT brand is a massive critical success. The territory is overseen by Paul Levesque, aka Triple H, and the wrestlers in NXT consider him something of a father figure. The one-hour taped weekly TV show airs on the WWE Network and Hulu, and is a simple, old-school, logically booked show that never offends and often produces some of the better wrestling matches of the week. The quarterly TakeOver specials almost unanimously get rave reviews and feature some of the best wrestling in the entire company.

Of course, comparing developmental today to developmental during any other period isn't really fair. OVW had to create guys from scratch. NXT's modus operandi is to take the best workers from the independent scene, put them in "developmental," and run shows that are competition to Ring of Honor and the top

U.S. indies. Because the TakeOver shows feature five matches and usually run less than three hours, you only get the absolute cream of the crop at TakeOver, so it's no surprise TakeOvers get better reviews than the main roster shows.

But it's not all roses. Vince McMahon runs *RAW* and *SmackDown* and doesn't watch NXT, so with rare exceptions, one call-up after another has flopped on the main roster. McMahon starts virtually all call-ups from scratch, and usually has no idea why they got over on the NXT roster in the first place. But it won't be like this forever. At some point the man behind NXT will be the man behind WWE proper. While there are myriad reasons that you can't run *RAW* and *SmackDown* like NXT, it does give fans great hope for the future.

60 Paul Heyman

Paul Heyman is among the most fascinating characters in wrestling history. He started out as a photographer, then became a manager, then a booker, then a wrestling promoter, then a commentator and storyline writer, and finally a storyline "advocate" for Brock Lesnar when Vince McMahon decided he hated the word "manager." He's one of the greatest talkers and creative minds in wrestling history. And yet what he's most famous for is a promotion that changed pro wrestling forever but was a financial failure.

In 1993, after a seven-year career as a wrestling manager largely for Jim Crockett Promotions and then WCW, Heyman took over the book for Eastern Championship Wrestling. He was taught booking by Eddie Gilbert, who was in charge of creative at the time. Tod Gordon, who ran ECW, fired Gilbert and gave Heyman the book. Heyman took the ball and ran with it.

Eastern Championship Wrestling, which became Extreme Championship Wrestling, took the underground wrestling world by storm. Heyman introduced hardcore wrestling concepts from Japan and Memphis, the latter of which was where he originally broke in. While people remember ECW for broken tables and barbed wire and sundry insanity, that was only part of what made ECW different. He scoured the world for the best unsigned wrestling talent, guys like Rey Mysterio Jr. and Chris Benoit and Dean Malenko and Eddie Guerrero, and gave them a platform upon which to show their talents. They ran shows in the 1,800-seat ECW Arena in Philadelphia, sometimes making a little profit, sometimes losing money, sometimes breaking even.

Heyman was a master of psychology. He understood that packing a small building made for a significantly better atmosphere then running a larger building that was half empty. He pushed to his die-hard loyalists—and that included both the fans and the wrestlers—that they were part of a revolution (at the height of this so-called revolution, the company was secretly being financed by WWF). Compared to the painfully sterile WWF and the nothing-happenin' WCW of 1994, to those in the area and to tape traders around the country, ECW seemed like the hottest promotion in the world.

But it wasn't. It was all an illusion. The company, from 1993 through 2001, lost millions of dollars. Countless wrestlers saw checks bounce; many of them never got paid everything they were promised. Heyman at one point had to file for personal bankruptcy.

The hardcore style probably led to many wrestlers ending up with serious substance abuse problems (although to be fair, this was industry-wide), and some died. Some ended up with chronic injuries. None became rich. But somehow, largely through his backstage oratory, Heyman was able to convince the wrestlers to keep fighting the good fight, that they were part of history, something bigger than all of them.

It was WWF and WCW copying ECW concepts that led in part to both WCW's success early in the Monday Night Wars and WWF's success later with the Attitude Era. ECW's high-flying stars lit WCW undercards on fire. ECW's hardcore style strongly influenced WWF's style for a good decade-plus. As ECW sunk deeper into the money pit, WWF and WCW capitalized on what Heyman had started.

ECW officially died on April 4, 2001. However, the actual death took place a month earlier when Heyman debuted as a *RAW* commentator, replacing Jerry Lawler, who had quit after the company fired his girlfriend, Stacy Carter. It was pretty clear ECW was dead at that point, but a few wrestlers still refused to believe it, clinging to the notion that this was just part of the master manipulator's plan, and that at the last moment he was going to swoop in and save the company. ECW Living Dangerously, after all, was scheduled for PPV on March 11, and Tommy Dreamer was insisting it would take place, even though they'd run their final house show back on January 13 in Pine Bluff, Arkansas, and there hadn't been a single show since.

The PPV never aired. ECW was indeed dead.

Years after "ECW wrestlers" were used in storyline as part of the WCW Invasion angle, WWE relaunched ECW as its own separate brand in 2006. A year earlier, a DVD called *The Rise and Fall of ECW* was released and did tremendous business, so that June WWE promoted an ECW: One Night Stand PPV, filled with former ECW stars and headlined by the Dudley Boyz vs. Tommy Dreamer and Sandman. It was a critical and financial success, and between the DVD and the PPV, Extreme Championship Wrestling made more money in one night than it had made in its entire existence, four years after it officially went out of business. The following year, ECW was officially relaunched following a second

One Night Stand, and the brand was given a TV show on the Syfy network. Suffice it to say, the WWE version of ECW on Syfy was the furthest thing from a critical success. Following an absolute disaster of a PPV, ECW December to Dismember on December 3, 2006, Heyman and WWE parted ways for six years.

Heyman returned in 2012 as the "advocate" (manager) for Brock Lesnar, who had returned to WWE after a very successful UFC career. He has remained in this role ever since. As a mouthpiece for both Lesnar and CM Punk, he's been responsible for many of the best talking segments in WWE of the 2010s. While not an official booker or writer, he has had influence on various storylines involving Lesner, and has also helped work with Ronda Rousey since her signing with WWE in 2017. While he and WWE had a very volatile relationship for years, for the most part stories of major issues between the two sides have largely quelled since his latest return. A student of the sport his entire lifetime, he remains among the more influential figures in wrestling history and is looked up to today by the younger wrestlers as a creative genius.

61 Read *Hitman*

Bret Hart's *Hitman: My Real Life in the Cartoon World of Wrestling* is arguably the greatest book ever written by a pro wrestler.

In 1985, Bret bought a small hand-held recorder, and from that point forward he recorded virtually every major detail of his career, and many minor ones. Unlike a lot of other wrestling memoirs—written by those whose memories are faulty or who conflate stories, misremember details, or flat-out lie—Bret's book feels as historically accurate as any story of his entire pro wrestling career could be written.

His approach was to write a book that would appeal to people who were not fans of wrestling, knowing that pro wrestling fans were going to love whatever he wrote anyway. It clocks in at a massive 592 pages and covers his childhood, his time growing up as a member of the famous Hart dynasty, his Stampede career, his WWF career through the Montreal Screwjob, the death of his brother Owen, his failed WCW run, his stroke, and his post-retirement struggles.

The only real downside to the book is that the original, unedited version would have run several thousand pages, and it had to be greatly condensed to create what the publishers felt would be a detailed yet readable book. But every base is covered, and if you're part of WWE's demographic and grew up with Bret Hart as one of your wrestling idols, you'll put the book down knowing everything you could ever want to know about his career, plus tons of details about both WWF during its hottest period ever and WCW during its demise.

Bret's book is available in multiple formats on Amazon.com, where it retains a five-star rating with more than 350 reviews.

62 Attend an NXT TakeOver Event

The best WWE show of WrestleMania weekend usually isn't WrestleMania or the *RAW* or *SmackDown* held immediately afterward. It's almost always the Saturday night NXT TakeOver event.

NXT runs TakeOvers four or five times per year in association with the bigger PPV events, including WrestleMania, SummerSlam, and Royal Rumble. Like a major WWE show, TakeOvers feature the culmination of many months' worth of storylines and usually feature the biggest angles and title changes. They're almost always spectacular and almost always feature among the better WWE matches of the year.

But wait, you say: why are TakeOvers so much better than the main roster shows if NXT is supposed to be WWE's developmental territory?

As noted elsewhere in this book, NXT is technically considered "developmental," but it features some of the best wrestlers on the planet. There are a handful of superstars who started out with WWE and went on to become good workers and big stars on the main roster—Roman Reigns and Charlotte come to mind. But the vast majority of the NXT names who move up to the main roster were big stars and great workers before they ever came to WWE. Probably 80 percent of the "NXT graduates" on the main roster fall into this category. Shinsuke Nakamura, Samoa Joe, Kevin Owens, Sami Zayn, Daniel Bryan, and many others were big indy stars before they ever stepped foot in the WWE Performance Center. So, TakeOvers don't really feature matches between "developmental" wrestlers; they feature incredible matchups of former independent stars with the added benefit of weeks and months of television to build up their programs.

Unlike *RAW*, which runs live every week, NXT tapes weeks in advance. The belief in pro wrestling is that live is better than tape, but history doesn't really back that up. Although bookers fear that a taped show will suffer poor ratings because spoilers will get out and people won't bother to tune in, taped shows almost always pull ratings just as good or sometimes even better than live shows. There are benefits to going live. If WWE is live on Monday and someone gets hurt at a house show on Friday night, they can be written out of his or her storyline the following Monday. If you tape six weeks in advance and someone gets hurt three days after you finish taping, you can't write them out of storyline for five more weeks, which can be very problematic. There are also negatives to going live, one of which is that Vince McMahon is constantly changing his mind, so it's tough to do long-term storylines when the guy in charge can show up on Monday and decide to switch everything around. When you tape six weeks in advance, you have to plan out six weeks' worth of storylines, and once you tape they're set in stone.

That's one of the reasons TakeOvers are usually so well received. NXT's Wednesday night show on the WWE Network is a very simple one-hour show with storylines that build up programs between great wrestlers that pay off at TakeOvers in excellent matches. The in-ring wrestling is obviously at a high level on a TakeOver, but the right storyline going in can enhance a good match and make it great, and that's something that NXT does better than the main roster. NXT also benefits from having wrestlers who only stay with the brand for a year or two before moving up to the main roster, so they rarely feel stale to the audience.

Some of the best live shows I've ever seen have been NXT TakeOvers. Because of the spectacle, I'd probably recommend WrestleMania over TakeOver if you can only choose one on that particular weekend. But if you have the opportunity, I've never been to a bad NXT TakeOver, nor has one ever existed that fans haven't raved about. They're always among the best wrestling shows in the world in any given year.

Rey Mysterio Jr.

Rey Mysterio Jr. is an all-time legend who broke barriers wherever he went during his career, including WWE.

Mysterio, at 5-foot-2 and a little over 100 pounds when he debuted in 1989, was so small that he was right on the dividing line between a full-sized and a mini wrestler in Mexico. Had he been put in the mini's division, who knows how the history of wrestling might have changed. But he worked as a full-sized wrestler and within a few years was a sensation.

He first came to America in 1995 and blew people away with his matches against Psicosis and Juventud Guerrero in ECW. The following year, he was signed to WCW. On June 16, 1996, he was scheduled to face Dean Malenko at the Great American Bash PPV in Baltimore. Behind his back, everyone was laughing at this tiny guy, sitting around in his trunks thinking he could be a pro wrestler. He then went out with Malenko and tore the house down.

Mysterio opened the door for smaller wrestlers in this country. Prior to his superstardom, if you were 5-foot-6 and under 200 pounds, you had to be among the best and most charismatic workers in the world to get a chance, and even that wasn't enough in many places. Today, combined with the effects of WWE's Wellness Policy, undersized wrestlers are commonplace.

Mysterio was a star in WCW, but never really pushed at the top level. He won the cruiserweight title five times, the tag team titles, and the cruiserweight tag team titles. He was always positioned well in WCW, first in undercard matches that stole the show, and later as part of the Filthy Animals with Konnan, Kidman, Eddie Guerrero, and others. But he was never a true main-eventer.

His most famous match in WCW was a mask vs. title match with Guerrero at Halloween Havoc 1997, which was a legitimate five-star bout. He was supposed to lose his mask that night. He and all of the Mexican wrestlers were totally against it, but Eric Bischoff insisted. The night of the show, cooler heads prevailed. In hindsight, it would have been better to have lost it here in a five-star match, because Bischoff didn't give up and ultimately unmasked him in a nothing match on a nothing show, SuperBrawl IX on February 21, 1999, where Mysterio and Konnan lost to Scott Hall and Kevin Nash in a mask vs. hair tag team match (Konnan had neither mask nor hair).

Bischoff's argument was that nobody cared about masked wrestlers (the oldest wrestling promotion in existence, CMLL, has been built around masked wrestlers since 1933), and that Rey would be more marketable without it (unmasking him gave them one less thing to market, and when he put it back on in WWE, he likely sold tens of thousands of masks). During his run, Bischoff unmasked Rey, Psicosis, and Juventud Guerrera, and Guerrera was probably the only one you could argue was better off without it.

When WCW died, WWF picked up the contracts of 24 wrestlers. Rey, despite being very popular, was not among them. He was "too small." More than a year after WCW went under, WWE finally signed him. He was asked to wear the mask again, which violates Lucha Libre tradition, but he was given the blessing of the community due to the circumstances in which he dropped it. He was renamed "Rey Mysterio," dropping the "Jr." The original Rey Mysterio was not his father but rather his uncle, and he never worked for the WWF.

Following the death of Eddie Guerrero, Rey was made the world heavyweight champion in 2006. Vince McMahon was still very much against the idea; the smallest wrestler he'd ever put the title on was Guerrero, who was much larger than Rey. The creative team pushed and pushed and pushed, and Vince pushed back and pushed back and pushed back. Finally, he agreed, with one caveat—Rey could win, but damn it, he was quickly going to lose it.

And that's what happened. Worse, although he was given a big push leading into his championship reign—winning the 2006 Royal Rumble en route to pinning Randy Orton in a three-way with Kurt Angle at WrestleMania 22 to win the title—Vince, apparently bitter that he'd acquiesced against his better judgment, proceeded to beat Rey in countless non-title matches. It is doubtful any WWE champion in history ever lost more matches than Rey Mysterio. On July 23, 2006, three months after his win, he lost the belt to King Booker.

Mysterio is a three-time world champion for WWE. The other two occasions? He won the world title from Jack Swagger in 2010…and lost it five weeks later when Kane cashed in his Money in the Bank briefcase. Later that year, he won the WWF title in a tournament…and lost it later on the same show to John Cena.

Despite Vince's hesitance to fully commit to him, Mysterio was a gigantic Hispanic television and house show draw and sold an incredible amount of merchandise. He was more than just a small, high-flying luchador. He had a charisma that nobody else had. The company spent years trying to create another Hispanic superstar, pushing everyone from Alberto Del Rio, who had the size and the look, to Kalisto, who was almost pushed as a Mysterio clone, to Sin Cara, who was raided from Mexico where he had been the biggest star in the entire country in the mid-2000s. None of them made it. Even in 2018, when the United States indy scene was crawling with talented luchadors, Vince went back to the 43-year-old Rey Mysterio.

Mysterio is an all-time great who changed the landscape of American wrestling. Even though he made millions and was always pushed as a big star, he has still never received his just due.

 **Ric Flair**

When Ric Flair debuted for the WWF in 1991, he showed up with the NWA world heavyweight title after he'd been fired from WCW without dropping the belt. Bobby Heenan, who was set to be his manager, came on TV with the title and announced that the "*real world's heavyweight champion*" was on his way to the company. WWF at the time never acknowledged any other promotions or wrestlers, and they didn't here either; the storyline was that Flair was some guy coming in with a fake belt, and he was given no credibility as a legitimate champion until he won the WWF world title in the Royal Rumble.

When his WWF career was over, he was pushed as the greatest wrestler of all time, largely for things that he did outside of WWE.

While WWE does love to write its own history, in this case it's true—Ric Flair will almost certainly go down in history as the greatest wrestler of all time. He was one of the great workers in history, so good that you can count on one hand the number of people he couldn't have a three-star match with. He was one of the greatest promos ever. He was a "legitimate" world champion (i.e. one taken seriously) no fewer than 19 times and probably closer to 23 times. (Wrestling history was a weird thing even in the late 1990s and early 2000s, and when Flair won the title for the final time in WCW, the "official" number that someone came up with was 16, and so WWE just adopted that number and the rest is history. But there are title changes not counted, and even if someone becomes a 17-time, or 24-time, or even 50-time world champion, because of the way that titles are treated today as opposed to pre-1999, Flair will still almost certainly be forever considered the greatest wrestling world champion of all time.)

Flair spent only nine years of his incredible 40-year wrestling career as an active WWF/WWE wrestler. His first two decades were spent as the perennial NWA world heavyweight champion, the leader of the Four Horsemen stable, and one of the greatest workers and promos there has ever been. Nobody could play the role of world heavyweight champion better than Ric Flair. He legitimately lived the gimmick; he made and lost millions, was the personification of the larger-than-life living-in-excess decade of the 1980s, decked out in custom suits and gold chains, driving the nicest cars, flying the nicest jets, seducing the hottest women.

He first jumped to the WWF in 1991 after a falling-out with Jim Herd, the man in charge at the time of Jim Crockett Promotions. Herd bungled his departure so badly that Flair didn't even drop the NWA title on the way out. He showed up with it on WWF television, which led to a lawsuit. WWF gave him a tag belt and then an NWA replica title belt, both blurred out on television, and to solve the legal problems they eventually just made him WWF champion. He won the title at the legendary 1992 Royal Rumble, where he entered at No. 3, went all the way to the end, and captured the vacant title, last eliminating Sid Justice and Hulk Hogan.

Flair was never used to his full potential post-1990, and maybe even a couple years earlier. WWF gave him the title but he was positioned underneath Hogan. Because he was pushed as a pretender and not the legitimate claimant to the world title of WWF's biggest rival, the Hogan vs. Flair series, which should have done monster business since it pitted the two top champions of the two biggest promotions in the 1980s, quickly fizzled out. After almost a decade of wrestling magazine fantasy booking, they never even headlined a WrestleMania.

Flair returned to WCW in 1993 and remained there until the company closed down in 2001. While he was given the world title several more times, he was never pushed as the face of the

The Nature Boy, Ric Flair.

company; he put over other guys who WCW thought were going to be big stars, most of whom flopped in that position (this was the story of Flair's career in the 1980s as well). By the mid-1990s, he was portrayed as a crazy old guy on television, humiliated in the Carolinas on a regular basis by Eric Bischoff, taken off TV, sued in real life, buried in the desert in storyline, and worse. But no matter how badly he was abused by the company he worked for, the fans loved him and tuned in to see him on TV to a level surpassing nearly everybody else. And while it wasn't best for business, his crazy Flair 1990s promos were artistically awesome, but in a totally different way from his money-drawing Four Horsemen promos of the 1980s.

Flair returned to WWF in 2001. Again, he was pushed as a legend but not the top guy, and as great as he still was, he was in his early 50s and that shouldn't have been his role. In the early 2000s he had some heart issues and was put on medication, and a side effect was that the seemingly ageless Flair aged 10 years very quickly, including losing his world-famous hair. Vince McMahon has never been a fan of old people on television, but Flair, because he was so talented, managed to last longer than most. He played various roles both inside and outside the ring, including as the "co-owner of WWE" and the manager of Evolution, a stable which helped launch the careers of Dave Batista and Randy Orton.

But McMahon ultimately decided Flair's time was up and booked a storyline where the next match he lost would be his last. It would have made sense and been a great moment to make him the WWE champion one more time, but McMahon wouldn't have it. His final match—at the time—took place at WrestleMania XXIV when he did the honors for Shawn Michaels, who idolized him growing up. In everyone's mind, this was his real-life retirement match. He was honored with a Ric Flair Appreciation Night edition of *RAW*, which, given the state of *RAW* these days, will almost certainly go down as one of the great *RAW*s of all time.

But Richard Fliehr, after decades of living the gimmick of Ric Flair, was unable to come to terms with the end of his career. It devastated him. He had always done promos vowing that he would never retire, and he probably figured that one day he was just going to die in the ring. But his career had been ended for him, and it didn't sit well. So, the first thing he did when his contract expired in 2009 was return to wrestling. Privately, this really bothered Michaels for years afterward. Flair wrestled independently and then signed with TNA, where he wrestled on and off for the next several years. (Here's a trivia note: his actual final match took place on September 12, 2011, for TNA. His opponent? Sting.)

Flair returned to WWE in 2012, where he has remained in an ambassador role ever since. His daughter Charlotte is one of the biggest female stars in the company, appropriating some of her father's gimmick, such as the robes, the strut, and the "Woo!" catchphrase. She became a wrestler to honor her brother Reid, who died at the beginning of what looked to be a promising wrestling career of a drug overdose on March 29, 2013. Flair himself nearly died in August of 2017 after complications from bowel surgery. He was given a 20 percent chance of survival but made a miraculous recovery.

He was the consummate pro wrestling world champion, standing out above them all. There will never be another Ric Flair.

65 Ronda Rousey

On the surface, Ronda Rousey was a very popular UFC fighter who suffered a couple of losses, decided she wanted to become a pro wrestler, and became a WWE superstar.

But that doesn't even scratch the surface of what she has meant to WWE, long before she ever signed or debuted.

Contrary to WWE's recent version of history, there was women's wrestling in this country before Stephanie McMahon decided to #givedivasachance. And we're not just talking mud wrestling matches or evening gown matches or whatever stupid stuff WWE scripted its female performers to do over the years. Women have been wrestling in WWE—actually exchanging holds—for decades. While it was mostly terrible in the ring, the "Rock 'n' Wrestling Connection," which shot WWF into the mainstream in the early 1980s and led directly to the first WrestleMania, kicked

Few performers have garnered more mainstream press for WWE than Ronda Rousey.

off with a Wendi Richter vs. Fabulous Moolah wrestling match that drew, at the time, the highest rating in the history of MTV, a 9.0, bigger than any *RAW* ever. There were all-women teams wrestling on the first Survivor Series show in 1987. Chyna won the men's Intercontinental title, the only woman ever to do so in history, in 1999. Trish Stratus and Lita headlined *RAW* in a great match in 2004.

But women have historically been treated as second-class citizens in WWE outside of the examples above and precious others. And while WWE is hiring more women today than ever before and giving them opportunities they rarely had in the past, they still love to push attractive blondes in revealing outfits and generally treat them as sex symbols. WWE's narrative—that they're paving the way for women in sports—is preposterous if you know anything about female sports stars in the mainstream. But that narrative did start as a result of Rousey becoming, for a time, the biggest money-drawing star in UFC, outperforming all of the men.

Rousey's historic UFC run and the eventual WWE Women's Evolution dates back to a Gina Carano vs. Julie Kedzie MMA fight on February 10, 2007. Promoter Gary Shaw of EliteXC had a battle with Showtime management the night of the show, the latter of whom were violently opposed to airing a women's fight on TV. Both sides compromised; the fight would air, but if it was a disaster, Shaw was never to ask about women fighting again. As it turned out, the fight stole the show. Carano, a beautiful woman with a great smile, became a massive ratings draw, though her career didn't last all that long before she retired and went into acting.

Rousey was signed to Strikeforce in 2011 and brutalized women right out of the gate. UFC bought Strikeforce in 2012, and several months later announced that Rousey, the reigning Strikeforce bantamweight champion, was being awarded the UFC bantamweight title. If you include amateur fights, in five years Ronda went 15–0, with every fight except one ending in the first round. She became a massive sports superstar who transcended UFC. Her 2013 fight with Miesha Tate was built up so well that it broke 1 million buys. In the following two years against non–Miesha Tate opponents, she went from drawing 340,000 on PPV to 1.1 million for both of her final two fights. But she was defeated in those final two fights. Dating back to her days in judo, including the 2008 Olympics, she never took losing well. The first loss, to Holly Holm, was devastating to her, and the second, to Amanda Nunes, ended her career.

Rousey had been a wrestling fan for a long time. She had trained with Judo Gene Lebell, who also trained Roddy Piper, which is where she got the "Rowdy" nickname. She'd done an angle with WWE at WrestleMania 31 that appeared to set up a match between the Rock and Rousey vs. Stephanie and Triple H the following year, but that never happened. With her MMA career over, she came to terms with WWE in 2017 and began training at the company's Performance Center. She debuted at the 2018 Royal Rumble and went undefeated from that point forward, leading to her winning the *RAW* women's title at SummerSlam.

In 2018, with the WWE Network having largely cannibalized WWE's PPV business, and with the WWE brand always positioned as bigger than any wrestlers, virtually nobody is a business-mover outside of John Cena when he worked a full-time schedule. But Rousey brought something to the table more valuable than any other business metric—mainstream credibility. While there were obviously other factors involved, in speaking with representatives at FOX (which carried UFC programming for years) there is no question that Ronda being on WWE television played a part in the company signing a $2.3 billion television deal with USA and FOX in 2018.

At WrestleMania 35, Rousey dropped the *RAW* women's title in a three-way match with Charlotte Flair and Becky Lynch. It was widely speculated afterward that she was stepping away from the WWE in the interests of starting a family with husband and UFC fighter Travis Browne.

66 Rowdy Roddy Piper

Roddy Piper, like Ric Flair, is promoted as an all-time great by WWE despite the fact that he only wrestled full time for the company for a relatively short period of time. But unlike Flair, whose greatest moments happened outside the company, Piper's greatest moment happened within WWF and helped change pro wrestling forever.

Piper was a huge star for the Portland territory and Jim Crockett Promotions early in his career. Whenever people talk about Piper being an all-time great heel, they're talking about his pre-WWF work, since his days as a full-time top heel ended at WrestleMania II in 1986. He was a tremendous talker and top draw in both places before Vince McMahon raided him from Crockett in the early 1980s as part of his national expansion. Unlike most wrestlers who were given a great offer by McMahon and snuck out the back door, Piper went to Crockett and told him he was leaving. Crockett, unaware of the scope of Vince's ambitions, told Piper to take the offer, and had so much respect for him that he didn't even beat him around the horn on the way out.

When he first broke in around Western Canada in 1973, first as Roddy the Piper (because he played the bagpipes) and later as the simpler Roddy Piper, he was downright skinny. He had put on a lot of weight by the early 1980s but was still very small by WWF standards, so at first, despite his reputation as a talker and a legitimate money draw, he was mostly a manager and only wrestled sparingly. But during a tag team match with Andre the Giant he displayed his Golden Gloves boxing skills, and Andre, who had been a friend of Piper's for years, sold huge for him. The place went crazy. His days as a manager and occasional wrestler were over, and soon he was the top heel in the territory.

His most famous early angle was on his talk show, Piper's Pit, where he clonked Jimmy Snuka in the head with a coconut, causing Snuka to crash through the set and igniting a red-hot feud. In those days, angles took place fairly infrequently, unlike modern episodes of *RAW* and *SmackDown* where they shoot a half dozen forgettable angles every week. As a result, an angle that would be forgotten by the end of a show today is remembered as one of the greatest angles of the 1980s.

As noted elsewhere, Piper was a pivotal part of the "Rock 'n' Wrestling Connection" and the build toward the first WrestleMania, which he headlined. Piper attacked Lou Albano after he lost to Hulk Hogan via DQ at the War to Settle the Score on February 18, 1985. The show drew a 9.0 rating on MTV, the highest in the history of wrestling, unbroken to this day, and it was the angle that led directly to the first WrestleMania.

Despite headlining WrestleMania in a tag match, Hogan and Piper never had a singles match at WrestleMania, and for years they were largely kept away from each other. The company was better off with each man headlining a different house show tour, back in the days of 1,000 live events per year, plus there was the issue of Piper refusing to ever lose clean to Hogan. Throughout his career Piper had made demands to promoters and gone into business for himself to various degrees, and while others would have been fired, he was such a huge draw that he got away with it. Piper correctly identified the WWF formula: a threatening heel was brought in to feud with Hogan, they'd travel around the horn with Hogan hitting the Legdrop of Doom in every city for the pin, and then when the feud was over the heel was moved down the card and eventually fired. So, Piper figured, if he never lost to Hogan, they couldn't phase him out. And that's what he did, which led to a very lucrative five-year run with the company.

In Piper's mind, he was going to retire after WrestleMania III following his hair match with Adrian Adonis. He did leave wrestling afterward to try his hand at acting and did a lot of it over the next two decades, perhaps most famously in John Carpenter's *They Live*.

In 1989, Piper was back, and for the next 22 years he appeared as an attraction for WWF, WCW, and TNA. He won his first singles title in WWF, the Intercontinental title, at the 1992 Royal Rumble, but lost it at that year's WrestleMania in an excellent match with Bret Hart. It was probably the last excellent match of his career. His in-ring work had peaked before he ever came to WWF in 1983, and an intense house show schedule in very hard rings had wrecked his body. He needed hip replacement surgery in his 40s, and by the time he got to WCW during the Monday Night Wars he was practically immobile. But even then he was considered an all-time legend, and his subsequent matches with Hollywood Hogan, despite being atrocious in the ring, drew big money.

Probably the saddest period of his career was during the TNA years from 2002 through 2005. He couldn't move and his promos were terrible. But when he returned to WWE for his final run a few years later and they actually scripted promos for him, the magic was back. He "wrestled" matches for WWE through 2011, and even won the tag titles with Ric Flair at one point in that final run.

I met Piper in the early 2000s when I was wrestling for "the new Portland Wrestling." Frank Culbertson had restarted the promotion and gotten TV time on the local WB affiliate, KWBP-TV. One day at a show, Piper, who had a home in Hillsborough, Oregon, showed up. To the older wrestlers he was just Roddy, but to the younger guys it was like Jesus had walked through the door. He knew I "worked for Dave Meltzer." I didn't, but Meltzer and I did do an Internet radio show together on Eyada.com. Anyway, Piper pulled me into a bathroom, locked the door, lit a lighter and held it under his face, and in a low voice told me to tell Meltzer, "If he ever writes anything about my family again, I'll burn his fucking house down." To say I was surprised would be an understatement. For the record, Dave was unable to figure out what he'd ever written about Roddy's family, and it can be confirmed that Roddy did not, in fact, burn Dave's fucking house down. I went and told my good friend "Moondog" Ed Moretti about the situation. He told me not to worry about it. And sure enough, at the end of the show, as I was getting ready to leave, I ran into Roddy again. He stopped me, smiled warmly with that Roddy Piper twinkle in his eye, shook my hand, and said, "Thank you for everything, brother, it was great to meet you tonight." And that was that.

That was Rowdy Roddy Piper.

67 Watch *Beyond the Mat*

Beyond the Mat, produced and directed by Barry Blaustein, was among the first documentaries to really pull back the curtain on pro wrestling.

Blaustein, a longtime pro wrestling fan who wanted to do for wrestling what *Pumping Iron* did for bodybuilding in the 1970s, worked on the film for several years prior to its 1999 release. The film centers around the lives of three wrestlers, Jake "The Snake" Roberts, Terry Funk, and Mick Foley. Roberts was a huge star in the 1980s and early 1990s who had then fallen on hard times and was working small shows to help fund his very public drug habit. Funk was a legend of the sport who, in his early 50s, needed knee surgery but refused to retire, still doing crazy spots like moonsaults off ladders. Foley was one of WWF's biggest stars and was contemplating retiring himself.

Notably, Vince McMahon gave Blaustein full backstage access to WWF—at least initially. WWF had been struggling coming out of the mid-1990s, so McMahon was open to any sort of publicity he could get. WCW, which had been riding high from 1995 through 1998, refused to cooperate, feeling the company was above such a thing.

The film is famous for many moments: Darren Drozdov, who wrestled as Droz and Puke in WWF, displaying his talent backstage to McMahon, who excitedly screams, "He's gonna puke!"; two aspiring young wrestlers from All Pro Wrestling, Mike Modest and Tony Jones, getting a tryout with the company but not getting signed; Jake Roberts in a crack-induced stupor after a disastrous meeting with a daughter he barely knew; Mick Foley rambling incoherently in the aftermath of being tossed off the Hell in a Cell cage; and, most notably, footage of Foley's wife and children sitting in the front row at Royal Rumble 1999 where the Rock brutalized Foley with a dozen unprotected chair shots to the head in a very famous "I Quit" match. The children, who had been told that the Rock and their daddy were friends, were in complete hysterics and had to be dragged backstage by their mother.

Despite agreeing to cooperate, when the McMahon family, particularly Linda, saw the final cut, they were horrified. Vince immediately clamped down, refusing to air any advertising for the film and not allowing any of his wrestlers to speak about it publicly. The film still debuted theatrically and was a critical success. It grossed $2 million at the box office, four times its budget.

Beyond the Mat is one of the greatest documentaries ever produced on wrestling and captures an era prior to the PG-rated, corporate wrestling that operates today. Watching with modern eyes, it makes it very clear that while older fans might find today's wrestling boring, it's a significantly more humane business than it was in years past.

68 Edge and Christian

Edge and Christian will forever be linked in WWE history, even though Edge had a far more successful singles career.

The two were childhood friends, training and wrestling together in the mid-1990s before making it big in WWF. Edge worked for the company for two years before being brought up with a vampire gimmick alongside Gangrel. Eventually, Christian joined up with them as Edge's storyline brother. The Brood is one of those gimmicks from the 1990s that everyone remembers, but it was an act with cool music and little shelf life beyond that.

Around this same period the Hardy Boyz, Matt and Jeff, were also starting to pick up steam as a tag team. They did an angle where Gangrel turned on Edge and Christian and picked up Matt and Jeff as members of the New Brood. Nobody was getting over as part of the Brood. Later, Terri Runnels showed interest in both teams and created the Terri Invitational Classic (the "TIT"— welcome to 1990s WWF) where the winning team would get her managerial services as well as, completely at random, $100,000. They had a best-of-five series that culminated with a ladder match at the No Mercy PPV. You had four young guys getting their chance to wrestle a big-time match on a WWF PPV event and they tore the house down, nearly killing themselves in the process. The fans gave them a standing ovation after the match. For the record, Matt and Jeff won but that hardly mattered. The careers of all four were made with that match, and the following decade of insane stunt shows—ladder matches, TLC matches, etc.—kicked off with a vengeance.

At WrestleMania 2000, in another legendary match, the Hardy Boyz, Edge and Christian, and the Dudley Boyz worked a wild three-way ladder match, which saw Edge and Christian win to become WWF world tag team champions for the first time. In the immediate aftermath they became more of a comedy duo, at which point they introduced their soon-to-be-famous pre-match ritual of comedy, including the "five-second pose."

Ultimately, in the company's eyes, Edge was going to be a future singles star, since he was taller, better looking, and had better hair. Christian, at the time, was the far better worker of the two, but that ranked below the other qualifications on WWE's talent-judgment scale. The team eventually split, and with his future prospects not looking great, Christian left WWE and spent a few years in TNA.

Edge's singles career took off on a fluke. At WrestleMania 21 he won the first Money in the Bank ladder match. The winner got a briefcase that could be cashed in anytime, anywhere, for a WWE championship match, but it had to be done within one year's time. For nearly a year, Edge carried the briefcase around while working feuds with stars such as Ric Flair and Matt Hardy. The latter became extremely personal; in real life, Matt's girlfriend, Lita, left him for Edge. Edge's wife, his second, found out and divorced him. She went on a public tirade, saying that without steroids he'd be nothing but a skinny guy with a gut. Edge's car was defaced, and whether Matt was responsible or not, the company may have believed he was, and he was fired. Eventually, Matt was brought back and WWE turned it into a shoot-style storyline where their off-camera relationships were acknowledged, including Matt referring to Edge and Lita by their real names, Adam and Amy. It culminated with a very physical and bloody ladder match at SummerSlam. Edge won to end the feud; Matt was sent to *SmackDown* so the three of them wouldn't have to travel together. Edge tore his pec and was on the shelf for several months, at which point he began his own talk show, the Cutting Edge, and began referring to himself as "The Rated R Superstar."

On January 8, 2006, Edge, still the Money in the Bank holder, returned and wrestled Ric Flair at New Year's Revolution. They'd been feuding on the Cutting Edge, with Edge ridiculing Flair for his real-life issues with alcohol. Flair won via DQ. The main event was an Elimination Chamber match, won by WWE champion John Cena.

Since Edge only had three months left to cash in his Money in the Bank briefcase, and with the WrestleMania plans locked in place and Edge not a part of the main event picture, Vince McMahon had two options: Edge either had to cash in and win the WWE title briefly, or he had to cash in and fail. Obviously, to get the Money in the Bank gimmick over on a long-term basis, the first person who won it had to win the title. So, Vince made the call that after Cena came out of the Chamber battered and bloody, Edge was cashing in. The fans went crazy as Edge hit the ring, cashed in his briefcase, and immediately beat Cena to win his first WWE title.

The plan was for a short title reign that would end at Royal Rumble a few weeks later. But something unforeseen happened: the title change got over huge. Fans went crazy, particularly the next night on *RAW*, when Edge and Lita celebrated on the Cutting Edge with what was billed as a live sex show. No, they didn't actually get naked or have sex, but it was extremely risqué and one of the more infamous moments of the Attitude Era. The *RAW* rating blew up, the highest in a year. Every time Edge was on TV as champion that month, ratings spiked. But McMahon had his mind made up, and Cena beat Edge to regain the title at the Rumble as planned.

It didn't matter. Due to Edge's success during that three-week period, he was a made man. Six months later he won the title for the second time and became the face of *SmackDown* for several years. In a way, he was treated similarly to Ric Flair; whenever WWE didn't have anyone else to put the title on, it put it back on Edge. When he retired, he'd won the world title a record seven times, the WWE title four times, Money in the Bank, King of the Ring, the Royal Rumble, and also held the Intercontinental, the U.S., and the world tag team titles for a total of 31 different titles during his career.

The end of his career represented a catch-22. His over-the-top performances in ladder matches had put him on the map; the whole Money in the Bank title win began with a ladder match that he'd initially told Vince McMahon privately he didn't want to be a part of. But it was those performances that took a serious toll on his body. On April 3, 2011, at WrestleMania XXVII, he retained the world title with a win over Alberto Del Rio. But he'd been suffering numbness in both of his arms and occasional uncontrollable trembling and underwent an MRI the following week. The news was bad. Edge's neck, which had already undergone two-level spinal fusion surgery in 2003, was now in the midst of full-blown stenosis. He was told that one bad bump could leave him paralyzed or dead. He would never wrestle again.

Christian, who got a big push in TNA based on the fact that he was a former WWE star, twice winning the NWA world heavyweight title, returned to WWE in 2009. He became an upper mid-card WWE star, winning the ECW title on his return and the world title twice, the second in the wake of Edge's retirement. His career ended in a somewhat similar manner; on March 24, 2014, in a four-way match with Del Rio, Sheamus, and Dolph Ziggler to determine a No. 1 contender to Big E's Intercontinental title, he suffered a concussion. It was far from his first but it was his last, as he was never cleared to compete again.

Today, the childhood friends have a podcast together, *E&C's Pod of Awesomeness*. Edge went into acting upon retirement and has over a dozen film and television appearances under his belt, many of which are recurring roles. They still make special appearances with WWE to this day.

69 Goldberg

The story of Goldberg in WWE is a fascinating one.

Goldberg was WCW's biggest star during the company's peak. Granted, Hulk Hogan helped jump-start the resurgence of WCW in 1994 and 1995, and his pairing with Scott Hall and Kevin Nash helped ignite the Monday Night Wars. But WCW's two hottest years, 1997 and 1998, were all about the Goldberg phenomena.

It's incredible in hindsight to chart Goldberg's ascent. While the company was on fire at the time, as early as the spring of 1998 it was clear that the wheels were falling off the cart. Both Dave Meltzer and I wrote articles in our respective newsletters about all of the warning signs, and this was during a period where WCW had set its consecutive sellout record and was destroying WWF in the ratings. Suffice it to say that tons of mistakes were being made throughout 1997 and 1998, yet in the midst of all of that WCW did not screw up Goldberg until the very end of 1998. To me, it's one of the most amazing stories to come out of the Monday Night Wars.

The Goldberg character was simple: he was Bill Goldberg. No fancy gimmicks. No fancy ring gear. No fancy promos. On the surface, WCW was trying to clone WWF's most popular character, Stone Cold Steve Austin. But besides the look—bald head and goatee, black trunks, and black boots—the two had little in common. Austin was supremely charismatic, a great talker, and a great worker. Goldberg didn't even talk for quite a while, he absolutely wasn't a great traditional worker, and he had a totally different kind of charisma. He was a former football star turned pro wrestler. Calling him clumsy would be inaccurate, but he wasn't smooth. He was a wild animal in the ring. When he got in there, fans could expect one thing—carnage.

I've gone back and re-watched Goldberg's career week-by-week for one of our most popular podcasts at wrestlingobserver.com, the *Bryan & Vinny & Craig Show*. The biggest takeaway is that Bill Goldberg was the perfect "Goldberg." When I was younger, perhaps I thought he should be a better talker. I'd have been wrong. Perhaps I thought he should have been a better worker. I'd have been wrong. Everything he did was perfect for the Goldberg character, and it's why he got over the way he did. He was totally different from anyone else in the company, and he provided you with something that nobody else in the business did: pure, unadulterated violence and mayhem.

His matches went about a minute. He'd get in there, run roughshod on some poor fool, maybe sell for a few seconds, and then fire up, spear them in a horrifying manner, and then hit them with the Jackhammer, a suplex turned into a power slam, for the pin. No matter how good or bad *Nitro* was otherwise, the fans would go absolutely nuts for his music, his entrance, the match, and the aftermath. The key to his success was that he was not a great, smooth worker. He was an animal. Fans were not naïve enough to think that he was shooting on his opponents, but for three to five minutes they could believe that Goldberg was more "real" than anything else in pro wrestling.

Of course, because he wrestled for WCW it was inevitable that they'd eventually mess him up. Nash ended Goldberg's win streak at Starrcade 1998 after Hall zapped Goldberg with a cattle prod. This was followed by the famous Finger Poke of Doom spot a few weeks later, where Hulk Hogan returned for a match with Nash, but instead of wrestling, Hogan poked him in the chest, Nash took an exaggerated bump like he'd taken a shotgun blast, and then Hogan pinned him to win the title and they all celebrated together (don't ask). We'd gone from the extreme of wild, seemingly uncontrollable Goldberg massacres to the fakest of fake pro wrestling spots. It was all downhill from there.

After WCW died, WWF had the opportunity to sign Goldberg and a number of other top stars if it was willing to spend seven figures to buy them out of their WCW contracts. The company opted not to do so, claiming it wasn't financially viable and that it wasn't worth upsetting its current salary structure. Goldberg did sign with WWE, in 2003, two years too late. The less said about his first run, the better. It was clear that Vince McMahon had either never watched a Goldberg match in his life or was unable to fathom what it was that made Goldberg such a phenom. The very first thing they did was an angle where Goldust put a wig on his head. Then they wanted him to work like everyone else, doing long matches, cutting promos, and in general not being Goldberg. He was still a main-eventer and they still put the world title on him for a period. But he never recaptured his early WCW magic, and his two-year run ended in sad fashion when he faced Brock Lesnar at WrestleMania XX in 2004. Goldberg's contract was expiring, and Brock was leaving to try his hand at football. The fans knew both guys were leaving, so they booed them out of the building the entire match, not even giving them the opportunity to put on a good performance. Since it really didn't matter who won, Vince made the call that Goldberg was getting his hand raised. He won with the spear and Jackhammer.

Goldberg then disappeared from wrestling for years. It appeared he'd be remembered as a guy who had a hot run for a few years but then had his career tarnished by a poor WWE run.

In 2016, 2K Sports announced that Goldberg would appear as a character in the new WWE 2K17 video game. As had been the case several times, 2K had made an outside deal with someone who WWE wasn't on good terms with. But the fans' positive reaction led to the company opening up discussions and ultimately bringing them in.

Following an ESPN interview where Paul Heyman challenged Goldberg to show up on *RAW*, Goldberg did appear on the October 10 episode. The story was simple: Lesnar had gained revenge on everyone except one man, the man who had beaten him at WrestleMania XX. Goldberg issued the challenge for Survivor Series, saying Brock wasn't just next (his catchphrase had always been, "You're next!") but he was also last.

At the time, the plan was for Brock to indeed be last. The original idea was for Goldberg to come in, face Brock at Survivor Series, and that would be his swan song. However, as is often the case in WWE, plans change.

Goldberg's return got over huge. The guy who was never renowned as a talker came back, cut from-the-heart promos as William Scott Goldberg, and the fans went absolutely nuts for him. Vince approached him and encouraged him to ride the wave. And so, in a massive shocker, Goldberg faced Brock at Survivor Series and utterly destroyed him, winning the match in 1:26.

This led to the Royal Rumble 2017, where the winner would get a shot at the universal title held by Kevin Owens at WrestleMania 33. Goldberg vowed to win. Heyman entered Lesnar in the Rumble as well so he could take out Goldberg and get revenge. But Goldberg eliminated him, ran roughshod, and was a phenom again before finally being eliminated by the Undertaker.

Lesnar, furious, showed up on *RAW* the next night and challenged Goldberg to a match at WrestleMania. Goldberg accepted, and also challenged Owens to a universal title match at the Fastlane PPV. He won that match and the title in 22 seconds after an attempted distraction by Owens' partner Chris Jericho backfired. So, the main event of WrestleMania was set—Goldberg vs. Lesnar for the WWE universal title.

Bill Goldberg was 50 years old when he went into the ring at WrestleMania 33. While he had trained consistently all of his life, it took an incredible amount of hard work and dedication to get into "Goldberg shape" one last time. He was hurting all over. Outside of the Royal Rumble, his two singles matches had gone less than three minutes combined. And since he and Brock were the WrestleMania co-main event, the expectation was they'd have to put in some time.

In the end, the match went 5:35. Goldberg suffered an injury to both his groin and quad, both of which turned black in the days following the match. While that sounds like a disaster, the match itself was phenomenal, one of the greatest five-minutes matches in wrestling history. It was a wild battle from bell to bell, ending when Lesnar gave Goldberg an F-5 for the win. In a career that began in 1997 and saw Goldberg pushed as the top star in WCW and a main-eventer twice in WWE, it was the first time ever that he had been beaten clean in the middle of the ring.

Goldberg's second WWE run will go down in history as one of the greatest comebacks of all time, and totally rewrote a legacy which had been badly tarnished by his first WWE run. Like in the early days of his WCW push, it couldn't have gone more perfectly. Goldberg remains associated with WWE to this day and was inducted into its Hall of Fame in 2018.

AJ Styles

One of the greatest wrestlers in WWE history and a multi-time champion for the company, AJ Styles almost never became a star there.

Styles, real name Allen Jones (hence the "AJ"), first had a tryout match for WWF in 2001. The company felt he was too small to even bother offering him a developmental contract. So, he went on his way.

Over the next 14 years he became one of the best wrestlers in the world. Shortly after his WWF tryout he was among the standout performers in the All Pro Wrestling King of Indies tournament in Northern California, where he lost to Christopher Daniels in the second round. Rob Feinstein, Doug Gentry, and Gabe Sapolsky got hold of a tape of the show and determined that there was enough great, unsigned talent to start their own promotion, and Ring of Honor (ROH) was born.

Within a year, Styles was a main-eventer for ROH and a star for another newly formed promotion, Total Nonstop Action (TNA). He went on to hold 19 different titles in TNA, including the NWA title three times when it was the company's main championship, and later the TNA world heavyweight title twice. He worked in both the heavyweight division and X Division (a strange grouping which, based on the time period, included both smaller wrestlers and wrestlers of any size, and the rules changed regularly). He was acknowledged as one of the best wrestlers in the world for over a decade—impressive given that he wasn't even a wrestling fan growing up—but the rep on him remained that he was too small to be a star in WWE and didn't have the charisma or the speaking ability.

TNA had a tumultuous run—that's being polite—and in 2013, after 11 years with the company, Styles was asked to take a 60 percent pay cut. He declined. He returned to the independent scene with Ring of Honor, and then, in 2014, debuted with New Japan Pro Wrestling. In his very first appearance he attacked IWGP heavyweight champion Kazuchika Okada, and then, in his first match for the company under contract, he beat Okada to win the title, the top prize in New Japan. As the new leader of the Bullet Club (replacing Prince Devitt, who went to WWE as the rebranded Finn Bálor), Styles had classic matches with New Japan's top stars and best workers, including future WWE rival Shinsuke Nakamura.

His two-year run in New Japan was so acclaimed that for the first time in 14 years, WWE was interested in AJ Styles again. He signed and debuted in the 2016 Royal Rumble. The belief on the WWE side was that fans probably wouldn't know who he was, but instead the fans went crazy for him during the match and he was immediately brought up to the main roster. The guy who was allegedly too small and didn't have any charisma or the ability to cut promos was suddenly an average-sized guy in the overall much smaller WWE, and his speaking ability and charisma shocked those who thought he possessed neither. He was protected, put in meaningful programs, and 15 years after the company wouldn't even offer him a contract after his first dark match, AJ Styles beat Dean Ambrose on September 11, 2016, to become the WWE world heavyweight champion. He went on to become the longest-reigning champion in *SmackDown* history, and in 2017 was voted into the Wrestling Observer Hall of Fame.

71 Sit in the Front Row

If you're reading this, you've almost certainly attended a live WWE event. Perhaps even a *RAW*, *SmackDown*, or PPV event. But once in your life, you should spring for the money to sit ringside.

Going to a show is always fun but being in the front row is something everyone should experience at least once. You'll see things you'll never see otherwise. Wrestling is an art form, and if you're watching two great workers perform up close, you'll be amazed at how smooth and effortless they can make things look.

Wrestling is very different on TV, with the rapid camera cuts and incessant zooming. Up close, it's like watching a combination of a stage play and a gymnastics competition. You'll hear the chops and the forearms, the bumps are louder than ever, and sometimes you'll even get a glimpse behind the curtain and see someone miss a punch or catch the wrestlers calling their spots.

It's also fun to see the actual size of the performers and their environment. On TV, everything looks larger than life. When you walk into an arena to see a wrestling show for the first time, almost everyone's first thought is, "The ring looks so much smaller than it does on TV." You'll be amazed seeing the wrestlers close up. Sometimes someone you thought was a giant really isn't that big after all; you'll also be stunned to see those who are truly gigantic, such as Braun Strowman. And, more often than not, you'll be stunned to see how relatively small some of the women are in real life, much smaller than they appear to be on television.

You don't need to get front row tickets all the time. Live wrestling events are always fun, and unless you get an obstructed view and sit behind a giant fake palm tree at WrestleMania (this happened to me once), any seat is a decent seat. But, just once, treat yourself to the front row.

72 Chyna

The so-called Ninth Wonder of the World (the eighth being Andre the Giant), Chyna was a product of her time and place.

While today's WWE trumpets a Women's Evolution, one thing you'll never see is the men beating up the women. But in the mid-to-late 1990s, thanks in large part to the rise of Extreme Championship Wrestling and a fan base of testosterone-fueled male teenagers, men beating up women was all the rage. That's not how Chyna's WWF career started, though that is how it ended up.

Real name Joanie Laurer, the future Chyna broke into wrestling after training with Killer Kowalski in 1995. A year later, she met future Degeneration X members Shawn Michaels and Triple H, the latter of whom she had a real-life relationship with upon being signed to WWF. She was a bodybuilder, probably in the 200-pound range, and she worked as a valet for Triple H, a heel at the time. The psychology was simple: she was gigantic and would kick the asses of the male wrestlers. But she was also a woman, and despite her size, the storyline was that the men couldn't bring themselves to hit a woman.

The pairing of Hunter, Chyna, Rick Rude, and Shawn Michaels as the original DX in late 1997 was the spark that lit the fire under Triple H, and it made Chyna a star as well. For a while, her gimmick was that she was a strong mute who had befriended these two juvenile delinquents (played by a 32-year-old and a 28-year-old at the time), and she was the level-headed, responsible one. Fans loved to see her beat up the men.

As Hunter gained power in 1998 and 1999, Chyna's push increased to the point that they began to put her in matches with the men. Today, when WWE does the Mixed Match Challenge, for example, the women are allowed to hit spots on the men but the men are not allowed to touch the women. In 1999, the Rock would punch Chyna in the face and Jeff Jarrett would smash guitars over her head. Her push led to a feud with Jarrett, who was doing a woman-hater gimmick, culminating in a match at the 1999 No Mercy PPV where she beat him in a "Good Housekeeping Match" (your basic hardcore match) to become the first and only woman to win the WWF Intercontinental title.

While the fans cheered her as a babyface in the feud with Jarrett, there was something about a woman winning the Intercontinental title that didn't sit well with some of them. After Jarrett left for WCW (he held up WWF for somewhere in the neighborhood of $200,000, since his contract expired and they hadn't taken the title off of him yet), Chris Jericho was put in Jarrett's spot feuding with Chyna over the title. Jericho was so talented on the mic and the resentment toward Chyna had built to the point that Jericho was cheered by the fans as their chosen babyface in the feud.

It was all downhill from there. Her boyfriend, Triple H, had an affair with Stephanie McMahon. Chyna found out about it and complained to Vince McMahon, apparently unaware that he had given Stephanie and Triple H his blessing. She was still involved in some memorable storylines, including a pairing with Eddie Guerrero that propelled Eddie to stardom for the first time, but her run with the company was coming to an end. She won the women's title at WrestleMania X-Seven in a two-minute squash of Ivory, the idea being that she'd get a dominant win and then put over Lita, the new up-and-coming female superstar. But that never happened. Everything came to a head and she was taken off TV and released in November of 2001. She never dropped the title.

Her life was full of ups and mostly downs from that point forward. She was a mainstream celebrity based off her wrestling fame and appearances in two hot-selling issues of *Playboy*. But she also suffered from drug and depression issues, stemming from both her time in wrestling and a rough upbringing, and the word in wrestling was that the formerly nice and sweet Joanie Laurer had totally changed after the *Playboy* issues came out. She made sporadic wrestling appearances, first in Japan and later for TNA. For a while, she moved to Japan and taught English. She began an adult film career. She was involved in an extremely volatile relationship with former DX stablemate Sean Waltman. She appeared on various reality shows. Many times, when appearing in public or on various shows, she'd slur her speech and show signs of substance abuse.

On April 20, 2016, she was found dead in her home, an autopsy later revealing a mix of alcohol, diazepam, nordazepam, oxycodone, oxymorphone, and temazepam in her system. Her death was ruled an accidental overdose. She was cremated, with her ashes scattered over the Pacific Ocean.

73 Gorilla Monsoon

Middle-aged fans will remember Gorilla Monsoon as one half of one of the funniest duos in WWF history alongside Bobby Heenan on *Prime Time Wrestling*, as well as a television commentator and later WWF figurehead president in the mid-1990s. He was all of those things. But before he became the friendly, grandfatherly straight man who younger fans of the period loved, he was the fearsome Manchurian Giant, the 300-plus pound monster Gorilla Monsoon.

Real name Robert James Marella, Monsoon's reign of terror as a wrestler began in the early 1960s. He'd been a high-level wrestler in college, a football star, and proficient in both shot put and the discus. As a multi-sport star, he seemed a natural babyface and began his pro wrestling career as the friendly "Gino," who would sing before his matches. Fans liked him, but because of his great size (he was 6-foot-5 and around 350 pounds, which was enormous for that era), it was tough to be the babyface; he towered over everyone and it was difficult to believe he could be beaten. So, after going to work for Vince McMahon Sr. he underwent a transformation, growing a long beard, calling himself Gorilla Monsoon—one of the great names in wrestling history—and taking on a manager, Bobby Davis, who claimed he'd discovered Monsoon wading naked in a stream in Manchuria.

Gorilla was a star and made a lot of money in the 1960s as a heel feuding with the likes of Bruno Sammartino in the WWWF and Giant Baba in Japan. He twice won the United States tag team titles, but that was the extent of his WWF championship accomplishments. He turned babyface later in the decade, coming to the aid of his old rival Sammartino. From that point forward, he was an upper mid-card babyface, mostly used as a setup guy for all of the monster heels to beat en route to matches where they'd lose to Sammartino. Gorilla worked another decade or so, often just winning undercard squashes but occasionally feuding with top stars like Ernie Ladd and WWWF champion Superstar Billy Graham.

During the mid-1970s he worked for and owned a portion of the newly created World Wrestling Council in Puerto Rico. Because he'd bought into the World Wide Wrestling Federation in the 1960s, he was a part-owner of two very successful wrestling companies at the same time.

As a wrestler, he was most famous for an incident in June of 1976. Muhammad Ali was getting ready for a boxer vs. wrestler match with Japan's Antonio Inoki. While it seems preposterous today, at the time your average person thought it was impossible that a wrestler could ever beat a boxer. Since McMahon Sr. was helping to promote the event, he figured they needed to do something to prove to fans that the opposite was true. So, at a WWWF TV taping in Allentown, Pennsylvania, Ali was in attendance and introduced to the crowd. During a Monsoon vs. Baron Mikel Scicluna match, Ali suddenly hit the ring and started throwing jabs at Monsoon. Monsoon responded by grabbing him, hoisting him up on his shoulders, twirling him around in an airplane spin, and dropping him to the mat. Ali sold it huge, and clips were played on every sports and wrestling program all over the country.

A few years after retiring from the ring (he lost a match to Graham after claiming he'd retire if he lost, and believe it or not, with the exception of four special attraction appearances, he kept his word), he sold his WWF stock to McMahon Jr., who had purchased the company from Vince Sr. In return for the stock he received a 10-year deal that gave him a percentage of every house show the company ran, which in the 1980s was often nearly 1,000 shows per year. He was also given a commentary job on WWF television, usually seconded by Jesse "The Body" Ventura or Heenan.

What you think of Monsoon as a commentator largely depends on a number of factors. If you were a longtime fan during his heyday, you probably thought he was terrible. He was a bundle of clichés ("They're hanging from the rafters!"), talked incessantly about body parts (including ones he made up like the "external occipital protuberance"), and was blatantly pro-babyface to the point where he'd kill the drama by saying things like, "He will never give up!" during submission holds. He won Worst Television Announcer six times in the Wrestling Observer Newsletter Awards, as voted upon by readers. On the other hand, if you were a young fan who didn't grow up listening to guys like Gordon Solie, or if you were strictly a WWF fan in the mid-1980s and never watched guys like Jim Ross on WTBS, he was a funny, friendly guy whose banter with heels Ventura and Heenan made them a lot of fun to watch. And if you're a younger fan today, you'd probably look back and think, "Well, he wasn't great, but he's a hell of a lot better than almost anyone calling main roster WWE today."

He was phased out of commentary in the early 1990s when WWF hired Jim Ross. He later became the figurehead WWF president, replacing Jack Tunney, occasionally making babyface rulings and even sometimes doing physical angles, including one where, in his late 50s, he was destroyed by the debuting Vader.

Monsoon passed away on October 6, 1999. Vince McMahon paid tribute to him on *RAW*, calling him "one of the greatest men

I have ever known." On the other channel, Tony Schiavone and longtime real-life best friend Bobby Heenan paid tribute on *Nitro*. Heenan was able to hold it together through a brief speech, but then broke down on camera as Schiavone moved forward to talk about what was coming up next.

To this day, the area right behind the curtain (originally, before the referees had earpieces, it was in front of the curtain so the ref and wrestlers could see visual signals) is known in most wrestling promotions as the "Gorilla Position," since Marella ran it for the WWWF starting in the mid-1970s when he began transitioning to an office position.

74 Watch Every Royal Rumble

The WWE Network makes it easy to binge watch anything you want out of the WWE archives, and the Royal Rumble matches are a very good place to start.

The very first Royal Rumble took place in 1988 and was won by Hacksaw Jim Duggan. The concept was the brainchild of Pat Patterson, based on the fact that the battle royal was always one of the best-drawing events during his main event run in San Francisco in the 1970s. A traditional battle royal starts with a certain number of wrestlers in the ring, and wrestlers are eliminated once they've been thrown over the top rope to the floor; the last man standing wins. The Royal Rumble was different. Two men started, and a new man entered every two minutes. (Well, the actual time between entrants has ranged from 60 seconds to 90 seconds to two minutes. If you watch the shows with a stopwatch, particularly as the years go by, the time between entrants seems somewhat random.) After all 30 men had entered, the last man standing was declared the winner.

A few years ago, I watched every Royal Rumble in order, one per week. It was a ton of fun. In the early Royal Rumbles, the winner received a trophy. In one of the most famous Royal Rumbles ever, the 1992 version, the vacant WWF title was on the line and was won by Ric Flair, who entered at No. 3. In 1993, it was determined that it would be cool, since the Rumble was in January and WrestleMania was in March or April, to add a stipulation that the winner of the Rumble would get the main event championship match at WrestleMania. This didn't always happen. Sometimes the winner would get the title shot. Sometimes the winner would get the title shot but then lose it at a subsequent PPV. Sometimes, there were ties. Sometimes there were screwjobs. When you're running a Royal Rumble every year for 30 years, you've got to mix up the formula every now and then.

Some of the Rumbles were super exciting. As a kid I loved the 1990 Royal Rumble, where Hulk Hogan and the Ultimate Warrior faced off in advance of their WrestleMania VI clash. Often, when you look back at what you loved in your childhood, things don't always hold up. But I was overjoyed to see that the 1990 Rumble remains, in my opinion, one of the greatest Rumbles of all time.

Another cool thing about watching all the Rumbles in order is that they're only an hour long, so unlike trying to watch every WrestleMania, you can catch up on a year's worth of storylines in just an hour at a time. Since the Rumble includes 30 wrestlers, if you watch every Rumble in order on a weekly basis, in 30 weeks you can watch the complete history of the WWF over the past 30 years. There are so many interesting things to watch out for. Crowd reactions to various wrestlers year-to-year. Babyface and heel turns. Who had longevity and who did not. The size of the wrestlers based on the era. Big stars coming back years after they'd been at their peak for nostalgia pops. You see certain guys who, for whatever reason, were ridiculously popular for a short period of time, like Santino Marella, and then a few years later they're not even in the company anymore. You can see bizarre things like Roman Reigns getting cheered like crazy in a Royal Rumble before fans decided that they hated him because he got a push they wanted Daniel Bryan to get.

Yes, you'll have to sit through some ungodly boring Rumbles during certain years, but if you're a longtime fan of WWE, there is no quicker and easier way to relive your fandom then watching all of the Rumbles in order.

75 Sometimes Matches Are Scripted, Sometimes They're Not

Let's get this out of the way first: when I say a match is "not scripted," I'm not talking about a match where the two wrestlers are actually fighting. Those have happened at points throughout wrestling history but they're very rare. Despite what people like to believe, they had pretty much died out by the 1890s.

In this entry, "scripted" means the match is laid out move for move from beginning to end. "Not scripted" means the two wrestlers get in the ring and improvise as they go along.

Whenever I talk to anyone about wrestling who has either never watched it or only seen it occasionally, one of the first questions I get is about scripting. In 2018, almost nobody ever asks if the action is real or not; they mostly just want to know how the matches are put together. And the simple answer is, it depends. It depends on the wrestlers involved, the time and place, the promotion they're working in, and the time period in which the match took place, among other factors.

The loosest form of working involves "calling it in the ring." This means that two wrestlers go into the ring with almost nothing planned, perhaps just the finishing sequence, and they improvise from beginning to end. Sometimes, if they've worked together a lot, they can improvise large portions of the match without saying a word to each other. Often, they will whisper spots to each other during holds or while tied up in the corner. In the old days, wrestlers would call spots in "carny," a pig latin–style language derived from the carnivals; that way, if someone in the crowd heard them talking to each other, they wouldn't understand what they were saying. Sometimes, if two guys really trust each other and it's not all that important a show, they'll go into the ring with nothing and just end the match when they feel the crowd has reached its peak.

In WWE, the short television matches are usually scripted move for move. For longer matches, the key points are scripted but the longer segments are called in the ring. Obviously, if a wrestler is green or inexperienced, the matches might be more scripted than not. Ronda Rousey, for example, went to the WWE Performance Center and practiced her PPV matches for a week in advance of actually performing. Veterans, like John Cena, are usually given much more leeway to call it in the ring.

In the past, scripting matches was frowned upon; it was considered, for lack of a better term, cheating. But some of the greatest wrestlers in history scripted out their greatest matches, including what was for years considered the greatest match in WrestleMania history, Ricky Steamboat vs. Randy Savage at WrestleMania III. Savage scripted the entire match and assigned each move a number; he would quiz Steamboat prior to the match by throwing out a number and expecting Steamboat to name the corresponding move. In WCW, Diamond Dallas Page had a poor reputation among many wrestlers for insisting on scripting out his matches, even trying to fax the scripts to guys who wanted nothing to do with scripting. (In DDP's defense, he had some of the best matches of the era.)

No matter what some veteran might insist is the "right way" to do things, the "right way" is actually "whatever works."

76 Randy Orton

Randy Orton is a third-generation wrestler who is also among the first generation of wrestlers whose careers followed a completely different arc than anyone else's in more than 140 years of wrestling history.

Orton's grandfather, Bob Orton, wrestled in nearly a dozen different promotions throughout his 49-year career, from the AWA to Central States, various NWA territories, Big Time Wrestling, St. Louis, and more. Randy's father, Cowboy Bob Orton Jr., was even more prolific, wrestling in every major U.S. territory, Japan, and throughout the world for 47 years and counting. He still makes sporadic indy appearances today.

Randy Orton trained in WWF developmental in 2000, debuted in WWF in 2002, won more than 17 WWE titles during his run, won WWE Royal Rumbles and WWE Money in the Bank briefcases and everything else, main-evented countless WWE shows, and will one day retire, go into the WWE Hall of Fame, and probably be involved in some capacity with WWE until he dies. He will have never worked for another wrestling company in his entire career; based on how WWE runs its developmental system today, he won't be alone.

Every year when it comes time for readers to vote wrestlers into the Wrestling Observer Hall of Fame, Orton's name rarely gets much support. I'm sure I sound biased, but the Observer Hall of Fame is the only wrestling Hall of Fame voted on by hundreds of current and former wrestlers (some of whom are among the biggest names in wrestling history), reporters, and historians, and you must get 60 percent of the vote in a given region to go in. In the first three years that Orton was on the ballot, he got 15, 17, and 23 percent of the vote. That's a long way from 60.

As far as his WWE career is concerned, he's absolutely a Hall of Famer. While he was never the face of the company, during his entire run on the main roster there have only been two guys really pushed as the face of the company, John Cena and Roman Reigns. Steve Austin and the Rock were on the way out when he started. Cena was the top babyface for a decade and the company was dead-set on following him up with Reigns. But Orton was always a main-eventer. He's been a top rival for Cena; they had so many matches that toward the end of their feud they had to promise the fans that this was the last time you'd ever see them in the ring again (it wasn't). He was the youngest world champion in company (but not wrestling) history, and he won the company's main title (or one of them) 13 different times. He was in a championship match at five different WrestleManias and closed out the biggest event of the year twice. He was also part of two famous stables during the new millennium, Evolution and Legacy. And while he didn't always have the most exciting matches, he was a tremendous worker, praised by all of his peers.

He also had a lot of issues. Before he even got into wrestling, he went AWOL from the Marines and was dishonorably discharged. He wasn't always the most fun guy to be around, and wrestlers have gone on record claiming he defecated in people's bags or took out his genitals in front of writers. The WWE Wellness Policy "rehabilitation program," where you can have one of your strikes wiped out, was created in the wake of Orton having two strikes during a period when they were pushing him as a top guy and wanted to avoid having to fire him. There were also incidents, such as when his name came up as part of the Signature Pharmacy scandal (almost two dozen current or former WWE wrestlers were listed as having purchased steroids and other drugs from the online pharmacy in 2007), which probably should have resulted in a strike but didn't. He was far from a model employee, and more than once Triple H has talked about having to sit down with him and tell him to get himself together.

In putting this book together, I've tried not to just list everything that every wrestler did in their career. For many of these names, a full book would be needed; plus, you can get all of that information online. Instead, I have tried to encapsulate their careers and concentrate on the things that made them stand out, the defining moments in their career, or their legacies. With Orton, as big a superstar as he was and remains, as many titles as he's won, as many shows as he's main-evented, the truth is that he doesn't have that defining, business-changing moment on his résumé. His legacy is largely that he was a very famous WWE star, and among the first of a new generation who never worked anywhere else.

This reads harsher than I mean it to. I'm a big fan of Randy Orton, and on our radio shows Vince Verhei and I have created a "Hall of Awesome" to recognize performers who we believe may not be all-time greats (although some are) but were awesome in one way or another. Orton is in it. I think he's an awesome performer. But I don't think he's an all-timer.

77 Subscribe to the Wrestling Observer Website

A cheap plug! But, as with *The Death of WCW*, I'd have included this even if I didn't own the website.

The Wrestling Observer/Figure Four Online website is the largest subscription wrestling news website in the world. It has roots in both Dave Meltzer's *Wrestling Observer Newsletter*, which he launched officially in 1983 (although he'd been writing about wrestling since 1971), and my own *Figure Four Weekly*, launched in 1995.

I began wrestling in my own backyard promotion, the Youth Wrestling Federation, in 1991. By 1994, the YWF was running regular shows at Cascade Elite Gymnastics in Lynnwood, Washington, and running television shows weekly on Seattle Public Access Channel 29. We'd amassed a large following and, with the help of a wealthy donor, were sending out a free print newsletter to members of our fan club, alerting them to upcoming shows, storylines, etc.

By 1995 we had become too big to be small and too small to be big. Our shows and our roster were growing, and CEG became concerned that one of the wrestlers could get hurt. They wanted us to provide insurance for the shows. We couldn't afford it, and that was the end of the YWF.

I had graduated high school two years earlier. At 19, I had two goals in life: to be a wrestler and to be a writer. I took English and creative writing (and karate) classes at Shoreline Community College, aced them, and figured since I aced English and creative writing and I didn't need any sort of degree to write books, I might as well quit. So, I dropped out.

I was coaching gymnastics and trying to think of a way to start my own business and become rich. I read all sorts of books on business and mail order. As a wrestling fan, I subscribed to the *PWI Weekly* newsletter, a four-page publication put out by *Pro Wrestling Illustrated* magazine. At the time I'd never heard of the *Wrestling Observer Newsletter* or the *Pro Wrestling Torch*, the two largest wrestling newsletters at the time. I looked at *PWI Weekly*, with its two pages of news and two pages of results from around the country that I never read, and I thought to myself, "I could do better than this."

And my life changed forever.

I sent out a note to everyone in our fan club saying the YWF had been forced to shut down, and that the newsletter was no more. But, I said, I was going to start my own weekly wrestling newsletter, and if anyone wanted to subscribe, they could send $39.95 for 52 weekly issues. I believe 37 people took me up on the offer. My grandmother Gladys (the famous Granny from the *Bryan & Vinny Show*) helped finance my first laptop ($3,000 dollars in 1995, a ridiculous price for computing power that an iPhone would put to shame). My aunt Lynne allowed me to print the newsletters on her work printer. And my mom, Valerie, helped set up the business end. I was off to the races.

Those first issues sucked. Absolutely horrible. The worst. But I didn't give up. Soon I discovered the *Torch* and *Observer*, and being able to read professionals helped up my game. I saved up money working at the gym to buy ads in *Wrestling World* magazine, which increased my subscriptions to the point where the newsletter started doing pretty well. The wrestling war was on, and interest in wrestling was reaching its peak. Business was good.

About a year in, after reading a book about how to get rich with a 1-900 number, I opened up my own premium wrestling news hotline. I advertised it in the newsletter and in *Wrestling World*. It started slowly but began to build. I experimented with different prices to see what the happy medium would be. After a few months it started to bring in substantial money. But then, it all hit the fan. The deal with 900 lines was that you'd get paid, say, 40 percent of the revenue and the phone company would receive the other 60 percent. However, if someone complained to his or her phone company that they hadn't made the call, or that their child made the call without their permission, they wouldn't have to pay. And instead of having to return only the 40 percent that the operator received as a percentage, the operator would have to return the entire 100 percent to the phone company. One month, a fan who I knew rang up thousands of dollars on the hotline and his parents refused to pay. I was hit with the entire "chargeback" bill and I couldn't afford it. The 900 line was finished, and I was facing what was for me at the time a rather severe financial calamity. Thankfully, Granny stepped in and called the company, claiming she "represented" me (she never claimed to be my lawyer, but that's what she wanted them to think). In the end, they agreed I wouldn't have to pay back all of that money, but the line was shut down permanently.

The *Observer* had its own 900 line. I'd never talked to Dave Meltzer in my life. I sent him a fax—yes, a fax—asking if he needed a replacement, since one of his regulars was leaving. He said sure. I started immediately on option four of the Wrestling Observer Hotline. I wasn't making as much as I was on my own line, but I'd never have to worry about chargebacks again.

In 1999, Bob Meyrowitz launched Eyada.com, the first streaming Internet radio station. Meyrowitz was the co-creator of the Ultimate Fighting Championship, knew Dave well, and wanted him to host a wrestling show on Eyada five days a week. Dave agreed. The first week was rough, so he asked me if I wanted to co-host the first segment of the show, talking about the news. A longtime fan of Art Bell who of late had dreamed of someday having his own paranormal radio show, I said sure. I could only do the first segment, however, since I had to get to the gym to coach gymnastics to supplement my income. Ultimately, as much as I thought I absolutely sucked, our pairing worked out and I eventually became the full-time co-host. After almost two years of working for free, I was finally put on the payroll, making $250 per week. I thought I was rich.

Unfortunately, Eyada was an idea before its time. They had a studio in Times Square—yes, Times Square in New York—and were spending tens of millions of dollars. Internet streaming then was hardly what Internet streaming has become today, and while our show was wildly successful and really the only show that anyone listened to in large numbers, the station couldn't make money and Eyada.com went out of business in 2001.

Around that time, Dave launched the first Wrestling Observer subscription website, but it was also an idea before its time. The online Observer wasn't making great money, and worse, online piracy was affecting his print newsletter business, and Dave made the decision to shut it down.

For several years, we worked together as co-hosts on *Wrestling Observer Live*, which had moved to Ron Barr's Sports Byline USA Radio Network after the death of Eyada. We continued publishing our separate newsletters.

The early 2000s were a terrible time for pro wrestling, with the death of WCW, the death of ECW, WWF's botched Invasion storyline and Steve Austin heel turn, plus the departure of the Rock for Hollywood. My newsletter business was starting to slowly dwindle, and by 2005 I was considering, at the age of 29, whether it was worth it to continue. One day, while watching a UFC PPV at my brother-in-law Tony Leder's house, I asked him how hard it would be to offer the newsletter via email, which would save money on the rising costs of printing and postage.

Tony said the following words, which changed my life again: "Why don't you just start a website?"

Tony, taking on the role of webmaster, proceeded to design f4wonline.com. The idea was that subscribers could put in their username and password and access the newest issue of *Figure Four Weekly* for just $6.95 per month. The $6.95 was a big value for them, and since there was no postage or printing, it would be all profit for the two of us as partners. Within a few weeks, I came up with the idea of recording "hotline" reports, similar to those on the old 900 lines, and uploading the audio for subscribers. "We should just do a podcast," Tony said. I'd never even heard the term. He set us up with a podcast through iTunes, and we put out one of the first pro wrestling podcasts in history. The podcast proved to be a bigger draw than the newsletter. We would provide members-only podcasts daily, and then once a week put out a podcast on iTunes for free, which included information on how to subscribe to f4wonline.com for daily exclusive content. Business completely turned around, and I went from contemplating my future to making a fairly good living virtually overnight. Of course, it wasn't really overnight; as I'd once read in a book, it took me 10 years to become an overnight success.

When it was clear this was a successful business model, we went to Dave with the idea of either creating a website for him, which we'd help run, or a merger with f4wonline.com. Because of the nightmares he had with the first Wrestling Observer website, he wasn't interested. So, for three years we built up f4wonline.com, adding more podcasts and more newsletters to the growing archives.

Finally, in 2008, in part because his workload had become ridiculous and in part because of our success, Dave finally agreed to a merger. *Figure Four Weekly* launched on my 20th birthday, June 12, 1995. Figure Four Online launched on my 30th birthday. And on my 33rd birthday, Figure Four Online/WrestlingObserver.com was officially launched. The rest is history.

In 2005, I was contemplating quitting and doing something else with my life. Today, the website provides full- or part-time jobs to more than a dozen contributors around the world. It provides breaking news every day, which ends up getting reposted on most other wrestling websites. Every audio show we have ever done dating back to 2005 is archived, an astounding 10,000-plus shows, covering every major story of the last decade-plus, as well as thousands of interviews with everyone from the most obscure independent name to the biggest stars in wrestling history. The newest issues of *Figure Four Weekly* and the *Wrestling Observer Newsletter* are posted every week, a new back issue is added to the archives weekly, and at some point in the 2020s every single issue of the *Wrestling Observer Newsletter* ever published will be made available. In terms of the written and oral history of pro wrestling, it is the most invaluable resource available on the Internet.

One last thing: it's a cliché, but my life proves that if you put your mind to something, you can achieve anything. I dropped out of community college after one year. I never had a literary agent, I never had any formal journalism or broadcasting training, and I've been in a legitimate radio studio exactly once in my entire life. But today, I run a very successful business and have lived my dream of becoming a bestselling author and a podcaster/terrestrial radio show host, not to mention a jiu-jitsu black belt and part-time pro wrestler who has had matches he's very proud of. I never should have enjoyed anything approaching this level of success but I did, because I wanted it and I never quit.

78 Mike Tyson

Mike Tyson was one of the pivotal figures in creating WWF's hottest babyface star of the 1990s and the biggest short-term draw in company history, Stone Cold Steve Austin.

To understand the story, we have to go back to the late 1980s. Tyson had become the undisputed world heavyweight champion of boxing, unifying the WBA, WBC, and IBF titles. He was a gigantic star and massive pay-per-view draw, riding high with a string of KO and TKO victories and a 41–1 record. And then, on February 10, 1992, he was convicted of raping 18-year-old Desiree Washington. Six weeks later, Tyson, 25, was sentenced to six years in prison with four years of probation.

Tyson only served three of the six years and was released in March of 1995. He immediately resumed his boxing career. He won four straight bouts before running into Evander Holyfield. Holyfield was given virtually no chance to win, but he did, in the 11th round via TKO. It was a shocking upset. The Tyson camp complained of headbutts during the match.

The rematch, on June 28, 1997, was one of the most infamous fights in boxing history. Tyson would later claim that he was once again being headbutted repeatedly and thus couldn't help but do what he did, which was bite Holyfield. He actually bit him twice. The first time, referee Mills Lane paused the fight and gave Tyson a warning. The second time, Tyson bit a piece of Holyfield's ear off, resulting in the first boxing DQ in more than 50 years and a small riot in the building. Fans at home were furious and it made international headlines, given the PPV was purchased by a whopping 1.99 million homes, a record it would take decades to break. Tyson was subsequently banned from boxing, although the Nevada State

Athletic Commission ruled that it would not be permanent—after all, the dude made a lot of money for the state—and therefore he would be allowed to return in October of 1998.

In the interim, Vince McMahon came up with an idea. Tyson would be hired to be a regular character on *RAW* from January through WrestleMania XIV. He'd get the company huge publicity. After all, he was a household name, a massive PPV draw, and the WWF had successfully used outsiders throughout history to attempt to give the rub to its superstars. The first WrestleMania was a massive success built off the back of Mr. T, who was incredibly famous in the 1980s, though not quite as famous as Tyson was in 1997. They contacted the NSAC, which told them that Tyson's pro wrestling activities would have no bearing on his suspension from boxing. It was a fairly easy sell to the Tyson side, for two reasons. First, Tyson was a huge WWF fan. And second, the idea was to babyface him at WrestleMania; align him with Austin, the hottest star in the company; and attempt to rehab his public image. Plus, they'd pay him $3 million.

And that's exactly what happened.

Tyson appeared on the January 19, 1998, edition of *RAW* in what became one of the hottest angles in company history. McMahon called him and his entourage down to the ring and was preparing to announce what his role would be at WrestleMania when Austin interrupted. Austin flipped Tyson off, Tyson shoved him, a massive brawl broke out, and tons of referees, WWF officials, and cops all swarmed the ring to keep them apart. McMahon, who came out of the night almost as hated as Tyson, was screaming at Austin that he'd ruined everything. It was an incredible TV moment and drew headlines all over the world.

McMahon later announced that Tyson was being assigned the role of special guest enforcer for the WWF title match at WrestleMania, Shawn Michaels defending against Austin. About a month before the show, they shot an angle where Michaels was going to interview Tyson, they teased getting into a fight, but then Michaels tore off Tyson's shirt to reveal—a DX shirt. Tyson, the special referee for Michaels' title match against Austin at WrestleMania, had joined Michaels' own stable, seemingly guaranteeing that Austin had no chance to win.

But, you say, didn't they want to turn Tyson babyface? In wrestling, one of the best ways to turn someone babyface is to make them as hated as possible before the big turn (this also works in the reverse). Tyson came in as a heel and they first made him an even bigger heel—best buddies with the most hated man in WWF at the time—and put him in a position to screw the top babyface in the biggest match of the year. But then, in the end, it was all a swerve.

Michaels, who had a terrible back injury that would interrupt his career for four years, was touch and go about whether he'd do the match. In the end, he gutted his way through what was a massive disappointment; after the match, Austin walked through the curtain and told McMahon, "That sucked!" to which McMahon told him not to worry about it, that everything started fresh the next day (he was right). At the end of the match, referee Mike Chioda took a bump. Austin hit Michaels with the Stunner, but there was nobody to count. Tyson, the outside ring enforcer, hit the ring, fast-counted Michaels (he wasn't supposed to count so fast but presumably he was excited), and declared Austin the champion. Austin and Tyson celebrated afterward and Tyson, who got a massive ovation for his turn, laid out Michaels with a punch after Michaels confronted him.

And that was the end of Tyson's run in WWF. Austin got the rocket strapped to him and became a gigantic megastar, and Tyson returned in January of 1999 to wrap up his boxing career.

In 1998, everyone wanted Tyson to work an actual match with Austin, which would have done gigantic business. It never happened. But Tyson did appear on *RAW* on January 11, 2010, as a guest host, and found himself in the ring as an official participant, teaming with Chris Jericho to face Shawn Michaels and Triple H. He didn't do anything outside of punching Jericho at the end and reuniting with DX, but officially, without even being advertised, Mike Tyson wrestled for WWE on free TV 12 years after everyone would have paid massive money to see it.

Sunny and Sable

Sunny and Sable were two of the three biggest female stars of the 1990s (the other being Chyna), megastars during an era when children and teenage boys were watching in droves. They served as the prototypes for the WWE's portrayal of women into the mid-2010s.

Contrary to the story WWE would like to tell you, women's wrestling has existed in this country for almost as long as men's wrestling has. Josephine Schauer, a renowned strongwoman in the late 1800s, is remembered historically as the first women's world champion in pro wrestling. Cora Livingston dominated the title in the 1910s, and the biggest names of the 1930s are still known to hardcore fans today, women such as Clara Mortenson, Mildred Burke, and June Byers. Women's wrestling had a boom period in the 1950s, corresponding with the rise of wrestling on national television via the DuMont Network. Fabulous Moolah won the NWA version of the women's world title in 1956 and allegedly held it for 28 straight years. In reality, that belt—which WWE takes credit for dating back to 1956 despite the fact that the WWWF wasn't even formed until 1963—changed hands many times over the years on untelevised events.

While a lot of male wrestling fans throughout the 20th century watched the women wrestle solely to see them in their swimsuits,

Sunny on the cover of the WWF Magazine *in 1996.* (© WWE)

the women themselves took their craft seriously and did, in fact, have wrestling matches where they exchanged wrestling holds. Yes, there was a seedy underground subculture, and obviously longtime fans remember the ads for women's "apartment wrestling" videos in the wrestling magazines. But for the most part, at least publicly and on the posters, the women were portrayed as athletes competing for money and titles. Women won titles, sometimes they wrestled and beat men, they were the headline act for the MTV special that helped kick off WWF's 1980s boom period, they competed in the first Survivor Series match, and sometimes they outshone the men. And that's only in America. In Japan, there were periods when it was generally accepted that the best women wrestlers were superior to the best male wrestlers.

This all changed in the 1990s.

WWF was in the doldrums following a steroid scandal and the loss of several top stars, including the hottest act of the 1980s, Hulk Hogan. WCW couldn't get anything going year after year. The territories were all but dead, and a few larger regional promotions were attempting to gain traction. The kids who loved wrestling in the 1980s had moved on to other forms of entertainment. The business had changed drastically following Vince McMahon's national expansion, and not for the better.

And then it all turned around. Extreme Championship Wrestling gained a cult following in the Tri-State area, with Paul Heyman promoting a mix of great wrestling and wild, hardcore action that you couldn't see anywhere else in America. Eric Bischoff talked Ted Turner into giving him a Monday night time slot and launched *Nitro* head-to-head with *RAW*. *Nitro* featured the hottest young talent from around the world having great matches on the undercard, and the stars of the 1980s coming back to work main events. McMahon thought guys like Hulk Hogan and Randy Savage were too old to headline. He was wrong. They got over huge, and many of those kids from the 1980s who'd quit watching wrestling remembered Hogan and Savage and wanted to relive their childhood. This led to the hottest six-year period in American wrestling history.

There were also plenty of new fans, kids and teenagers who were watching wrestling for the first time. And unlike today, when a kid with unfiltered Internet access can view a thousand lifetime's worth of scantily clad women in an instant, the kids of the 1990s had to rely on scrambled cable channels and whatever they could manage to see on television. And what they saw on *RAW* were Sunny and Sable.

Tammy "Sunny" Sytch came first. She broke in as a manager for Jim Cornette's Smoky Mountain Wrestling, working alongside her boyfriend at the time, wrestler Chris Candido. She was incredible given her nonexistent level of experience, displaying great talking ability and charisma, plus she was gorgeous. WWF hired her to do backstage interviews, but that lasted a whopping one month before they had to put her on television as a manager. She was given the name Sunny, and started out managing Candido, now known as Skip, and Tom Prichard as a tag team named the Bodydonnas. Over the next few years she bounced around from one tag team to another. WWF fans couldn't get enough of her, so she was added as a host for some of the B-level shows, and also did segments where she'd come out wearing skimpy outfits on *RAW*, advertising whatever merchandise happened to be hot at the time. WWF sold tons of Sunny calendars and such, and when the Internet began to rise, she was one of the most popular downloads; this back when it would take 15 minutes to download one photograph. AOL named her the most downloaded woman on the Internet in 1998.

Meanwhile, another blonde woman was rising in the ranks. Sable, real name Rena Mero, was wrestler Marc Mero's wife. Mero was signed by the WWF, but as has happened many times before and since, management took one look at his wife and wanted to give her the push that had been planned for her partner. Sable, with her slim physique and breasts that seemed to enlarge on a monthly basis, was rocketed to superstardom, playing a role similar to Sunny's. The jealousy was inevitable. Sable ended up outlasting and supplanting Sunny, largely because Sable was willing to bare far more of herself on television (including an incident where she won a bikini contest by coming out topless with body paint covering her nipples), and also because Sunny had fallen into a battle with substance abuse that would last for most of the following two decades.

Because of Sable's massive popularity, she was given the WWF women's title despite having zero wrestling experience. This was largely the beginning of the end of this title being considered a serious belt. It went from being held by legitimately great wrestlers like Alundra Blayze, Bull Nakano, and Jacqueline, to women like Sable, Fabulous Moolah (a woman by then in her 70s), Debra (no experience, blonde), Miss Kitty (Jerry Lawler's girlfriend, no experience, blonde), and Stephanie McMahon (Vince's daughter, no experience). Eventually the title did start to return to actual wrestlers in the early-to-mid-2000s, but wrestling had lost tons and tons of viewers following the death of WCW and the botched WWF/WCW Invasion storyline, and so most fans' memories were that women couldn't wrestle and were only there because of how they looked.

Sunny and Sable took different paths outside of wrestling. Sunny had personal issues which often surfaced publicly due to her desire to hang on to her wrestling fame. After leaving WWF she bounced around from ECW to WCW to XPW and everywhere in between. For a while she was making money producing private adult videos for fans. Beginning in 2012 she had one legal issue and arrest after another and spent time on and off in jail. She was jailed for five months on a probation violation stemming from three DUIs in 2015 and was arrested again for a DWI in 2019.

Sable, on the other hand, went on a totally different path. After suing and settling a $110 million lawsuit against WWF for sexual harassment in the 1990s, she laid low for four years before returning to WWE in 2003 for a second run. During this period, she and Marc Mero divorced, and she began dating Brock Lesnar. The two were largely inseparable from 2004 on and married two years later. Outside of a few appearances managing Lesnar for New Japan Pro Wrestling in 2006 and 2007, she left the business altogether in 2004. She and Lesnar remain married to this day.

80 The Hardy Boyz

Matt and Jeff Hardy are one third of the trio that revolutionized tag team wrestling in the early 2000s, the other two teams being Edge and Christian and the Dudley Boyz. They've been superstars in wrestling for more than two decades; Jeff, the one who many figured would be most likely to kill himself wrestling, outlasted many of his contemporaries and continues to work a full-time WWE schedule today.

The real-life brothers were originally self-taught and ran their own backyard promotion in the early 1990s, first billed as the Trampoline Wrestling Federation and later OMEGA, or the Organization of Modern Extreme Grappling Arts. As teenagers they did jobs for WWF, two skinny kids put in there to take big bumps and make the superstars look good. In 1998 they signed contracts with the company and underwent some official training with Dory Funk Jr. They were a fairly popular mid-card tag team, largely just doing matches to fill time.

That all changed in late 1999 when they had a best-of-five series with Edge and Christian as part of the Terri Invitational Tournament. The busty Terri Runnels was offering her services and $100,000 to the winners. The two teams battled to a draw, so at No Mercy that year they squared off in a tiebreaker, what became a legendary tag team ladder match where they damn near killed each other but got a standing ovation afterward. It was a turning point in their careers.

In 2000, Lita, who had just been turned on by Essa Rios and powerbombed through a table, joined up with the Hardyz. Lita played a tomboy character who wore baggy pants, did the same sorts of crazy moves the Hardyz did, and was pushed as one of the boys. Unlike all the other larger-than-life superstars such as the Rock and Steve Austin, the newly dubbed Team Xtreme were characters fans could relate to; young, skinny kids like themselves who just happened to be living the dream. The act got over big. In real life, Matt and Lita, real name Amy Dumas, began dating.

After feuding with Edge and Christian for a year, the Dudley Boyz were added to the mix, leading to a three-way tag team ladder match at WrestleMania X-Seven and a three-way TLC match (tables, ladders, and chairs) at that year's SummerSlam. Both matches were completely insane. The six wrestlers raised the bar and the expectations for ladder and TLC matches to the point that they became exceedingly dangerous; it would be hard to argue these matches didn't take years off the careers of Edge and Christian, and, to a lesser extent, Matt Hardy.

Unfortunately, being young wrestlers in the late 1990s and early 2000s with no drug policy and a tendency to do crazy things in the ring caught up with both brothers. Jeff was fired for the first time in 2003 and jumped ship to TNA, where his lifestyle did not seem to improve. He was fired from TNA three years later, and in what was a shocker at the time, WWE hired him back. A year earlier, Matt had been released from the company due to personal issues with Lita after he discovered she was cheating on him with Edge in real life. A few months later he returned, and they turned their personal lives into a rather uncomfortable storyline that ultimately led to Lita's departure from the company.

The Hardy Boyz reunited for another tag team run, but the magic of the early 2000s was gone. They did, however, remain a popular act, and continued to beat up their bodies in high-risk matches.

They left the company again in the late 2000s after WWE tried to do an angle where they split up and feuded (this was tried several times in various promotions throughout their careers but fans never wanted to see the brothers fighting each other). Both worked for

TNA on and off for the next six years, but it wasn't always pleasant. Jeff was fired in March of 2011 for an incident at the Victory Road PPV where he came out for the main event in no condition to perform, and Sting had to shoot on him and pin him in seconds to end the match. Matt was fired later in the year following a DWI.

Both had major personal issues in the early 2010s, to the point where many fans thought tragedy was inevitable for either or both at any time. But thankfully, both did what needed to be done to clean themselves up. While there have been setbacks since, for the most part, it appears the worst is behind them.

Both eventually returned to TNA for a remarkably creative period: their creation of the Broken Universe, where Matt portrayed an insane rich guy with an oddly unexplainable accent. His brother, Nero (Jeff's middle name), was, well, Jeff Hardy, and they surrounded themselves with other wacky types, including Matt's gardener (and real-life father-in-law), Señor Benjamin; his wife, Reby; his son, King Maxel; and his drone, Vanguard 1. With the help of executive Jeremy Borash, they created a series of mini-movies that were simultaneously completely preposterous but also by far the most popular things on Impact Wrestling. After a falling-out with Anthem, the new parent company of Impact, they parlayed that success into a jump back to WWE at WrestleMania 33, where WWE amazingly allowed them to use slightly altered versions of the same gimmicks they'd created on the competition's TV show. Due to an ongoing legal battle over ownership of the Broken Universe concept, Impact essentially allowed them to leave without even dropping the Impact tag team titles, at which point they won and lost the ROH tag team titles prior to returning to WWE and winning the tag team titles at WrestleMania. In other words, they became the only tag team in history to win the tag titles of the three biggest wrestling organizations in America in the span of one month.

In late 2017, Anthem, taking great blowback from fans over their legal battle with the Hardyz, changed its policy and announced that all of its wrestlers would be allowed to take their gimmicks with them if they left. Matt then trademarked all applicable terms, giving him permission to use all of it in WWE if he so desired. WWE, for trademark purposes of its own, allowed him to do the gimmick, but changed it from Broken to Woken. They spent a year essentially re-creating many of their gimmicks from Impact. At the *SmackDown* after WrestleMania 35, the Hardy Boyz defeated the Usos to become tag team champions once again, nearly 20 years after winning their first titles.

81 Play WWE Video Games

I'll be honest, I don't play video games. I haven't touched a video game console since 1990. But video games are a very big deal to my generation, and WWE video games have been extremely popular over the years. Therefore, I shall hand this entry over to an expert in the field, my co-host on the Bryan & Vinny Show *and Football Outsiders' assistant editor, Vince Verhei:*

Most everyone who has ever watched a WWE show has dreamed at some point of being a WWE superstar. Only a tiny fraction of them will ever try to make that a reality, and only a tiny fraction of those will find any measure of success. Thanks to the magic of technology, however, anyone can see those dreams come true. The following list highlights some of the best video games for WWE fans through the years.

Pro Wrestling (Nintendo, 1987)

One of the first wrestling video games to hit consoles is also one of the best. Pro Wrestling for the original Nintendo Entertainment System was years ahead of its time, with a referee in the ring, commentators in the crowd, and a cameraman on the floor. Colorful characters—such as the luchador Starman, the Japanese hero Fighter Hayabusa, and the strange and terrifying Amazon—each had their own unique look and special moves. It would be more than a decade before a better game came along.

WCW/nWo Revenge, WWF WrestleMania 2000, WWF No Mercy (AKI, 1998, 1999, 2000)

We're cheating a bit here by listing three games at once, but each of these three titles is built around the same basic engine, and your preference will be based on whichever bells and whistles suit your taste. The simple gameplay can be picked up in minutes, making these excellent party games, while also adding enough variety to keep dedicated gamers coming back for more. The first two editions will let you relive the heyday of the Monday Night Wars, while No Mercy's Create-a-Wrestler mode opened infinite roster possibilities.

SmackDown vs. RAW 2006 (Yuke's, 2005)

Every new year brings a new WWE game. Some are good, some are bad, but often they can run together. What separates SvR 2006 from the pack is its General Manager mode, where two players compete not to win matches but to win fans, drafting wrestlers to their respective shows and putting together the best cards they can. It's not the only game with this feature, but it is the one Xavier Woods chose for his competition with Tyler Breeze on his UpUpDownDown YouTube channel.

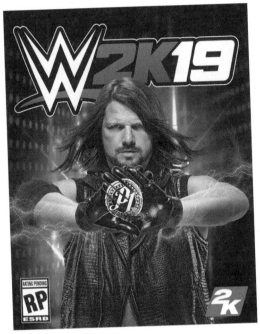

*AJ Styles graced the
cover of WWE 2K19.*
(© 2K Sports)

Fire Pro Wrestling World (Spike, 2017)

There are certainly prettier games, but for die-hard fans of the art of wrestling, there's no beating this title, produced in Japan but available worldwide on PCs and PlayStation 4. The Fire Pro Wrestling series lets you edit not only each wrestler's appearance and moveset, but how he paces and puts together a match. Is he a fast starter, or does he save his big moves till the end? Will he counter his opponents' moves, or conserve energy for a wild flurry? With thousands of wrestlers readily available for download, any match you can dream of can quickly be brought to life.

WWE 2K19 (2K Sports, 2018)

The lights and fireworks. The music and explosions. The arenas and the stadiums. For pure spectacle, there is nothing in sports entertainment that can touch WWE, and no game has ever managed to re-create that spectacle like their newest offering, WWE 2K19.

Gameplay modes like MyCareer (where you start on the indies and work your way up to WWE), Showcase (in which you re-create the historic rise of Daniel Bryan), and 2K Towers (offering new daily and weekly challenges) will give a player plenty to do, but the game is so gorgeous that sometimes you'll just want to sit back and enjoy the extravaganza—and that, after all, is what being a WWE fan is all about.

It's me, again. I would like to add that although I don't play video games, my favorite period every year is when the new WWE 2K video game is released and I get to watch videos on Twitter of the most hilarious game glitches, where wrestlers levitate or get their heads sucked into the canvas. Sometimes I laugh because I think that as goofy as these glitches are, some of them are less goofy than things I have seen in pro wrestling over the years.

82 Attend a WWE Hall of Fame Ceremony

One of the more annoying questions I get asked on a regular basis is, "Why isn't so-and-so in the WWE Hall of Fame?" Another one is, "Do you think so-and-so belongs in the WWE Hall of Fame?"

As you will learn over and over in this book, WWE has a segment of hardcore fans who want to believe certain things regardless of the truth behind them. They want to believe that WrestleMania III really drew 93,173 fans. They want to believe that Andre the Giant was really 7-foot-4. And they want to believe that the WWE Hall of Fame is a real thing.

Granted, I will be accused of bias, but the most legitimate Hall of Fame in pro wrestling, which WWE will never acknowledge, is the Wrestling Observer Hall of Fame. Dave Meltzer designed it after researching baseball's Hall of Fame, and more than 100 reporters, historians, and active and former wrestlers cast a ballot every year on who they believe should go in based on a list of qualifications (drawing power, influence, longevity, working ability, etc.). A person must get 60 percent of the vote to get in. This is a very difficult hurdle to overcome, and it has led to a Hall of Fame where only the truly deserving get in.

The WWE Hall of Fame is a marketing device. So-and-so isn't in the WWE Hall of Fame because Vince McMahon has decided that there is no way to market them this year or perhaps any year. Does so-and-so deserve to be in the WWE Hall of Fame? Sure, why not? Anyone and everyone can go in, all based on the whims of one guy.

WWE's Hall of Fame does include some of the biggest stars in wrestling history, including Hulk Hogan, Ric Flair, and Bruno Sammartino (and it took years for Sammartino, one of the all-time most important names in the history of the company, to get in, due to his decades-long heat with McMahon, and he only agreed to it because he met with and liked Triple H). It also includes—God bless them—folks like James Dudley, who was Vince McMahon's limo driver, the Godfather, and Hillbilly Jim, none of whom would ever be legitimately voted into any pro wrestling Hall of Fame.

WWE's Hall also has a "celebrity wing," which is its way of getting celebrities to attend the event. Some of them are quite deserving, including Mr. T (whose importance in making the first WrestleMania a success cannot be understated) and, yes, Donald Trump. Others, like Kid Rock, are there largely because they performed songs on WrestleMania shows. Low bar.

The ceremony itself has had its ups and downs over the years. I have attended during years like 2008, when Ric Flair was allowed to talk for so long that I thought they were going to bring out the old Vaudeville hook to get him off stage (and they sort of did). I've been there during years like 2009, when the Funks—Terry and Dory, two of the biggest legends in pro wrestling history—stepped on stage and a giant "4:00" clock appeared on the TitanTron and counted down the 240 seconds that both men had to discuss their careers. And I've been there during years when it was a combination of both, where folks often hit their cues, but others rambled on for 30 minutes or more.

The one thing I can say that is a positive every year is that, for the most part, the wrestlers who are chosen for the Hall of Fame either believe or have convinced themselves that this is a real Hall of Fame and they are deserving entrants. They accept the honor, and their gaudy Hall of Fame rings, as if it is one of the great achievements of their lives, and the fans usually respond largely in kind with respectful applause and the usual chants, either "You deserve it!" or something from their wrestling career (including chants such as, "You suck!" as a phrase of endearment for Kurt Angle).

You should go. You should know it's not really all that real, and you shouldn't be concerned about who is in and who isn't in, and who deserves it and who doesn't. If you never get a chance to attend, you can find many of the Hall of Fame ceremony broadcasts on the WWE Network.

Attend a Cauliflower Alley Club Banquet

The Cauliflower Alley Club—named for the gnarled ears possessed by longtime amateur wrestlers, and a badge of honor among many pros of the past—was founded by wrestler and actor "Iron" Mike Mazurki more than 50 years ago. Originally, it was an exclusive annual gathering of boxers and pro wrestlers, but over the years it has opened its membership up to wrestling fans as well. The first banquet kicked off at Baron's Castle Buffet Restaurant in Los Angeles in 1965. It has moved locations many times over the years, of late settling into the Gold Coast Hotel & Casino in Las Vegas, Nevada.

If you're a wrestling fan, young or old, attending Cauliflower Alley is an incredible experience. There are numerous historical exhibits; often a wrestling show featuring independent talent; at least two banquets, including the Baloney Blowout (named for an old-school pit stop during long road trips between towns); and, of course, the chance to run into wrestlers all over the hotel. You'll see everyone from the very top stars of the past like Tully Blanchard, Arn Anderson, and Kevin Von Erich to journeyman wrestlers only the hardest of the hardcore will recognize to stars from the Attitude Era like Trish Stratus and Stone Cold Steve Austin. WWE offers the Club its support and sends members of its own Hall of Fame every year.

The highlight of the week is the annual awards banquet, where a multitude of stars are honored, the top winners being given time to speak in front of the hundreds in attendance. Among the prizes are the Iron Mike Mazurki Award (the Club's top honor), the Lou Thesz Lifetime Achievement Award, Men's and Women's Wrestling Awards, a Posthumous Award for deceased stars, and the James C. Melby Historian Award. Stars who have attended and been awarded during the Club's existence, some of whom remain regular attendees, include current CAC president B. Brian Blair of the Killer Bees, Shawn Michaels, Harlem Heat, Kevin Von Erich, Trish Stratus, Dave Meltzer, Paul Orndorff, Lance Russell, Larry "The Axe" Hennig, Diamond Dallas Page, Demolition, Gail Kim, Beth Phoenix, Jimmy Hart, Terry Funk, Michael Hayes, Ivan Koloff, Paul Bearer, Mick Foley, Sgt. Slaughter, the Honky Tonk Man, Ted DiBiase, Jim Ross, Nick Bockwinkel, Bret Hart, Pat Patterson, Ronnie Garvin, Harley Race, Verne Gagne, Jack Brisco,

Bobby Heenan, Antonio Inoki, Stu Hart, Kurt Angle, and Lou Thesz.

Back in the day, you could expect some sort of minor scandal, usually a shouting match between drunken wrestlers over some issue that should have long since been forgotten, but things have mellowed in recent years. Sometimes the speeches go longer than they should, and it's pro wrestling, so you're not always going to get the historical truth. But you'll always hear great stories, make great memories, and experience a great deal of respect for wrestling's past.

# Donald Trump

Yes, *that* Donald Trump.

The 45th president of the United States is not only a WWE Hall of Famer in the "Celebrity Wing," but he's more deserving than some of the wrestlers who have been honored.

Trump's relationship with WWF began when his Trump Plaza in New Jersey hosted WrestleManias IV and V, the latter of which was the most successful WrestleMania ever up to that point in time, built around the climax to the legendary Hulk Hogan vs. Randy Savage feud. Had Trump's run with WWF ended as merely a host for two WrestleManias, he'd have been just another random, nothing-happening celebrity placed into the WWE Hall of Fame. But along came WrestleMania 23 in Detroit.

In real life, Donald Trump was feuding with comedian and TV personality Rosie O'Donnell. It started when Tara Conner won the title of Miss USA in 2006. After winning the crown she ran into all sorts of trouble, including allegations of underage drinking, drug use, and more. People called for her to be stripped of her crown but

Trump stood up for her, saying he believed she was a good person and that everyone deserved a second chance. O'Donnell, at the time a co-host on *The View*, disagreed and buried Trump, calling him a snake-oil salesman who had gone bankrupt and cheated on his wives. Trump told *People* magazine he planned to sue. "Rosie's a loser," he said. "A real loser. I look forward to taking lots of money from my nice, fat little Rosie." (He never sued, by the way.)

Vince McMahon decided to capitalize on this, presumably since Trump and Rosie were cutting promos on each other like they were pro wrestlers. He booked a segment for *RAW* where a fake Donald Trump faced a fake Rosie O'Donnell in a wrestling match, and Trump won. Three weeks later, who should show up on *RAW* but the Donald himself.

The story was that Vince McMahon was an evil billionaire and Donald Trump was a friendly billionaire (he dropped real money from the ceiling during *RAW* to cement that fact). The two finally agreed to have a "match" of sorts at WrestleMania—more of a bet. Each man would choose a wrestler; if Trump's wrestler, the heroic patriot Bobby Lashley, won, Vince would shave his head. If Vince's wrestler, the savage Umaga, won, Donald Trump would shave his famous and intensely questionable hairdo.

It was a simple stipulation, one that has been done count-less times, particularly in Mexico but also in companies all over the world. But because the hair in question belonged to Vince McMahon and Donald Trump, the show did monster business. And don't let anyone fool you; nobody cared at all about Umaga vs. Bobby Lashley, or the other matches on the card. John Cena vs. Shawn Michaels (which went on last) and the Undertaker vs. Batista were solid matches, but the undisputed biggest draw of the night was the Battle of the Billionaires. Trump won the match, Vince's hair, and also the bragging rights to being one half of the most lucrative WrestleMania up to that point in history. The show drew $5.38 million at the gate, breaking the previous record by more than $1.5 million, and drew a record-breaking 1.2 million PPV buys, a number that wouldn't be topped until the Rock faced John Cena five years later.

Two years later, Trump returned to WWE for an angle where he appeared to purchase *RAW* from Vince. He claimed that it was the smartest business decision WWE had ever made, and that the following week he was going to do something Vince had never even dreamed of doing; he was going to air the entire show commercial-free and also refund the ticket price of everyone who showed up.

What happened next, I could not make up. Even though it should have been obvious to anyone with a brain that this was a goofy wrestling storyline, *the WWE stock price tumbled because people thought that Donald Trump had really purchased RAW from Vince McMahon.* Two years earlier, WWE had shot an angle where Vince allegedly got blown up in a limo and killed, and there had been discussions about "hiring other people" to allegedly "take over *RAW.*" Vince at the time had said that he liked the idea but was concerned it would hurt the stock price. It sounded ridiculous, but sometimes truth is stranger than fiction. The week after Trump allegedly bought it, they shot an angle where Vince "bought *RAW* back" for double the price Trump paid for it, putting over Trump in the end as the master manipulator.

Interestingly enough, as revealed by Triple H years later, when WWE shot the angle where Vince McMahon blew up in the limo (an angle that was immediately scrapped after Chris Benoit killed his wife and family later that week), Donald Trump called WWE to make sure that Vince was okay.

85 Vince Russo

Vince Russo remains one of the most controversial figures in WWE history, which is pretty incredible given he only worked there for a few years in the 1990s.

Russo bought a video store in the late 1980s with help from his parents, who mortgaged their house to finance it. The store was a success and they soon opened up a second location. Unfortunately for him and his family's finances, Blockbuster Video had opened up two years earlier and was soon opening up one new location per day around the country. Locations opened up across the street from Russo's store. By 1991, business was in the toilet.

Russo was a huge wrestling fan and used to promote autograph signings with stars at the video store. John Arezzi, who ran the *Pro Wrestling Spotlight* radio show on Long Island, walked into the store one day, said his show was struggling, and asked Russo if he'd be interested in advertising. Russo, who was looking for a way to get into the business, jumped at the opportunity. They moved the show to the 50,000-watt WEVD in New York at a cost of $1,500 a week, which Russo helped pay for through video store profits and the launch of a *Pro Wrestling Spotlight* newsletter, which they promoted throughout the show. He also started training under Johnny Rodz at Gleason's Gym, largely in an attempt to become a manager.

At the time, Vince McMahon was embroiled in his steroid trial and Arezzi was all over the story. Russo claimed he wanted nothing to do with trying to take down McMahon, since he'd been a fan his entire life, but he was sponsoring the show and understood that Arezzi covering it in his controversial style would be great for listenership. Arezzi then appeared on *The Phil Donahue Show* for a panel which included Dave Meltzer, McMahon, Bruno Sammartino, Barry Orton, and Superstar Billy Graham discussing the WWF steroid and sex scandals that had rocked the company. The show, and Arezzi's participation, left a very bad taste in Russo's mouth.

Russo called WWF and asked to attend its upcoming steroid symposium. Afterward, he became incensed at a column Phil Mushnick (who wasn't there) had written about it in the *New York Post*, feeling Mushnick exaggerated and took quotes out of context based on material fed to him by Arezzi. This led to a split between the two, at which point Russo and WWF came to an agreement where the company would pay for the *Pro Wrestling Spotlight* show if Russo took over as solo host. WEVD chose to stick with Arezzi, so Russo went back to Arezzi's original station, WGBB, and started his own wrestling variety radio show, his influence being another idol of his, Howard Stern. He closed down the video store and took a job at an appliance store to help pay for the radio time. He was still struggling to make it, so as a Hail Mary he contacted Linda McMahon of all people and sold her on the idea of hiring him to do freelance work for *WWF Magazine*. Within a year the original editor was fired, and Russo applied for and got the job.

Long story short, Russo went from editor of the magazine to being asked to sit in on booking meetings, to eventually impressing McMahon enough with his ideas that he became one of the major creative forces of the Attitude Era.

And that's where the controversy comes in.

Russo was, without question, a very creative person. But pro wrestling is a very nuanced enterprise, much more complex than it appears on the surface. You've got to come up with ideas that are logically sound and put storylines together in a way that gets fans excited to pay to see two guys get in the ring and fight. In Russo's defense, both WWF and WCW put too much emphasis on ratings during the Monday Night Wars, because that was one thing that you could look at every Tuesday to find out who was "winning."

While everyone obsesses about ratings to this day, it doesn't matter how many times *RAW* won or lost the ratings war. What matters in the end is WWF won, because it stayed in business, and WCW lost, because it went out of business.

Russo and his fandom of Howard Stern led to an era in WWF rife with raunchiness, which helped draw a huge audience of children and teens. But as someone who has lived through the Attitude Era twice now—I've watched the shows live in the 1990s and again on the WWE Network week-to-week in the 2010s—the reality is that WWF turned its business around based on the success of Stone Cold Steve Austin, the Rock, and Vince McMahon. When Russo jumped to WCW in October of 1999 and took all of his craziness with him, WCW business did not rise to new heights and WWF business did not sink. On the contrary, WWF business grew significantly larger after he left. With the exception of a lame duck edition of *Nitro* that did a terrible rating, WCW under Russo stayed even for his first run (which, to be fair, is to his credit since it had been sinking for months before he showed up). The problem was—and again, this is more on WCW than Russo—his contract had escalators based on ratings and not on any of the other revenue streams, so in a desperate attempt to keep ratings strong, the company's other income generators, most notably pay-per-view and house show business, collapsed. Russo returned for a second run, which led to a further decline in the company, and by 2001, partly due to his run and partly due to mistakes made by everyone else who was in charge before and after he came along, the company was out of business. WWF, two years removed from his leaving, had its biggest year in history by a substantial margin.

Russo managed to stay in wrestling for over another decade, largely working for TNA. The company had its ups and downs but never came close to the success that WCW had experienced even in the dying days of 2000 and 2001. At one point in the early 2000s, WWE announced that Russo was returning. He appeared for one creative meeting, threw out a bunch of wild ideas including stripping everyone of all of their titles (which was how he normally wanted to reset shows), and exhibited no knowledge of the current product. Everyone in the meeting complained to McMahon, and within a few weeks Russo was gone again.

He remains on the periphery of the business today, running a podcast out of his home. He's spent much of the last two decades defending himself from his detractors and claiming responsibility for all sorts of things during the Attitude Era, most of which have been refuted by others who worked there at the time. There is no point in arguing about what he was and was not responsible for. The fairest analysis of him is this: he was a creative guy who had some good ideas and a lot of bad ideas that McMahon filtered out. He was an incredibly hard worker who did help change WWF business in the mid-1990s, aiding in the company's rise from its worst business period since McMahon's national expansion. But he wasn't the sole driver; he was a cog in a larger wheel, and he was exposed in WCW as someone who was better off with an editor who understood the nuances of pro wrestling. And, for better or worse (and often worse), he deserves credit for being driven enough to work full time in pro wrestling for more than 20 years, something that not everyone in wrestling history has been able to do.

86 Follow WWE Around the Loop

Following WWE as far around a loop as you can is about as close as you can get to living the life of a WWE superstar without actually being one.

A loop is a series of towns that WWE will hit in a given week, all in somewhat close proximity. Usually, WWE will provide a plane ticket to the first stop and another one home from the last stop. It is up to the talent to get their own rental cars and travel from town to town. Usually wrestlers will carpool together, although some, like Randy Orton and the Big Show, have tour buses to ease the misery of travel. Usually, if a town is more than 300 miles from the previous town, the talent will get a plane ticket as opposed to having to drive. A sample loop would be a tour that began on Saturday in Oakland, California; traveled 90 minutes to San Jose for a Sunday PPV; then two hours to Sacramento on Monday for *RAW*.

To fully experience what the wrestlers experience, instead of waiting for a loop in your area you'd fly to another part of the country, rent cars to take you through the loop, and then fly back home afterward.

Doing so will give you a glimpse of the profoundly unglamorous side of life on the road. Traveling sucks, and unlike you, the casual fan, the wrestlers can't sit in the stands and enjoy the show that night. They have to arrive early, hang out backstage, and then go out and work a match and entertain the fans, then return backstage, pack everything up, and jump in the car for the drive to the next city, many of which are much farther apart than the cities in the California loop I mentioned above.

Even re-creating a loop won't give you the full effect; for that, you'd have to do a loop approximately 50 weeks a year. Once wrestlers arrive home, they've got three days before they're on the road again. If you cut out a half day for travel on the way in and out, you're looking at 48 hours with your family per week on average.

Traveling as a fan is fun because you can also see how WWE matches change and don't change during a given tour. Sometimes the men and women wrestle the same people in largely the exact same matches every night, usually if they're preparing for a PPV match. Sometimes they mix and match in tag teams and singles matches so it's not exactly the same. House shows are looser than television and the wrestlers usually enjoy working them more, because they get a little more freedom. But there is only so much creative freedom to be had working for WWE.

Whatever you think about *RAW* or *SmackDown* or the PPVs or the WWE product in general, spending a few days on the road doing what can be done to re-create the lives the wrestlers live will give you a new appreciation for what they do day after day, week after week, and year after year, both to entertain the fans and provide for their families. It's nowhere near as glamorous as it appears on television.

87 Watch Every Five-Star WWE Match

Aside from the Slammy Awards, WWE doesn't regularly award Match of the Year honors, and even if it did, like everything else, the winners would be whoever or whatever made most sense in whatever storyline happened to be running at the time. Therefore, to see the best of WWE, Google "Wrestling Observer Five-Star Matches" and watch every one featuring the WWE.

At press time, those include, in order: Razor Ramon vs. Shawn Michaels from WrestleMania X; Bret Hart vs. Owen Hart from SummerSlam 1994; Bret Hart vs. Steve Austin from WrestleMania 13; Shawn Michaels vs. the Undertaker from Badd Blood 1997 (the same day Brian Pillman was found dead); CM Punk vs. John Cena from Money in the Bank 2011; Andrade Cien Almas vs. Johnny Gargano from NXT TakeOver, January 27, 2018; Gargano vs. Tomasso Ciampa from NXT TakeOver, April 7, 2018; and the six-way ladder match from the same show. (That TakeOver is the only show in WWE history to have two five-star matches on the same card, and Gargano is the only wrestler in WWE history to appear in two in the same year.)

Yes, it's a small list, and you can always go through the same Google links and watch everything above 4.5 as well. Obviously, star ratings are subjective and have led to countless arguments about why a particular match got a rating either "too high" or "too low." But that list is a great place to start.

The biggest takeaway from watching the greatest matches in WWE history is confirmation of something that Eddie Guerrero's father, Gory, told him when he was young: wrestling will always change and you never know what it might become, but if you are a great wrestler there will always be a place for you. Obviously, that does not always hold true, but looking back at these matches it's clear that when two men or women get in there and exchange wrestling maneuvers, utilize psychology, take the audience for a ride, and then pay it off in a satisfying way, they are still great matches years and decades later. The matches built upon gimmicks—cage matches, ladder matches, hardcore matches—well, they don't necessarily hold up as well, because over the years the bar has been raised to such a degree that they can seem downright quaint today.

88 WrestleMania VI

WrestleMania VI, held on April 1, 1990, in Toronto's SkyDome, is hardly a legendary WrestleMania, but it was headlined by a very famous match. You could almost say I am including it here for selfish reasons, since it was the first WWF PPV that I successfully convinced my parents to order.

You wouldn't be wrong.

But hear me out. I was born June 12, 1975. I was 14 years old for WrestleMania VI.

When *Nitro* premiered, I was 20 years old.

When Steve Austin won the WWF title, I was 22 years old.

When WCW died, I was 25 years old.

What's the point of this? Well, when *Nitro* launched, the average age of a pro wrestling fan, per the Nielsen television ratings, was approximately 20 years old. When Steve Austin won the WWF title, the average age was about 22 years old. And when WCW died, the average age was about 25 years old.

In other words, during the hottest era of pro wrestling in this country's history, the average wrestling fan was…me. Which means, in my opinion, that to the vast majority of fans who carried wrestling through the Attitude Era boom period, WrestleMania VI was a damn big deal to them, and the Ultimate Warrior vs. Hulk Hogan was the biggest match of their childhood.

I loved the match. The last time I watched it, all things considered, it was still a pretty decent match. That is a minor miracle, because neither Hogan nor the Ultimate Warrior were known for having good matches, and the two of them together sounded like a recipe for disaster. But they scripted the match out move-for-move, practiced it several times prior to performing it, and when

I watched it live as a starstruck 14-year-old—man, it was the most awesome thing ever. In some ways, you're reading this book right now because of that match.

Unlike today, where WWE builds up matches by having the two guys in the main event lose to each other on *RAW* or *SmackDown* repeatedly, the Ultimate Warrior vs. Hogan was the unstoppable force meeting the immovable object. Hogan had not been pinned clean since he returned to WWF in 1983. The Ultimate Warrior virtually never lost, and his most recent defeat, at the prior year's WrestleMania, was the result of his opponent Rick Rude's manager, Bobby Heenan, holding his foot down for the pin. The Ultimate Warrior regained the Intercontinental title at SummerSlam, so WrestleMania VI was WWF title vs. Intercontinental title. One of these behemoths was going to beat the other and leave with two belts. A young brain could hardly comprehend these ramifications.

The Ultimate Warrior won an epic battle when Hogan went for the Legdrop of Doom; in a stroke of genius, the Ultimate Warrior, like, moved, then hit his finish, the big splash, for the pin. It sounds goofy. To 14-year-old wrestling fans everywhere, it was the biggest moment in the history of sports.

The idea at the time was that the Ultimate Warrior would be Hogan's successor. Long story short, he wasn't. Historically, when a wrestling promotion successfully replaced its top star, it would do so with someone completely different than his predecessor. That was not the case with Hogan and the Ultimate Warrior. Even worse, even though Hogan's job was to put the Ultimate Warrior over, he manipulated the fans in such a way that they felt more sympathy for him as the longtime champion who lost, rather than celebrating the Ultimate Warrior's victory. WWF gave up on the Ultimate Warrior in less than a year and switched the title to Sgt. Slaughter, who was doing an incredibly tasteless Iraqi sympathizer gimmick to generate heat based on the Gulf War. It was all a setup for the American hero, Hulk Hogan, to beat Slaughter and regain the title at WrestleMania VII.

WrestleMania VI was the Ultimate Warrior's peak. He had a very volatile relationship with Vince McMahon, and by the end of 1992, he was gone. He returned very briefly in 1996 with the idea that he'd get a gigantic push, but only lasted about three months before another falling-out. He was hired by WCW in 1998, where he proceeded to have two of the worst PPV main events in history, a War Games match and a rematch with Hogan. Then he disappeared again (coincidentally, his WCW gimmick included the ability to, no joke, magically appear and disappear in a cloud of smoke). Aside from a single match in 2008, that was the end of his pro wrestling career.

In 2013, the Ultimate Warrior, real name James Hellwig, opened up a new relationship with WWE which saw him inducted into its Hall of Fame the following year. Despite the fact that during his downtime he'd maintained a controversial blog where, among other things, he had gone on hate-filled rants about homosexuals, celebrated the death of Heath Ledger, celebrated Bobby Heenan's cancer diagnosis, and ridiculed those affected by Hurricane Katrina, he was not only pushed as an all-time legend but they even created a "Warrior Award" given annually to those who "exhibited unwavering strength and perseverance, and who lives life with the courage and compassion that embodies the indomitable spirit of the Ultimate Warrior."

The Ultimate Warrior was inducted into the WWE Hall of Fame on April 5, 2014. The next day he appeared at WrestleMania XXX. The day after that he made his first *RAW* appearance in 17 years. He cut a weird promo, almost a eulogy to himself. People backstage said he appeared frail and was breathing heavily and sweating profusely. The next day, after attending the full WrestleMania weekend, I was boarding a flight from New Orleans home to Seattle. Just as the flight was about to take off, I got a text that said something to the effect of "Warrior died." I was floored. It was hours before we landed and I was able to get the news. The Ultimate Warrior had been walking from his hotel to his car that afternoon, clutched his chest, and died of heart failure. He was 54 years old.

Read *The Death of WCW*

Yeah, it's another cheap plug. But I would tell you to read this book even if I wasn't the co-author.

In 2004, R.D. Reynolds, the creator of WrestleCrap.com, approached me with the idea of writing a book about WCW. Originally, the idea was that we would make a comedic list of things that wrestling companies should not do if they want to remain in business. The comedy would be that these were all things that WCW did prior to imploding. As I began writing, I realized that I was writing a history of WCW, and so the plan changed.

While wrestling books flood the market today, even in 2004 it was tough to get a book published if you weren't a giant WWE superstar. The manuscript was enormous and a great deal of it had to be cut out. I was largely happy with the book but felt it could have been better. After all, how do you write the story of the rise and fall of WCW in just 80,000 words?

The book was a smashing success. We sold tens of thousands of copies and virtually everyone loved it—with the exception, of course, of the many people we painted as having a hand in its demise. They, of course, said none of it was true. The reality is that while it's probably impossible to write a book that is 100 percent accurate, I had followed and written about WCW on a weekly basis in my newsletter, *Figure Four Weekly*, from the birth of *Nitro* in 1995 through to its demise, and also sourced Dave Meltzer's *Wrestling Observer Newsletter*, which had done the same. Between the two of us, over six years, we'd written approximately 110 million words about pro wrestling, a fair percentage of which were about WCW. Between Dave and I, we had also interviewed the vast majority of the major and minor names in the promotion multiple times. In my opinion, the book was probably as close to the truth of the rise and fall of the company as could possibly fairly be written.

A few years later, Vince Russo, a standout name in the death of the company, wrote his own book and got it published by the same company, ECW Press. When I found out he was granted a hardcover edition, I was furious. I knew it wouldn't sell even a fraction of the number of books ours did, and I was right. This fact simmered in the back of my mind for years.

Nearly a decade later, R.D. and I were approached with the idea of writing a new and expanded edition. I jumped at the opportunity on one condition—the book had to be available in hardcover. Our wish was granted. We updated the book with tons of new information, re-inserted most of what had been cut from the original, and sourced some people by name this time (sourcing people on the record in 2004 was nearly impossible, since so many of them were still hoping to get a job in WWE). We could use information from books that other WCW stars had written over the past decade, as well as interviews with former WCW stars and employees from our website archive of 7,000-plus podcasts. The result was the version of *The Death of WCW* I'd always wanted.

As of mid-2018, the book remains what I believe is the best-selling non-WWE-promoted wrestling book in history. Nearly 85,000 copies have been sold worldwide and the book remains in print 13 years after it was first published. It's available in hardcover, paperback, a Kindle edition, and in 2014 I personally voiced the Audible.com audiobook, which because I'm a perfectionist was harder than writing the book itself. It remains the only book in history to win Best Book in the fan-voted Wrestling Observer Newsletter Awards twice (once for the original and once for the anniversary edition). R.D. and I are very proud of it, and I stand by my belief that if you want to know the true and unbiased story of WCW from beginning to end, there is no better book in the world and probably never will be.

If I have one regret, it is this: since publishing the expanded edition in 2014, I have gone back and re-watched, week-by-week, every single *Nitro* from the day it debuted. And it has become abundantly clear that if I ever have the opportunity to write a 25-year anniversary edition, I will probably have to do so, because I was not nearly hard enough on WCW. By the time it died, it was even worse than I remembered it being.

90 Read *Have a Nice Day*

You can thank Mick Foley's *Have a Nice Day* for the book you have in your hands.

I was a huge fan of pro wrestling as a kid. I also loved to read and always wanted to be a writer. I spent a lot of time at libraries looking for books, back in the days when there was no such thing as the Internet or Amazon or eReaders. If my daughters are reading this, they cannot believe how old I am.

Anyway, there were never any wrestling books to be found. Of course, books about wrestling did exist; the famous *Fall Guys: The Barnums of Bounce* came out in the 1930s, and I've got a book illustrating wrestling and jiu-jitsu holds that dates from the 1920s. But you certainly couldn't go to your neighborhood library and find much of a selection of wrestling books, if any at all, and you certainly weren't going to find any at the local bookstore. The feeling amongst publishers was that there was no market for books about pro wrestling.

This all changed in 1999 when ReganBooks took a chance on an autobiography written by Mick Foley. It wasn't a huge gamble, as pro wrestling was absolutely on fire in 1999 as a result of the Monday Night Wars. Wrestling topped the cable ratings, and at its peak drew more than 10 million viewers combined on Monday nights. Mick Foley was one of the WWF's biggest stars, and with *RAW* available as a vehicle to promote it, the book debuted at No. 3 on the *New York Times* bestseller list, and a few weeks later hit No. 1.

Foley wrote the book by hand; his typewriter broke and he had no idea how to use a computer. Originally, he was going to work with a ghostwriter but he didn't like how it was being written, and so he wrote it himself, by hand, page by grueling page. Any author who has ever poured their soul onto a computer screen can surely appreciate the hard work and dedication that went into writing what was originally a 760-page manuscript.

With the book a hit, the floodgates opened. A number of WWE biographies followed, many hitting the *New York Times* bestseller list, and Foley went on to write 10 more books, including more autobiographies, children's books, and even works of fiction.

Besides being a trailblazing book, it remains one of the best books ever written by a pro wrestler, detailing Foley's career from its start through the night he beat the Rock to win the WWF championship.

91 Attend WWE Axxess

WWE Axxess is an event that every pro wrestling fan should attend at least once. Personally, I feel if you've gone once, you probably never need to go again.

That probably sounds more negative than I mean for it to be. There is certainly nothing wrong with Axxess. It's WWE's annual fanfest done in association with WrestleMania, and if you're a big fan, it's a lot of fun. If you're an autograph-seeker, you'll have the opportunity to meet all of your favorite stars and get merchandise signed, provided you're willing to not only pay premium prices but wait in very long lines for your opportunity to talk to a superstar for a few moments. For the most part, reports we have received are that virtually all of the performers are really nice, and most people who pay up and wait are happy to have done so. WWE does make it clear that the wrestlers are only going to sign one piece of merchandise and will not take posed pictures.

But Axxess isn't just your opportunity to meet your favorite stars. If you love merchandise, Axxess includes a WrestleMania superstore selling everything you could ever want to buy, from T-shirts to replica belts to cups and beanies and bears and everything they can possibly pack in with the WWE logo stamped upon it. If you've ever dreamed of getting into the ring, you can get into the ring—sort of. They provide a life-sized WWE wrestling ring, complete with ropes, but the gimmick is there is no canvas. Rather, the hard part of the ring is replaced with a foam pit like you'd see in a gymnastics academy, so you can climb up to the top rope and attempt your own shooting star press into the pit without having to worry about killing yourself. Watching people do nutty things into the foam pit has been worth the price of admission every time I've gone.

Depending on the year they also have other fun little things like the opportunity to get your picture taken inside Hell in a Cell, or the ability to play color commentator and call a match, the DVD of which you can take home. Keep in mind, none of this is free, and for some of these things you'll pay top dollar.

Axxess also provides NXT wrestling matches. Sometimes they'll tape certain matches for TV, and sometimes they'll just provide matches for the fans' enjoyment. You're not usually going to get amazing action at an Axxess NXT event, but you will sometimes get to see wrestlers who either haven't debuted on TV yet, or are there to work matches but have not yet signed with the company (stars such as Keith Lee had their first matches at Axxess before signing with WWE, and others have wrestled at Axxess but not gone on to sign deals).

In addition to matches, you can also catch in-ring Q&As with NXT employees or WWE Hall of Famers, including stars like Ricky "The Dragon" Steamboat.

My personal favorite thing about Axxess is the museum area. For years, WWE has discussed the idea of opening up a physical Hall of Fame. For the time being, the physical Hall of Fame travels to WrestleMania every year. If you're a fan of history, there is all sorts of cool stuff inside, including original historical championship belts from all over the world; ring-worn gear including famous pairs of boots, robes, or costumes worn by stars such as Ric Flair; masks worn by guys such as Rey Mysterio and Kane; and more.

92 Wrestling Is Dangerous

Wrestling matches in this country have been predetermined since at least the 1890s, and a portion of them prior to that. Two or more individuals get in a ring, work together to put on a show, and there are winners and losers.

Contrary to what some wrestlers will tell you—and I have been wrestling since the early 1990s—it is not true that "every bump hurts." In fact, if you know how to fall, most bumps don't hurt. You don't really get run headfirst into the turnbuckle, you don't really land on your head when someone gives you a piledriver, and for the most part nobody makes contact with their punches or kicks.

That said, wrestling is extremely dangerous, and throughout history many performers worldwide have been seriously injured or even killed. The most famous in-ring death in WWE history was that of Owen Hart, who fell from the rafters in a stunt gone awry in May of 1999 and died in the ring. Mitsuharu Misawa died in the ring in Japan after taking a suplex on June 13, 2009. Perro Aguayo Jr. took a drop toehold into the ropes to set up a 619 by Rey Mysterio in Tijuana, Mexico, on March 21, 2015. It was a fluke bad landing and his neck snapped and he died of a heart attack. And there have been dozens of others.

Statistically, given the number of matches held worldwide over the last 140 years, deaths in the ring are extremely rare. Injuries, however, happen every day. They range from relatively minor things like broken fingers, toes, and noses to more serious issues like concussions, torn muscles and ligaments, and neck injuries. Hardly a week goes by in WWE when someone doesn't go down with some injury or another. When wrestlers are working three to four days a week 50 weeks out of the year, things go wrong.

Of course, while injuries are inevitable, many of them are likely preventable. During the mid-2000s, one WWE star after another had to undergo neck fusion surgery as a result of the crazy ladder and hardcore matches that the company promoted from the late 1990s on. The company has toned those matches down in recent years, and thus you hear fewer stories of performers needing neck surgery. The number of muscle tears has gone up and down over the years, largely based around the drug testing policies of a particular time period. Steroid users are more prone to muscle tears due to the steroids building muscle at a faster rate than the tendons and ligaments that hold everything together. Steroids also build up all the muscle in the body, not just the "show muscles" like the biceps, pecs, and shoulders. The heart is a muscle, and rampant heavy steroid use led to many heart attack deaths to wrestlers under 40, with "left ventricular hypertrophy" (enlarged heart) listed on many an autopsy report.

There has been a disturbing trend in recent years of an increasing number of concussions. To be fair, there were tons of concussions in the 1990s and 2000s, but back then wrestlers often didn't report them and would continue to wrestle. Many of the stars of the Attitude Era will likely have very uncomfortable retirement years. Today, because WWE has a strict concussion protocol, you hear about more wrestlers being taken off TV for their own safety. So, it's probably unfair to say there are more concussions today than there used to be. Done properly, pro wrestling doesn't inherently carry the danger of concussions. Some wrestlers were able to work their entire careers without ever suffering one. Others, whether because of the way they work or maybe just the way their bodies were made, are more susceptible to them. It is rightly a huge concern.

Virtually no wrestler escapes their career completely unscathed. But everyone should remember that the entire point of pro wrestling is to make it appear as though you are beating up your opponent when the truth is you're barely touching them. The old-school wrestling handshake used to involve barely touching the other person's hand, a reminder that the concept of pro wrestling was to be as light with your opponent as possible. That is the art of wrestling as it was originally designed in the 19th century, and it's a mindset that, for the long-term health of every performer, should change.

WWE Action Figures

I've never bought a wrestling action figure in my life, but my longtime friend and pro wrestling historian Karl Stern, who works for both wrestlingobserver.com and whenitwascool.com, told me it would be a glaring omission not to write about them. So, as was the case with the video game entry, I enlisted help for this one from Karl himself:

The toy aisle at your local big box store has been famously volatile since the mid-1980s. There have been seasons of feasts and seasons of famine as trends have come and gone, yet there has been one constant on the shelves: WWE action figures.

The first line of action figures hit the shelves in 1984, produced by the LJN toy company. The line known simply as "Wrestling Superstars" left a lot to be desired as action figures. In fact, they had no "action" at all. Standing out of scale and proportion to the other hit action figures of the day from Star Wars, Masters of the Universe, and G.I. Joe, the static lump of plastic that was the

LJN Wrestling Superstar figure is nevertheless fondly remembered by fans, mostly due to their sculpting and variety. Virtually every WWF star from that time period had their likeness forever cast in rubber, from luminaries like Hulk Hogan to enhancement wrestlers like S.D. Jones to forgotten superstars like Ted Arcidi.

WWF action figures would shrink considerably and gain limited articulation and largely goofy action features once Hasbro obtained the toy license in 1990. Again, these were largely terrible action figures compared to others on the toy shelves in the early 1990s but the Hasbro line developed a cult following. Despite being in no way comparable to Teenage Mutant Ninja Turtles or G.I. Joe, which were the dominate toy lines of the time, the Hasbro WWF figures were fun and strikingly visual in their styling. Even today, the Hasbro lineup is highly collected and sought after by wrestling fans and toy collectors.

The next toy company to get the WWF license was Jakks Pacific. At least these action figures had, you know, action to them. WWE finally caught up with the rest of the toys on the shelves and added articulation, which greatly improved playability. While the early Jakks Pacific figures left a lot to be desired in sculpting (you could barely tell an Owen Hart from a Billy Gunn), Jakks would continue to improve during its 13-year run with the license. By the end of the Jakks era the WWE figures had improved dramatically and were carried by virtually every major department and toy store in America.

WWE finally hit a home run in the action figure department in 2010. Action figures, in general, had cooled off considerably since the 1980s. But WWE figures became staples on toy shelves across the country, with very well-rendered and playable action figures by the king of toy companies, Mattel. The Mattel toy license was so important that even WWE itself, who often had shown indifference to the other toy manufacturers who previously held its license, now treated Mattel with respect, going so far as to tame down some of its more risqué storylines and acts to placate Mattel.

Even now the toy aisle is a volatile place with action figures only making up a minor part of the toy retail market compared to its mid-1980s heyday, with seemingly one exception. Visit the toy aisle in your local major department store and you will see a considerable amount of shelf space still dedicated to WWE Mattel action figures.

Mattel is the best thing to ever happen to WWE toys. They have solidified their place in the toy market and the quality of the action figures are exceptional. Every WWE fan has probably owned one at some point, probably has their favorite era or line, and there seems to be no end in sight for the WWE merchandising juggernaut.

WWE Crown Jewel

Aside from Over the Edge 1999, where Owen Hart died in the ring and the show continued 15 minutes later, WWE Crown Jewel from Riyadh, Saudi Arabia, on November 2, 2018, is likely the most controversial event in company history.

With that said, to the audience that rabidly watched WWE at the time, it seemed like nobody really cared.

WWE signed a 10-year deal with the Saudi General Sports Authority in 2018. While the amount it's being paid was never made public, if you scan WWE's corporate earnings report it can be deduced that the amount is in the range of $50 million per year, or a half billion over 10 years. In 2018 they ran two shows, but it is believed it'll be one show annually going forward.

Wait, you say, $50 million a year to run one wrestling event in Saudi Arabia?

Yes. The Saudis have a lot of money.

The deal runs deeper, however. Saudi Arabia isn't just paying for the most expensive "sold show" in history. (A sold show is an event where the wrestling company is not booking an arena and trying to make money on ticket sales and PPV buys. The host, in this case Saudi Arabia, pays the company a flat fee and then sells all the tickets—a no-lose situation for the wrestling company.) They're paying for wrestling, yes, as Crown Prince Mohammed bin Salman Al Saud is a huge wrestling fan. But they're mostly paying for the propaganda.

Saudi Arabia is infamous for its treatment of women and homosexuals, its foreign relations, and its criminal justice system, which lacks jury trials and is known for harsh punishments, including abuse and torture.

But if you watched WWE's first PPV from Saudi Arabia, The Greatest Royal Rumble—hey, life in Saudi Arabia is awesome! Videos played throughout the show pushing what a wonderful and progressive country Saudi Arabia was, with shots of smiling women and children. The wrestlers gave interviews talking about how beautiful it was and how happy they were to perform there. To the uninformed WWE audience, it was interesting to see what life was like in a place they knew nothing about. To those who follow current events, it was considered everything from annoying to flat-out disgusting.

Fast forward to October of 2018 and the announcement of a second Saudi Arabia show for the year, Crown Jewel. The show was coincidentally (not) booked to occur just four days after WWE's first-ever women's-only PPV, Evolution. Zero women had been allowed in the Greatest Royal Rumble. Zero women were wrestling at Crown Jewel, although they did allow Renee Young to do commentary, provided she dressed head-to-toe in black with only her head showing.

While the Greatest Royal Rumble was controversial, it was worse with Crown Jewel. Weeks before the show, *Washington Post* journalist Jamal Khashoggi, who had been critical of the Kingdom, entered the Saudi consulate in Istanbul, Turkey. He was there to obtain documents for his upcoming marriage. He never left. Immediately reports surfaced that he had been killed and dismembered. The Saudi government denied it. It was two weeks before the consulate was examined. Nearly three weeks later, the Saudis admitted Khashoggi had been killed. They claimed a fight broke out and he was killed and "accidentally" dismembered. Shortly thereafter, they revealed that his killing had been premeditated, and all eyes fell on the Crown Prince.

The story, which made worldwide headlines and also opened the eyes of the world to the disastrous Saudi-led war that was decimating Yemen, was front and center as WWE prepared to head to Saudi Arabia. According to sources, WWE never considered pulling out of the show for fear of the money that would be lost and how it would affect its stock price. As soon as the Khashoggi news broke, the company removed all references to Saudi Arabia from its promotion of the event. It continued to build up "Crown Jewel," which was now a WWE Network special from an undisclosed location. Soon, mainstream media picked up on the story and debated WWE's decision to do the show. To a degree, the WWE audience was aware of the controversy, as often when the words "Crown Jewel" were uttered on WWE TV, the fans booed. But WWE continued to plug away.

In the week prior to the event, word broke that John Cena and Daniel Bryan were refusing to work the show. Despite appearing only rarely, Cena was WWE's biggest star and attempting to make inroads in Hollywood, and the feeling was with Saudi Arabia being such a controversial subject, working the show would not be good for his career. Bryan, who worked the first Saudi show, evidently felt he didn't want to have any part of this; being someone whose life isn't focused on money and who was fully prepared to leave WWE had he not been cleared and re-signed earlier in the year, he took a stand with little concern for the potential ramifications.

The Tuesday before the show, the U.S. State Department came very close to ordering WWE to cancel the show. Democratic senator Bob Menendez and Republican senator Lindsey Graham both urged WWE to end this relationship. But ultimately Vince McMahon was told he could make the call, and of course, the call was to go.

In a statement released the day before the event, the company did not mince words: "WWE has operated in the Middle East for nearly 20 years and has developed a sizable and dedicated fan base. Considering the heinous crime committed at the Saudi consulate in Istanbul, the Company faced a very difficult decision as it relates to its event scheduled for November 2 in Riyadh. Similar to other U.S.-based companies who plan to continue operations in Saudi Arabia, the Company has decided to uphold its contractual obligations to the General Sports Authority and stage the event. Full year 2018 guidance is predicated on the staging of the Riyadh event as scheduled."

And so, they went. There was a massive outcry on WWE's social media and in other areas of the Internet, with many claiming they were done with WWE, or that they were going to cancel their WWE Network subscriptions. WWE was unconcerned, since in the past, whenever something happened where fans online claimed they were going to cancel the Network, Network numbers actually increased.

Despite the claimed outrage, *RAW* the following Monday did an almost identical rating as the week prior. *SmackDown* the following night was actually up. There was zero statistical indication that anyone who watched WWE programming cared all that much that the company had gone to Saudi Arabia again.

For the record, there was zero propaganda at Crown Jewel. The audience appeared to have fun and the WWE cameras made sure to catch shots of smiling women and children. The words "Saudi Arabia" were never mentioned on the broadcast, although they did admit they were in "Riyadh." The belief is that WWE and the Saudi General Sports Authority agreed that it would be in the best interests of the relationship to dial it down for this show, presumably with the agreement that the propaganda would return when the heat died down in 2019.

95 WWE Stars Are Independent Contractors

Despite the belief of many that WWE wrestlers should be classified as employees, the reality is that WWE has been audited and investigated on a number of occasions, and every single time, the government has ruled that WWE wrestlers are, in fact, independent contractors.

There are a million arguments to the contrary. In so many ways, WWE stars are treated like employees. They have to sign exclusive contracts with WWE. They cannot work for Impact or New Japan or any other wrestling company without WWE's permission. They are told when and where to perform, how long to perform for, and exactly what to do in those performances. They are told what time they need to arrive for the show. They are told what to wear, both in the ring and, more importantly, outside the ring (yes, there is a dress code). They can be fined, they can be drug-tested (note that actual employees aren't drug tested, but the "independent contractors" are), and they aren't allowed to do outside appearances or media without it being cleared by the company (to this day, WWE stars are not allowed to do podcasts for our website or appear on *Wrestling Observer Live*, an over-the-air broadcast radio program).

Why is this important? As employees, WWE stars would have access to numerous benefits, including retirement/401k plans, health insurance for their families, group-term life insurance, and more. WWE does pay for surgeries and the treatment of injuries suffered inside the ring, and the wrestlers themselves are given insurance cards which they can use for personal injuries suffered on the job, but they must purchase their own health plans to cover outside-the-job injuries and illnesses, plus coverage for their families, which given their vocation can be difficult and expensive to get. They also must set up their own retirement accounts, pay for ground transportation and lodging on the road, and much more.

Still, every single time this issue has come up, whether it be via lawsuits or government investigation, WWE wins out in the end. Notably, when Linda McMahon was running for the Connecticut state senate in 2009, the state of Connecticut began an audit of WWE, seeking to determine, among other things, whether WWE was misclassifying its wrestlers. Linda believed the audit to be politically motivated. Nearly two years later, the audit concluded, and WWE was forced to pay $7,000 in underpaid employment compensation, which they did under duress. But they were not deemed to have misclassified the wrestlers.

96 Women Headline WrestleMania 35

WrestleMania 35 on April 7, 2019, from MetLife Stadium in East Rutherford, New Jersey, was historic for being the first WrestleMania headlined by a women's match.

Lost in all of WWE's hype for the historic nature of the match was the fact that 34 years earlier, the very first WrestleMania actually had a women's championship match as the semi-main event: Wendi Richter, seconded by Cyndi Lauper, beat Leilani Kai to regain the women's championship, the culmination of the "Rock 'n' Wrestling Connection" era that blasted WWF into the mainstream.

But in 2019, the official history of the WWE was that Stephanie McMahon decided to give women a fair shake in 2015 after decades of them being treated as sex objects on TV. (Or, as cynical fans might describe it, "Stephanie McMahon invented women's wrestling!")

As noted elsewhere in this book, nothing could be further from the truth.

The story of how the first WrestleMania main event featuring women came together is somewhat convoluted, but I'll try to keep it as simple as possible.

WWE signed Ronda Rousey after what appeared to be the end of her UFC career. She was pushed super strong right out of the gate, and in her very first match, at WrestleMania 34, she teamed with Kurt Angle to beat Triple H and Stephanie McMahon in what many regarded as the best match on the entire show. Few in history had ever debuted in such a high-profile match and put on as good a performance. On that same show, Charlotte Flair ended the win streak of Asuka to win the *SmackDown* women's title.

A lot of ideas were discussed, but by mid-2018 it appeared the plan for WrestleMania 35 was Ronda vs. Charlotte. Rousey won the *RAW* women's title shortly thereafter. Charlotte lost her title to Carmella, who won the 2018 women's Money in the Bank ladder match and cashed in her briefcase to win the belt.

Meanwhile, Becky Lynch, whose WrestleMania Moment™ in 2018 was being tossed out of the women's battle royal on the pre-show, quietly began a winning streak that summer on *SmackDown*. She defeated most of the women's roster, including Carmella in a non-title match. Her popularity was growing by the week and she was granted a championship match against Carmella at SummerSlam. Her fans were ecstatic.

Then, one day, she was attacked by Carmella, and Charlotte, who had been out of action for several weeks, returned and made the save. *SmackDown* GM Paige told Charlotte that if she could beat Carmella in a non-title match, she would be added to the SummerSlam title match. Charlotte won. Though Becky and Charlotte were friends, Becky made it clear that while she wasn't happy Charlotte had been added to her match, nothing would get in the way of their friendship.

Keep in mind, to the viewers at home, Charlotte had done little to deserve this opportunity. She'd lost the title to Carmella, she'd lost a rematch, she'd lost at Money in the Bank, and she'd missed weeks of television. The 2019 "You deserve it!" crowd determined that, in fact, Charlotte did not deserve it.

In their SummerSlam match, Charlotte—again, intruding on Becky's hard-earned title match—hit her friend from behind with her finisher (a heel tactic dating back to Cain and Abel) and pinned her, winning the title. Becky, furious at being wronged, beat the hell out of her as the audience went crazy. In an instant, Becky became the hottest babyface star on *SmackDown*.

And WWE was baffled.

The company was trying to turn Becky heel and could not understand why the fans would cheer Becky, even though to me and virtually the entire viewing audience it was inconceivable that she was the heel in this scenario. She earned a title shot, Charlotte did not, and then Charlotte hit her from behind and stole what the fans felt was Becky's title.

WWE doubled down. Becky went on TV and cut heel promos in the following weeks, during which she tried to blame the fans for not supporting her, an absolutely preposterous accusation. The fans, not buying any of his, cheered even louder. The harder WWE tried to push her as a heel, the harder the fans pushed back.

To its credit, WWE finally gave up; one day, Becky was just the top babyface on the brand again, and Charlotte ended up a heel.

By the fall of 2018, the plan was for two big matches: Ronda Rousey vs. Becky Lynch at Survivor Series, and Ronda Rousey vs. Charlotte at WrestleMania 35. There were rumblings that the plan was for Charlotte and Ronda to be the first women's match ever to close the biggest show of the year.

Fate intervened. Survivor Series was being promoted as *RAW* vs. *SmackDown*, so the week before the event, WWE shot an angle where the stars from *SmackDown* invaded *RAW*. Unfortunately, in the middle of the melee, Nia Jax reared back and carelessly punched Becky right in the face, concussing her. The company was hoping Becky could be cleared in time for the Rousey match that Sunday, but it was not to be. She wasn't cleared, and the match fans had been clamoring for was canceled. With Ronda needing an opponent, they shot an angle on *SmackDown* where Becky had to choose her replacement; lo and behold, she inexplicably selected her hated arch rival, Charlotte.

Nia Jax "breaking Becky's face" (she didn't, but they claimed she did to make it seem more serious) was a short-term disaster for Becky, but in the long run was the best thing to ever happen to her career. The image of Becky closing that episode of *RAW*, her face covered in blood, still fighting valiantly after Nia seemingly broke her nose open, got her over bigger than she'd ever been before. The crowd reaction to her being pulled from Survivor Series helped convince Vince McMahon that she needed to be in the WrestleMania main event.

But nothing is simple in WWE. The road to Ronda vs. Becky vs. Charlotte was so nonsensical that the match ended up a success in spite of itself. See if you can follow along: Asuka won a three-way ladder match against Charlotte and Becky in December to win the *SmackDown* women's title. The plan was for Charlotte to win the Royal Rumble to get the WrestleMania match with Rousey, and then Becky would have to fight her way in. At the last minute, Vince decided that Becky was so hot that *she* had to win the Royal Rumble instead. So, at that PPV, Becky lost clean via submission to Asuka early in the show—which ultimately made absolutely zero sense—then later returned and took Lana's spot in the Royal Rumble match itself, last eliminating Charlotte. But now there needed to be a rationale for Charlotte to be inserted into the match; since she was a heel, a long, uphill battle to get in, as had been planned for Lynch, wasn't going to work. Instead, Vince just came out on *RAW* and randomly announced that he was putting Charlotte in the match and was suspending Becky for a supposed knee injury. Becky then continued to show up on every show until Stephanie McMahon, who hated her in storyline, told her she could fight her way into the WrestleMania main event by beating Charlotte at Fast Lane. On that show, Charlotte beat the hell out of the supposed one-legged Becky until Ronda showed up and attacked…Becky, giving her the win via DQ. That painfully lame angle is how Becky ended up in the WrestleMania main event.

If you don't have a headache by now, you're a tougher person than I am.

WWE screwed up the storyline so badly that by the time WrestleMania rolled around, the hottest program in the company was Daniel Bryan vs. Kofi Kingston. But the company was determined to promote the first women's main event, and so it was announced the women would close the show to try to get as much mainstream publicity as possible. It didn't get nearly as much as they'd hoped.

In the end, Becky was victorious, pinning Ronda with a crucifix to win both Ronda's *RAW* title and Charlotte's *SmackDown* title (the match was promoted as "Winner Take All"). The first women's WrestleMania main event was ultimately a major letdown. The women did so much media leading up to the show that they didn't have time to practice the match as Ronda had done for every other one of their major PPVs. The match was average, nothing more. Worse, as a way to pad WWE Network viewership stats, WWE had been running longer and longer PPV events, and that led to WrestleMania 35 being the longest show in company history at a whopping seven hours and 25 minutes. The show started at 5:00 PM local time and the main event didn't begin until midnight; fans were exhausted. As the icing on the cake, Becky and Ronda screwed up the finish; Ronda's shoulder came up as the referee counted three anyway. It was a flat finish live, and on TV the announcers went on and on about how Ronda's shoulder wasn't down, effectively tainting Becky's crowning moment.

At the end of the day, WWE is a wrestling promotion and Vince is a wrestling promoter, and so they will hammer home the historic nature of this match into infinity, as well as the groundbreaking performances of Ronda, Becky, and Charlotte. At least we can agree on one thing: years from now, we will look back at this show as a pivotal moment for women in WWE.

97 The Gimmicks Vince McMahon Would Like You to Forget

I've handed over a couple of entries in this book, and here is one more. Who better to write an entry on some of the terrible gimmicks in WWE history than the co-author of The Death of WCW, *R.D. Reynolds, the man behind both the book and website* Wrestlecrap. *Wrestlecrap.com has been documenting the worst in pro wrestling for 20 years, so if this entry whets your appetite, you know where to go for more:*

In many ways, the Undertaker could be considered the greatest character to ever grace WWE television. I'm not saying the greatest in-ring performer, but rather the most outstanding persona in history, a character no one watching could ever forget. A legend in every sense of the word.

But consider the pitch that would have been made to Mark Calaway upon his meeting with Vince McMahon and his crew. In essence, he was told, "Okay, we want you to be a zombie. You will speak very little, and when you do, you will generally just say, 'Rest in peace.' Also, try to sound exactly like Lurch from *The Addams Family.* Oh, and we need you to roll your eyes back into your head when you pin someone, because we saw that in an old black-and-white movie once. In a few months we are going to give you a manager named Paul Bearer—get it?—who will carry around an urn from which you derive your power. Sound good? Great. Sign your contract here."

It sounds completely ridiculous, but somehow, some way, Calaway and WWE were able to pull it off in a spectacular manner, creating a character that has been one of the top acts in the business for nearly 30 years. While the Undertaker was by no means the first absurd character in professional wrestling, he became the gold standard by which all others are judged. Seeing his incredible success, it was obviously something to be copied, right?

Why not an evil tax man named Irwin R. Schyster (IRS)? How about a friendly garbage man named Duke the Dumpster? And the holidays are coming up, so what if we turned the fat man from the North Pole into a villain named Xanta Klaus who didn't give presents to children, but rather snuck into their homes on Christmas Eve and stole their toys instead?

All of those things, as well as all kinds of ridiculous ideas, have appeared in WWE rings. Let's have a voodoo priest named Papa Shango, whose black magic includes the ability to make shoes catch on fire, cause black ooze to drip from foreheads, and make people, such as the Ultimate Warrior, vomit on command? That just sounds like good television. While we're at it, how about a chicken man who pecks and struts while entering the ring? We can call him the Red Rooster, and he can tell all his fans ("Rooster boosters!") about how he is "Poultry in Motion"! A dastardly hockey player would sell tickets, too, I am sure; let's name him the Goon. Please tell the tailors in the back that his wrestling boots need to look exactly like hockey skates. We don't want him to look silly, after all.

These are just the tip of the iceberg. While goofball characters still show up from time to time, it's a far cry from the early 1990s, when WWF was flooded with horrific ideas. Evil baseball players (Abe "Knuckleball" Schwartz), clowns (Doink, and later his little buddy Dink), monks (Friar Ferguson), plumbers (T.L. Hopper), and dentists (Isaac Yankem—I. Yankem, get it?) all battled in WWF matches.

What did they have in common? They all failed miserably.

But hey, that Undertaker guy...he worked out great. You can blame him for all this lunacy.

And Vince. When in doubt, always blame Vince.

98 Mired in the Mid-card

Prior to the debut of *Monday Night RAW*, WWF had a hierarchy. There were the superstar main-eventers—your Hulk Hogans and Randy Savages and Ultimate Warriors—at the top. At the bottom were your jobbers, guys whose role was to go in there and get their asses kicked by the stars. Among the most famous jobbers in WWE history are the Brooklyn Brawler (the losingest jobber in company history), Barry Horowitz (who actually got a six-month run as a mid-carder after an upset win over Bodydonna Skip following four years of jobber duty), Duane Gill (who was also pushed as a comedy act and cruiserweight champion in the 1990s playing "Gillberg," a spoof of Goldberg), and Frank Williams (according to wrestling writer Chris Harrington, if your name is Frank, you are pretty much doomed to failure in WWE; nine Franks in history have a collective 15 percent of total wins).

In between the top and the bottom were the mid-carders.

Once the Monday Night Wars started, the traditional jobber match became a rare thing on television, with each company fearing that people would switch to the other channel during any squash matches. They were probably right, but I do know that some of my favorite guilty pleasure matches in history have been stars killing jobbers, and I wish there were more of them today.

As a result, over the last 20 years or so, in the WWE you were either a main-eventer or a mid-carder.

Granted, some mid-carders were hardly a step above jobbers. Guys like Evan Bourne, Kofi Kingston (prior to the New Day taking off), and Crash Holly were among the guys who were portrayed on TV as stars, but in singles competition on television they rarely did anything of note. Still, the key to the WWE mid-card is that if you were able to stay in the company long enough, you usually ended up with a title run or two. For years, the company did very little with Kingston and Bourne, but they did team up and win the tag team titles once; Kingston also won his first WWE championship at WrestleMania 35. Holly was a comedy guy, the "cousin" of Hardcore Holly who believed he was a super heavyweight, but he still won four different titles during his run, including the hardcore title 22 times.

The mid-card of the mid-card encompasses about 90 percent of the performers who have come through WWE. We're talking about guys like Tito Santana, Brutus "The Barber" Beefcake, Ricky "The Dragon" Steamboat, the Junkyard Dog, Greg "The Hammer" Valentine, Jake "The Snake" Roberts, the Honky Tonk Man, Hacksaw Jim Duggan, Dino Bravo, and Don Muraco in the 1980s; the Mountie, Owen Hart, Tatanka, Repo Man, Curt Hennig, Bam Bam Bigelow, Adam Bomb, Razor Ramon, and Savio Vega in the early 1990s; Marc Mero, Ken Shamrock, Terry Funk, Bart Gunn, Mark Henry, X-Pac, and D-Lo Brown in the late 1990s; William Regal, Raven, Lance Storm, Christian, A-Train, Rhyno, Test, Ron Conway, Rene Dupree, and Tajiri in the early 2000s; Mr. Kennedy, Fit Finlay, Tommy Dreamer, Elijah Burke, John Morrison, Carlito, and MVP in the late 2000s; Cody Rhodes, Santino, Wade Barrett, David Otunga, Big E, Fandango, and Cesaro in the early 2010s; and R. Truth, Rusev, Dolph Ziggler, and Erick Rowan in the late 2010s.

The upper mid-card has changed for WWE over the years. In the last decade or so, career mid-carders such as the Miz, Ziggler, Henry, Morrison, and even guys like Jack Swagger and Jinder Mahal have gotten title reigns, thanks mostly to WWE's brand split resulting in a world title of some sort on both *RAW* and *SmackDown* (and, for a while, on the ECW brand). Depending upon which brand is considered by the company to be dominant at the time or who the bigger star happens to be as champion, the "real" WWE title has alternately been the WWE championship, the world championship, or the universal championship. The other belt sometimes goes to guys as a thank-you for years of service, or because of a storyline designed to get the belt onto a bigger star, or due to other business considerations (Jinder Mahal and WWE's attempts to break into India, for example). Really, the secondary belt serves the purpose that the Intercontinental title served for many years, which has in many ways rendered the modern-day Intercontinental title largely useless.

Which is a great segue into our next entry.

99 The Intercontinental Title

For people my age—folks who grew up in the late 1980s and early 1990s and made up the bulk of the viewers in the Attitude Era—if you were a serious fan, someone who valued pro wrestling over the cartoon WWF world of Hulk Hogan and the Ultimate Warrior, the championship that meant the most to you was the Intercontinental title.

The title allegedly dates back to September 1, 1979. In storyline, the WWF North American champion Pat Patterson beat the WWF South American champion Johnny Rodz to unify the two championships into the new Intercontinental title. I'll bet you didn't know there ever was a WWF South American champion; that's because there wasn't. WWF made up the championship and the tournament.

The title was a secondary championship under the WWF title for several years. The match that really got the title over took place on March 29, 1987, at WrestleMania III, when Ricky Steamboat beat Randy Savage in what was for years considered the greatest match in WrestleMania history. Despite being in existence for eight years, it was the first time the championship had ever changed hands on TV outside of a tape-delayed switch on an episode of *Maple Leaf Wrestling* in 1984.

After the Steamboat and Savage feud, it became the centerpiece of the Honky Tonk Man's gimmick as he proclaimed himself the "Greatest Intercontinental Champion of All Time." HTM was only supposed to be a transitional champion between babyface champions Ricky Steamboat and Jake "The Snake" Roberts, but Roberts had drug issues and HTM remained champion for 454 days, a record that still stands; this despite the fact that he fluked and cheated his way into victories, and occasionally in real life just refused to do jobs. He and the company pushed the "Greatest Intercontinental Champion of All Time" moniker so many times over three decades that today, younger fans are under the impression that he was actually a great champion. He finally lost the title to the Ultimate Warrior, who went on to beat Hulk Hogan at WrestleMania VI in 1990 in a champion vs. champion match. Warrior was forced to relinquish the Intercontinental belt, which led to its most critically acclaimed period.

Note I did not say "most successful period"—its most successful period was the late 1980s when WWF was still riding the wave of Hulkamania. The early 1990s was the most trying period in the company's history, but the company being in a down period actually helped boost the prestige of the title. Every stupid gimmick under the sun seemed to debut during this time, and the top of the card was overtaken with the likes of the Ultimate Warrior vs. Papa Shango, a feud built around voodoo and vomit. But in the middle of all of this awful, surreal programming, the Intercontinental title was being defended in great matches by the likes of Mr. Perfect, Bret Hart, Roddy Piper, Shawn Michaels, and Razor Ramon.

The run began at SummerSlam 1991, when Bret Hart beat Mr. Perfect in one of my favorite childhood matches, which I remember almost move for move today. Hart beat Roddy Piper at the following year's WrestleMania in an excellent match, ending the only singles title reign of Roddy's WWF career up to that point. SummerSlam 1992 was headlined by the British Bulldog beating Hart for the title in another classic before what was, at the time, the legitimate biggest crowd in WWF history. Shawn Michaels beat Marty Jannetty to win the title at the Royal Rumble the following year, which was a good but not great match, but the one where Jannetty won the belt, on *Monday Night RAW*, was another all-time classic. WrestleMania X saw Razor Ramon beat Michaels in a ladder match, at the time a five-star match, to win the title.

The glory period of the Intercontinental title really only spanned from August 26, 1991, to March 20, 1994, just under three years, but to many fans it seemed like their entire childhood.

The title was still taken seriously and positioned as a secondary title to the WWF championship up through probably August 30, 1998, when Triple H beat the Rock to win the belt in a ladder match at SummerSlam. Hunter ended up vacating the title, and that, combined with the rise of Vince Russo and the acceleration of title changes at the peak of the Monday Night Wars, diminished the title's prestige. As a workhorse title, the belt had always changed hands with far more frequency than the WWF title. But then, in 1999, the belt changed hands a ridiculous 11 times, ending up on folks like the Godfather—best known for bringing strippers to the ring—and Chyna. At that point the company had also added a slew of other titles, including the European title, the hardcore title, and the light heavyweight title.

The Intercontinental title effectively died in 1999, but the real death took place when WWF purchased WCW and promoted the Invasion angle. The WCW championship became a part of WWF programming, and with that, the Intercontinental title lost its place as the company's secondary championship.

The title has waxed and waned in importance over the years, depending upon the whims of Vince McMahon. More often than not, it's a third-tier belt on par with the U.S. title, bounced around between mid-carders. Every now and then a star will win it and talk about how they want to bring the prestige of the title back. Usually, this leads to absolutely nothing. Probably the biggest game changer over the past two decades was a return to the classic design at the hands of Cody Rhodes in 2011; believe it or not, to a lot of fans that was a really big deal. The closest thing any secondary title has come to the glory days of the Intercontinental belt was John Cena's run as U.S. champion in 2015. Cena, a bona fide all-time Hall of Fame WWE superstar, not only lent immense prestige to the title just by holding it; he regularly defended it in long, great matches in what was probably the best run of his entire career in terms of in-ring action. It was that series of matches that convinced a lot of fans that John Cena was actually a pretty good worker, and it was the first thing that really helped quiet the incessant booing that had haunted him for most of his career.

Perhaps one day, the Intercontinental title can enjoy a similar renaissance.

100 There Is Wrestling Outside of WWE

I hesitated to include this entry for two reasons. First, this is a book about the WWE. Second, I'm confident that everyone reading this book already knows there is wrestling outside of WWE.

But it's important to underscore that WWE is not the only game in town, and that if the company isn't providing you with what you want as a fan, it's okay to look elsewhere.

This seems to be a very difficult concept for hardcore WWE fans to wrap their heads around. My job is to cover wrestling all over the world, including WWE, Ring of Honor, All Elite Wrestling, and Impact in the U.S.; CMLL and AAA in Mexico; New Japan; and dozens of other organizations. We even cover UFC and Bellator, which aren't pro wrestling but promote in a very similar way, and which at various points have seen pro wrestlers fight and even win championships, Brock Lesnar being the most famous.

But every day I get blowback from hardcore WWE fans who don't want to hear about other promotions they don't watch. They don't want to hear about five-star matches in New Japan. Sometimes they get irrationally upset that a match in New Japan that they didn't see was rated five stars in the Wrestling Observer, but a great WWE match that they loved only got four stars. Even though star ratings are subjective opinions, they accuse us of bias, making comments such as, "If that match had taken place at the Tokyo Dome, Dave Meltzer would have given it five stars."

I've never understood this attitude. Wrestling is wrestling, and there is great wrestling and great wrestlers all over the world.

Virtually every major star in WWE history, with very few exceptions, made their name somewhere else before coming to WWE. Many top stars of today, such as Seth Rollins, AJ Styles, Daniel Bryan, Samoa Joe, Shinsuke Nakamura, Finn Balor, and Kevin Owens, all headlined major promotions before coming to WWE. And while WWE doesn't release people all that often anymore—partly out of concern they'll become big stars elsewhere, as happened with the former CJ Parker, now Juice Robinson in New Japan; Cody Rhodes, now of AEW; and Kenny Omega—when it does, those wrestlers sometimes go on to become stars in the same promotions the WWE hardcores hate to hear about.

Enjoying another promotion is not "cheating on" WWE. It's not putting WWE in any sort of imminent danger. WWE, based on its television deals, stock price, and cash on hand, isn't going out of business anytime soon, and probably won't in our lifetimes. But if there is one thing that has motivated Vince McMahon to try different things and shake up his promotion, it's competition.

Today, there are so many different ways to watch wrestling from all over the world that no matter what style you prefer or who your favorites are, you can check them out with the click of a button. New Japan, the second-biggest promotion worldwide, streams all of its biggest events and many smaller shows on the New Japan World service at NJPWWorld.com. Japanese female wrestling promotion Stardom, Ring of Honor, and Impact each has its own streaming service, all for less than $9.99 per month. Independentwrestling.tv features shows from dozens and dozens of independent promotions around the world. FITE.tv and TWITCH stream PPV events and more, and worst-case scenario, YouTube features CMLL and select matches from pretty much every wrestling promotion there has ever been.

So open up the laptop or switch on your Apple TV, Roku, or however you watch on your big screen, and enjoy. You'll see great action from all over the world. You'll see incredible things you've never seen before. You'll be ahead of the curve on trends. You'll see big stars before they become big stars in WWE. And don't worry, you're not going to hurt Vince McMahon or World Wrestling Entertainment.

Wrestling Terms You Should Know

Pro wrestling has its roots in the carnivals, and thus it possesses its own special language, even to this day. While this is far from a definitive list of inside wrestling terms, here are a few that you will find throughout the course of this book.

Babyface: A crowd favorite, the hero.

Heel: The villain.

Tweener: Someone who falls in the middle between good guy and bad guy. One example is Stone Cold Steve Austin, who would regularly give the Stunner to babyfaces and heels alike.

Bump: To take a fall (as in, fall down, not a pinfall).

Gimmick: Used to describe a wrestler's character, e.g. the Honky Tonk Man worked an Elvis impersonator gimmick. It can also refer to some sort of foreign object (a table, a chair, brass knuckles, etc.).

Angle: A twist in a storyline. Often used incorrectly, an angle is not a storyline. An angle is when the storyline is running along and then something happens to change the direction of the storyline.

Heat: Negative emotion from the crowd. Beating a babyface will, in theory, put heat on the heel.

Finish: The end of a match, usually via pinfall or submission, but sometimes by disqualification, countout, referee stoppage, etc.

Book: The act of creating matchups or storylines. To book a feud is to create a storyline that explains why two people are wrestling each other.

Finisher: A wrestler's move that usually brings about the end of the match. Steve Austin's Stunner, for example.

House show: An untelevised event.

PPV: A pay-per-view event, nowadays usually referring to a WWE Network special.

Job: To take a loss.

Pop: Applause and cheering from the crowd. The popularity of a character can often be measured by the size of the pop that wrestler gets when he or she appears.

Program: The series of matches that make up a storyline.

Promo: A promotional monologue by a wrestler building up a future match.

Push: When a wrestling company begins to put its resources behind a wrestler, giving him wins and attempting to move him up the card and make him into a bigger star.

Shoot: Either to legitimately try to outwrestle an opponent in a fake match, or a term used to denote that something is real.

Spot: A move or series of moves in sequence, or a catchall term for an important moment.

Squash: A one-sided match.

Swerve: A very sharp turn in an angle, often but not always used in reference to an angle that doesn't actually make any sense.

Tap: To tap the mat, signifying that a wrestler is giving up.

Turn: The process of transitioning from a babyface to a heel or vice versa.

Worker: A pro wrestler. Also used to denote the skill level of a wrestler, i.e. a good worker or a poor worker.

Over: A state of being wherein a character is getting the desired response from the crowd. An over heel will be booed, while an over babyface will be cheered.

Indy: An independent wrestling promotion.

Blowoff: The last match of an ongoing feud.

Schmozz: A match that ends without a decisive finish.

Mid-carder: A wrestler who is treated by the promotion as less than a main event star, but better than a jobber.

Selling: The art of acting as though one's opponent has inflicted pain or damage.

Kayfabe: The curtain of secrecy intended to maintain the illusion that everything in pro wrestling is real.

Dark match: A match that occurs at a televised event either before or after the cameras are off.

Moveset: A wrestler's repertoire of holds.

Rub: A measure of affirmation, usually given by a major talent to a less-established talent.

Gone into business for himself: Putting one's goals or character above those of the opponent or promotion. In other words, making yourself look good at the expense of others.

Acknowledgments

First and foremost, I want to thank my family: my beautiful wife, Whitney, and two daughters. Mine is a very time-consuming job, requiring weird and sometimes way too many hours, working in strange places and at bizarre times, and traveling at inconvenient moments. (To hammer the point home, I'm writing this on what is supposed to be a family vacation in Hawaii.) They have stuck with me and supported me through it all, and I cannot properly express how much I love them.

I want to thank my parents, Carlos and Val, without whom there would not be a me. I want to thank the Ultimate Warrior, which quite frankly is somewhat painful to do given what you learn about your heroes later in life, but without him I probably would not have gotten interested in pro wrestling at all. I want to thank Granny and Lynne, without whom there wouldn't be a *Figure Four Weekly*. I want to thank the late Art Bell, without whom I might not have been motivated to pursue a career in radio/podcasting. I want to thank Ron Barr and Darren Peck at Sports Byline USA Radio Network, without whom there would not be a *Wrestling Observer Live*.

I want to thank Tony Leder, without whom there would not be a Figure Four Online. I want to thank Dave Meltzer, without whom there would not be a Wrestling Observer/Figure Four Online, or this book, or my radio career. I want to thank R.D. Reynolds, without whom there would not be *The Death of WCW*, or probably this book either. I want to thank Vince Verhei, Craig Proper, Mike Sempervive, Filthy Tom Lawlor, Lance Storm, and all the other hosts I have ever worked with, without whom I never could have hit 10,000 archived podcasts over the past 15 years. I want to thank all of our other hosts and contributors at f4wonline.com, who work very hard and don't get enough recognition. I want to thank Adam Motin and everyone at Triumph Books, without whom you wouldn't be reading these words right now, and everyone who looked over the manuscript and gave me great advice, particularly Vinny, Missy Hyatt, and Karl Stern. I want to thank all of my readers, listeners, subscribers, and friends who have allowed me to work on this and all of my other projects through the years.

Nobody ever truly does anything alone. There are hundreds, probably thousands of others without whom I would not be doing what I am doing today, and to all of them I am very thankful.